Uniform Securities Agent State Law Exam

Series 63

8th Edition

License Exam Manual

SERIES 63 UNIFORM SECURITIES AGENT STATE LAW EXAM
LICENSE EXAM MANUAL, 8TH EDITION
©2017 Kaplan, Inc.

Published in August 2017 by Kaplan Financial Education.

Revised January 2018.

Printed in the United States of America.

ISBN: 978-1-4754-6465-8

Contents

4   Communications With Customers and Prospects   113

5   Ethical Practices and Obligations   141

Introduction

INTRODUCTION

Thank you for choosing Kaplan for your educational needs, and welcome to the Series 63 License Exam Manual (LEM). This manual has applied adult learning principles to give you the tools you'll need to pass your exam on the first attempt.

Why Do I Need to Pass the Series 63 Exam?

State securities laws require most individuals to pass a qualification exam to sell securities within their states. Almost all states require individuals to pass the Series 63 exam as a condition of state registration.

Are There Any Prerequisites?

Although there are no prerequisites for Series 63, some states require you to pass a FINRA exam, which is a corequisite exam that must be completed in addition to the Series 63 before an individual can become registered with a state. You may take either exam first (we recommend taking the FINRA exam first) but must complete both satisfactorily before you are fully licensed.

What Is the Series 63 Exam Like?

The Uniform Securities Agent Law Examination consists of 65 multiple-choice questions. The questions are prepared by the North American Securities Administrators Association (NASAA). Applicants are allowed 75 minutes to complete the test. Of the 65 questions on the exam, 60 will count toward the final score. The remaining 5 questions are being tested for possible inclusion in the test bank for future use. These questions may appear anywhere in the exam and are not identified.

What Score Must I Achieve to Pass?

You need a score of at least 72% (43 of 60 correct) on the Series 63 exam to pass and become eligible for registration as a securities agent.

What Topics Will I See on the Exam?

As far as exam coverage is concerned, the official title of the exam tells the story. This is the *Uniform Securities Agents State Law Examination*. Almost every question will deal with some aspect of state securities laws and practices prohibited or required by those laws. There are virtually no questions about securities products, but you will need to know enough about them to understand their suitability for different clients.

The questions you will see on the Series 63 exam do not appear in any particular order. The computer is programmed to select a new, random set of questions from a very large test bank for each exam taker, selecting questions according to the preset topic weighting of the exam. Each Series 63 candidate will see the same number of questions on each topic, but a different mix of questions. The Series 63 exam is divided into several critical function areas:

	# of Questions	% of Exam
Regulation of Persons (broker-dealers, agents, investment advisers, and investment adviser representatives)	24	40%
Regulations of Securities and Issuers	3	5%
Remedies and Administrative Provisions	6	10%
Communication with Customers and Prospects	12	20%
Ethical Practices and Obligations	15	25%

PREPARING FOR THE EXAM

How Is the License Exam Manual Organized?

The License Exam Manual consists of five units (chapters) and unit tests organized to explain the material that NASAA has outlined for the exam. The introduction to each unit indicates the number of questions you can expect the exam to ask about that unit's material. For students attending one of our classes, live or OnDemand, the class lecture will follow the sequence of these units. There is a test at the end of each unit. These test questions have been selected to repeat and reinforce the information presented in the reading.

In order for the material to be properly explained, it sometimes happens that a term or phrase is used prior to its formal introduction in the course. In almost all cases, you can consult the glossary for the definition or the index to locate a more complete discussion.

In addition to the regular text, the LEM also has some unique features designed to help with quick understanding of the material. When additional emphasis is valuable to your comprehension, the follow-ing distinctions are made:

TAKE NOTE   These highlight special or unusual information and amplify important points.

TEST TOPIC ALERT   Each Test Topic Alert! highlights content that is likely to appear on the exam.

EXAMPLE   These give practical examples of the material just covered and convert theory into practice.

CASE STUDY   These are more detailed examples, generally incorporating two or more concepts.

QUICK QUIZ   Quick Quizzes provide a quick, interactive review of what you just read. These ensure you understand and retain the material.

Additional Study Resources

To accompany and supplement your License Exam Manual, your study package may contain additional study resources. Be sure to spend some time on your dashboard, view the best practices video, and understand all that is available to help you study.

SecuritiesPro™ Qbank

Coordinating with the LEM, the SecuritiesPro™ QBank includes a large number of questions that are similar in style and content to those you will encounter on the exam. You may use it to generate tests by a specific unit or a combination of units. The QBank also allows you to create weighted mock exams that mimic your test in terms of topical coverage. There is no limit on the number of QBank exams you can create.

One thing you should know about the SecuritiesPro™ QBank is that the answer choices are scrambled each time you take a test. That is, if the first time you saw a specific question, the correct answer was choice A, that statement might be choice D the next time. Please keep this in mind if you need to contact us regarding that question.

Another important point is that the online questions are "live." That is, unlike this manual, which, once printed, can't be changed, our questions can be updated with a moment's notice. This enables us to keep current with rule changes and, to the extent possible, with new topics as they are added to the Series 63 exam. When we author questions covering new material that is not in this manual, there will be an asterisk (*) placed after the reference number, indicating the general area where this topic belongs and that there is no specific information dealing with it other than this (or similar) questions and the Exam Tips and Content Updates link.

Practice and Mastery Exams

Depending on the study package purchased, you may also have a fixed Practice Exam or a fixed Practice and Mastery Exam. These exams are designed to closely replicate the true exam experience, both in terms of the degree of difficulty and topical coverage. They provide scores and diagnostic feedback, but you will not be given access to, or be able to obtain from Kaplan, correct answers or question explanations. The Practice and Mastery Exams are sound indicators of potential actual exam scores—the better you do on these exams, the more likely you are to pass your actual exam. These may only be taken once each.

Video Library

You may also have access to various topics from our video library. These short, engaging videos cover key topics from your manual. If your package includes access to our video library, please review the topics as you complete your reading assignments in the study manual.

Please note that these videos are used for other courses as well, specifically the Series 65 and Series 66 exams, and because those exams deal with federal as well as state laws, there will be information in some of the videos that does not apply to your exam. When viewing, move forward until you get to material covered in your LEM.

Exam Tips & Content Updates Link

Don't forget to monitor your Exam Tips & Content Updates (located on your dashboard)—when rules and regulations change, or when we want to share new information regarding your exam, it is posted there.

In addition, try as we may, in a text this large, errors are difficult to avoid. When we become aware of them, we acknowledge them in the **Corrections** tab, also located on your dashboard.

What Topics Are Covered in the Course?

The License Exam Manual consists of five units, each devoted to a particular area of study that you will need to know to pass the Series 63. Each unit is divided into study sections devoted to more specific areas with which you need to become familiar.

The Series 63 License Exam Manual addresses the following topics:

Unit	Topic
1	Regulation of Persons
2	Regulations of Securities and Issuers
3	Remedies and Administrative Provisions
4	Communications With Customers and Prospects
5	Ethical Practices and Obligations

How Much Time Should I Spend Studying?

Plan to spend approximately 40–60 hours reading the material and carefully answering the questions. Spread your study time over the month before the date on which you are scheduled to take the Series 63 exam. Your actual time may vary depending on your reading rate, comprehension, professional background, and study environment.

What Is the Best Way to Structure My Study Time?

The following schedule is suggested to help you obtain maximum retention from your study efforts. Remember, this is a guideline only, because each individual may require more or less time to complete the steps included.

Step 1. Read a unit and complete the unit test. Review rationales for all questions whether you got them right or wrong (time will vary based on the size of the unit).

Step 2. In the SecuritiesPro™ QBank, create a minimum of two 25-question exams for each unit as you go. Carefully review all rationales. Use the reference number to locate additional or related information on the test topic in your LEM if needed (about 2 hours per unit).

■ Do not become too overwhelmed or bogged down in any one unit. You don't want to lose sight of the finish line because you're having trouble with one hurdle. Keep moving forward. It's a steady pace that wins the race.

■ View rationales after each question initially and spend time studying each rationale in order to learn the concepts. Later, you will want to create exam scenarios in which scores and rationales are viewed at the end of each exam.

■ Perfection is not the goal during the reading phase; a score in the high 60s to low 70s is good initially.

Step 3. When you have completed all the units in the License Exam Manual, the unit tests, and several custom quizzes, you will be ready to begin creating simulated (weighted mock) exams that cover all of the units. Complete as many as necessary to achieve a score of at least 80–85%. Create and complete additional topic tests as necessary to correct problem areas (5–10 hours). There are more than enough questions in the QBank and, while just taking tests is not the secret to passing the exam, exposing yourself to as many of these questions as you can increases the likelihood that you will see familiar items when you take your actual exam. During this phase of testing, it is best to view correct answers and rationales only after the test is completed.

Step 4. The online Practice Exam (and Mastery Exam, if included) mirrors the actual test in number of questions, subject matter coverage, and overall difficulty. Questions included in this exam are unique from all other question bank products, so you will see only new questions. You should complete these exams while observing the time limits for the actual exam. Like the actual exam, you will not see the answer key and rationale, but the detailed diagnostic breakdown will provide you with clear guidance on areas that require further study (1.5 hours for each test).

How Well Can I Expect to Do?

The exams prepared by NASAA are not easy. You must display considerable understanding and knowledge of the topics presented in this course to pass the exam and qualify for registration.

If you study diligently, complete all sections of the course, and consistently score in the 80s on the tests, you should be well prepared to pass the exam. However, it is important for you to realize that merely knowing the answers to our questions will not enable you to pass unless you understand the essence of the information behind the question. Our practice questions are carefully crafted to simulate the actual exam. The wording must be somewhat different, but if you understand the subject matter, you will be able to find the correct response when you sit for the test.

SUCCESSFUL TEST-TAKING TIPS

Passing the exam depends not only on how well you learn the subject matter, but also on how well you take exams. You can develop your test-taking skills—and improve your score—by learning a few test-taking techniques:

- Read the full question
- Avoid jumping to conclusions—watch for hedge clauses
- Interpret the unfamiliar question
- Look for key words and phrases
- Identify the intent of the question
- Memorize key points
- Beware of changing answers
- Pace yourself

Each of these pointers is explained below, including examples that show how to use them to improve your performance on the exam.

Read the Full Question

You cannot expect to answer a question correctly if you do not know what it is asking. If you see a question that seems familiar and easy, you might anticipate the answer, mark it, and move on before you finish reading it. This is a serious mistake. Be sure to read the full question before answering it. Mistakes are often made when assuming too much (or too little).

Avoid Jumping to Conclusions—Watch for Hedge Clauses

The questions on NASAA exams are often embellished with deceptive distractors as choices. To avoid being misled by seemingly obvious answers, make it a practice to read each question and each answer twice before selecting your choice. Doing so will provide you with a much better chance of doing well on the exam.

Watch out for hedge clauses embedded in the question. (Examples of hedge clauses include the terms *if*, *not*, *all*, *none*, and *except*.) In the case of *if* statements, the question can be answered correctly only by taking into account the qualifier. If you ignore the qualifier, you will not answer correctly.

Qualifiers are sometimes combined in a question. Some that you will frequently see together are *all* with *except* and *none* with *except*. In general, when a question starts with *all* or *none* and ends with *except*, you are looking for an answer that is opposite to what the question appears to be asking.

Interpret the Unfamiliar Question

Do not be surprised if some questions on the exam seem unfamiliar at first. If you have studied your material, you will have the information to answer all the questions correctly. The challenge may be a matter of understanding what the question is asking. In almost all cases, you can eliminate at least one and maybe two of the choices, thereby increasing your odds of success if you have to guess.

Very often, questions present information indirectly. You may have to interpret the meaning of certain elements before you can answer the question. Be aware that the exam will approach a concept from different angles.

Look for Key Words and Phrases

Look for words that are tip-offs to the situation presented. For example, if you see the word *prospectus* in the question, you know the question is about a new issue. Sometimes a question will even supply you with the answer if you can recognize the key words it contains. Few questions provide blatant clues, but many do offer key words that can guide you to selecting the correct answer if you pay attention. Be sure to read all instructional phrases carefully.

Take time to identify the key words to answer this type of question correctly.

Identify the Intent of the Question

Many questions on NASAA exams supply so much information that you lose track of what is being asked. This is often the case in story problems. Learn to separate the story from the question.

Take the time to identify what the question is asking. Of course, your ability to do so assumes you have studied sufficiently. There is no method for correctly answering questions if you don't know the material.

Memorize Key Points

Reasoning and logic will help you answer many questions, but you will have to memorize a good deal of information. Some memorization will be automatic as you go over the material and answer questions; some you will simply have to do systematically.

Beware of Changing Answers

If you are unsure of an answer, your first hunch is the one most likely to be correct. Do not change answers on the exam without good reason. In general, change an answer only if you:

- discover that you did not read the question correctly; or
- find new or additional helpful information in another question.

Pace Yourself

Some people will finish the exam early and some do not have time to finish all the questions. If you don't finish, you greatly reduce your chances of passing. Watch the time carefully (your time remaining will be displayed on your computer screen) and pace yourself through the exam.

Do not waste time by dwelling on a question if you simply do not know the answer. Make the best guess you can, mark the question for *Record for Review*, and return to the question if time allows. Make sure that you have time to read all the questions so that you can record the answers you do know. The exam questions are presented in a bell-shaped curve of difficulty. That is, the test begins with easy questions, which gradually become more difficult through the middle portion and then ease up with the easiest questions at the very end (be sure to get there).

THE EXAM

How Do I Enroll in the Exam?

To obtain an admission ticket to a NASAA exam, you or your firm must file an application form and processing fees with FINRA. To take the exam, you should make an appointment with a Prometric Testing Center as far in advance as possible of the date on which you would like to take the exam.

You may schedule your appointment at Prometric, 24 hours a day, 7 days a week, on the Prometric secure website at **www.prometric.com**. You may also use this site to reschedule or cancel your exam, locate a test center, and get a printed confirmation of your appointment. To speak with a Prometric representative by phone, please contact the Prometric Contact Center at 1-800-578-6273.

What Should I Take to the Exam?

Take one form of personal identification with your signature and photograph as issued by a government agency. No personal items, food, or drink, including coffee and water, are permitted inside the testing room. Personal items include, but are not limited to, pens, pagers, cell phones, watches, hats, non-medical electronic devices, outerwear, purses, and wallets. Personal items must be kept in your assigned locker or returned to your car prior to the start of your exam. As the testing vendor is not responsible for any personal items, they encourage you to bring only your identification into the Center.

Erasable note boards & pens will be provided to you upon admittance to the testing room. If you need additional note boards or pens, please alert your proctor. The note boards & pens must be returned at the end of your exam. If you need a calculator for your testing session, please see the Test Center Administrator. You will be provided with a non-programmable, non-printing calculator.

Additional Trial Questions

During your exam, you will see 5 extra trial questions (that is why the test is 65 questions long). These are potential exam-bank questions being tested during the course of the exam. These questions are not identified as such and are not included in your final score.

Exam Results and Reports

At the end of the exam, your score will be displayed, indicating whether you passed. The testing center will print your results and affix its stamp as physical evidence of your passing.

The next business day after your exam, your results will be mailed to your firm and to the self-regulatory organization and state securities commission specified on your application.

1

Regulation of Persons

The Uniform Securities Act (USA) is model legislation designed to guide each state in drafting its state securities law. These laws are frequently referred to as *blue-sky* laws; the term comes from a case heard in Kansas in 1911. Questions on your Series 63 exam will be based on the 1956 version of the USA as well as the North American Securities Administrators Association's (NASAA) Statements of Policy and Model Rules. Although the USA is a template and not the law of any specific state, it is the basis for the questions on the exam.

In 1996, the U.S. Congress enacted the National Securities Markets Improvements Act (NSMIA), federal legislation designed to integrate securities markets and eliminate conflicting state and federal securities legislation. The definitions and regulations contained in this license exam manual reflect the changes to the USA required by the NSMIA. We will refer to the NSMIA from time to time, but the most important thing to remember at this time is that federal law (the power of the Securities Exchange Commission [SEC]) supersedes that of the state.

As the saying goes, "you can't tell the players without a scorecard." Neither can you understand the law without knowing the definitions of the key terms. In this particular unit, it is critical to know the four classes of securities professionals and how they are regulated. The four classes are broker-dealers, agents, investment advisers, and investment adviser representatives. After a brief introduction to the important terms used in this unit, we will come back to each of these four in greater detail.

The Series 63 exam will include 24 questions on the material presented in this unit. ∎

When you have completed this unit, you should be able to:

■ **recognize** that the Uniform Securities Act is the template for all states' securities laws.

■ **identify** what is and is not considered a person;

■ **describe** the differences between exclusions from definitions and exemptions from provisions of the USA;

■ **describe** the differences between broker-dealer, agent, investment adviser, and investment adviser representative;

■ **recognize** the difference between a federal covered and a state-registered investment adviser; and

■ **identify,** for each category of professional, the procedures and requirements for registration in a state.

1. 1   DEFINITIONS UNDER THE UNIFORM SECURITIES ACT

1. 1. 1   THE UNIFORM SECURITIES ACT OF 1956 (USA)

1. 1. 1. 1   The USA Is Model State Securities Legislation

With the enactment of numerous state securities laws, commonly referred to as blue-sky laws, the need for uniformity in securities laws among the states arose. In 1956, the **National Conference of Commissioners on Uniform State Laws (NCCUSL)**, a national organization of lawyers devoted to unifying state laws, drafted the original **Uniform Securities Act (USA)** as model legislation for the separate states to adopt. As model legislation, the USA is not actual legislation; the USA is a template or guide that each state uses in drafting its securities legislation. The securities laws of most states follow the USA very closely, and, in many cases, almost exactly.

TEST TOPIC ALERT   The exam will test your knowledge of the Uniform Securities Act, not the specifics of your state's securities legislation. The USA is periodically updated to adjust to developments in the securities markets through the passage of Model Rules. You will be tested on the **1956** version of the USA used by the **North American Securities Administrators Association (NASAA)**, the advisory body of state securities regulators responsible for the content of the exam. The Series 63 exam requires that you not only know what the USA says, but also are able to apply the law to concrete situations. General knowledge of the law is not enough to pass the exam; you will be asked to apply the law to situations that may arise in the course of business.

1. 1. 2   ADMINISTRATOR

Although some states may use other terms to describe this position, the exam will only use the word **Administrator** to refer to the office or agency that has the complete responsibility for administering the securities laws of the state.

Therefore, the Administrator has jurisdiction over virtually all securities activity that emanates from his state, as well as that which is received in his state. The Administrator has jurisdiction over the registration of securities professionals and securities. He has the power to make rules and issue orders. He can deny, suspend, or revoke registrations. Yes, there are some limitations on the Administrator's powers (which will be covered in this unit and Unit 4), but overall, this is one very powerful person.

When it comes to legal issues, terminology is critical. For example, there are three terms used in this section that can become quite confusing. Let's try to explain them here, and they will make more sense as you go through this manual.

1. 1. 2. 1   Cease and Desist Order

This is used by the Administrator whenever it appears that any registered person has engaged or is about to engage in any act or practice constituting a violation of any provision of the Uniform Securities Act or any rule or order thereunder. The Administrator may issue a cease and desist order, with or without a prior hearing, against the person or persons engaged in the prohibited activities, directing them to cease and desist from further illegal activity. Note that this only applies to registered persons, not securities.

1. 1. 2. 2   Stop Order

A **stop order** is used to deny effectiveness to, or suspend or revoke the effectiveness of, any registration statement. This applies only to securities, not professionals such as broker-dealers, agents, investment advisers, and investment adviser representatives.

1. 1. 2. 3   Summary Order (Acting Summarily)

The dictionary defines *summarily* as acting without prior notice. This is one of the powers of the Administrator with regard to registration of both persons and securities. There are three specific cases where this power applies in the USA:

- Postponing or suspending the registration of any securities professional pending a final determination of a proceeding related to a problem
- Postponing or suspending the registration of a security pending a final determination of a proceeding relating to a problem
- Denying or revoking a specific security or transaction exemption

In each of these cases, upon the entry of the order, the Administrator must promptly notify all interested parties that it has been entered, the reasons for the order, and that within 15 days after the receipt of a written request, a hearing will be granted.

1. 1. 2. 4   Final Orders

Regardless of whether we're referring to persons, exemptions, or registration, other than in the case of a summary order, no final order may be entered without:

- appropriate prior notice to the interested parties;
- the opportunity for a hearing; and
- written findings of fact and conclusions of law.

1. 1. 3   BLUE-SKY LAWS

The common term used to refer to state securities laws.

1. 1. 4   PERSON

The term **person** means any individual (sometimes known as a *natural person*), corporation, partnership, association, joint stock company, or trust where the interests of the beneficiaries are evidenced by a security, an unincorporated organization, a government, or a political subdivision of a government (sometimes known as a *legal person*). This is a very broad definition.

Although a wide variety of entities may be defined as persons, on the exam, there are only three nonpersons. Those are:

- minors (anyone unable to enter into contracts under the laws of the state);

- deceased individuals (but their estate would be a person); and

- individuals legally declared mentally incompetent.

1. 1. 5   BROKER-DEALER

The term **broker-dealer** means any person engaged in the business of effecting transactions in securities for the account of others or for its own account. When acting on behalf of others, they are acting as brokers; when acting on behalf of themselves, they are acting as dealers. For exam purposes, it is critical to remember that the primary function of a broker-dealer is making securities transactions. In almost all cases, broker-dealers register with both the SEC and the state(s). This term is sometimes abbreviated to BD on the exam.

1. 1. 6   AGENT

Agent means any **individual** who represents a broker-dealer or issuer in effecting or attempting to effect purchases or sales of securities. You must know that these are always individuals (natural persons), and their function is to be involved in securities sales or supervise those who do. On FINRA exams, these individuals are referred to as registered representatives.

These individuals almost always work for broker-dealers, but there can be instances when the individual is selling securities on behalf of the issuer of those securities.

1. 1. 7   INVESTMENT ADVISER

The term **investment adviser** means any person:

- who, for compensation, engages in the business of advising others, either directly or through publications or writings, as to the value of securities or as to the advisability of investing in, purchasing, or selling securities; or

- who, for compensation and as part of a regular business, issues or promulgates analyses or reports concerning securities.

Under the National Securities Markets Improvements Act of 1996 (NSMIA), investment advisers are registered with either the SEC (federal covered advisers) or the state (state-registered), but never both.

You may see the abbreviation IA on your exam.

1. 1. 8   INVESTMENT ADVISER REPRESENTATIVE

An **investment adviser representative** is any **individual** who represents an investment adviser performing duties related to the giving of or soliciting for advisory services. You may see the abbreviation IAR on your exam.

1. 1. 9   ISSUER

The term **issuer** means any person who issues or proposes to issue any security. Issuers primarily include corporations and governments. However, under the USA, there is not considered to be any issuer with respect to certificates of interest or participation in oil, gas, or mining titles or leases, or in payments out of production under such titles or leases.

1. 1. 10   NONISSUER

The term **nonissuer** means not directly or indirectly for the benefit of the issuer. Simply stated, a nonissuer transaction is one where the issuer does not receive the money because the seller of the security is someone other than the issuer. This is your basic, everyday trading on the stock markets.

1. 1. 11   SECURITY

The definition of **security** is quite broad and includes those items one normally thinks of as securities (e.g., stocks, bonds, debentures, mutual funds, variable annuities), but also includes a number of unusual items, such as an investment contract and a pre-organization certificate. We will cover securities in greater detail in the next unit.

1. 1. 12   EXEMPT SECURITY

First, you must understand the meaning of the term **exempt**. When something is exempt, it means that it is excused from certain requirements. When a security is exempt under the USA, it does *not* have to be registered in order to be sold, and there are no requirements to file advertising about the security with the Administrator. You will see more in Unit 2.

1. 1. 13   EXEMPT TRANSACTION

Under the USA, an **exempt transaction** is one in which the nature of the sale is such that registration with the Administrator and filing of advertising material is *not* required in order for that transaction to take place. More about this will follow in the next unit.

1. 1. 14   GUARANTEED

The term **guaranteed** means guaranteed as to payment of principal, interest, or dividends, but *not* capital gains. When used on the exam, it refers to a security with a guarantee from a third party other than the issuer of the security.

1. 1. 15   OFFER/OFFER TO SELL

The terms **offer** and **offer to sell** include every attempt or offer to dispose of, or solicitation of an offer to buy, a security or interest in a security for value.

1. 1. 16   SALE

The term **sale** or **sell** includes every contract of sale of, contract to sell, or disposition of, a security or interest in a security for value. In other words, the offer is the attempt; the sale is when it is successful.

1. 1. 17   FRAUD

The term **fraud** means an intentional effort to deceive someone for profit; this is not limited to common-law deceit.

1. 1. 18   SRO

This is the abbreviation for **Self-Regulatory Organization**. The most prominent of these is the **Financial Industry Regulatory Authority (FINRA)**, but there are others, such as the Municipal Securities Rulemaking Board (MSRB), the Chicago Board Options Exchange (CBOE), and the Investment Industry Regulatory Organization of Canada (IIROC).

1. 1. 19   SOLICITOR

The term **solicitor** means any individual who, for compensation, acts on behalf of an investment adviser in referring potential clients. In most cases, solicitors must be registered as investment adviser representatives.

1. 1. 20   ACCREDITED INVESTOR

The term **accredited investor** is found in Rule 501 of the federal Securities Act of 1933. It refers to a person who is not counted when computing the number of investors purchasing a private placement under Regulation D of that act.

Because it is a federal term and not one found in the Uniform Securities Act, on this exam, the term is basically used to confuse you, as you will see when you go through our practice questions.

1. 1. 21   REGISTRANT

The term **registrant** is used in legal circles to refer to those securities professionals (BDs, IAs, agents, and IARs) or securities issuers who are in the process of registering or who have registered with the Administrator.

1. 1. 22   INSTITUTION

The term **institution** would include banks, trust companies, savings and loan associations, insurance companies, employee benefit plans with assets of not less than one million dollars ($1,000,000), and governmental agencies or instrumentalities. The USA generally affords less protection to these investors, owing to their greater investment sophistication.

1. 1. 23 NATIONAL SECURITIES MARKETS IMPROVEMENTS ACT OF 1996 (NSMIA)

Congress enacted the NSMIA in 1996 to promote efficiency in capital formation in the financial markets. In effect, the act generally preempts states' blue-sky laws, eliminating the dual system of state and federal registration of certain securities and investment advisers.

1. 1. 24 STATE

The term **state** means any of the 50 states, any territory or possession of the United States (such as American Samoa and Guam), the District of Columbia, and Puerto Rico.

1. 1. 25 RETAIL CLIENT

Terminology is very important on this exam. A few questions use the term *retail client* instead of *noninstitutional client*. Look for it and remember that retail clients need far more protection than institutional ones. Also, individuals who meet the standard of accredited investor are still retail, rather than institutional, clients.

1. 1. 26 HOLDING COMPANY

A holding company is defined as a company whose primary business is holding a controlling interest in the securities of other companies. It is that element of control that differentiates holding companies from investment companies. The most common example on the exam is the bank holding company. A bank holding generally controls one or more banks and may also have subsidiaries registered as broker-dealers and investment advisers.

1. 1. 27 EXCLUSION FROM A DEFINITION

Exclusion means excluded from, or not included in, a definition. For the purposes of the Uniform Securities Act, if a person is excluded from the definition of an agent, that person is not subject to provisions of state law that refer to agents. Later in this session, we will learn when this particular exclusion applies.

1. 1. 28 EXEMPTION FROM REGISTRATION UNDER THE ACT

Exemption in the Uniform Securities Act means not being subject to a registration provision of the act. The most common example is when a security, although meeting the definition of a security under the USA, is exempt from the registration requirements of the act. Further examples of this will be covered in a later session.

1. 1. 29 WRAP FEE PROGRAM

A wrap fee program is a program under which any client is charged a specified fee or fees, not based directly on transactions in the client's account, for *investment advisory services* (which may include portfolio management or advice concerning the selection of other advisers) and *execution of client transactions*. Under a typical wrap fee program, a client will pay the sponsor a single fee (typically a percentage of the client's total assets held within the account) for management, brokerage commissions, custody, and other services provided under the program.

QUICK QUIZ 1.A

True or False?

_____   1. Under the Uniform Securities Act, the city of Atlanta would be included in the definition of the term *person*.

_____   2. The GEMCO Employees Retirement Plan currently has assets of $750,000. Under the Uniform Securities Act, the plan would be considered an institutional investor.

3. What is the official designation of the person or agency that enforces the USA in each state?
    A. Administrator
    B. Transfer agent
    C. Registrar
    D. Issuer

Quick Quiz answers can be found at the end of the unit.

---

1. 2   BROKER-DEALERS

The following four classes of persons are included under the jurisdiction of state securities laws:

- Broker-dealers (generally legal persons, such as corporations or partnerships)
- Agents (always individuals)
- Investment advisers (generally legal persons, such as corporations or partnerships)
- Investment adviser representatives (always individuals)

Most of the attention on your exam (18 of the 24 questions in this unit) will focus on broker-dealers (9) and agents (9), so we will begin with them. As you will see, there are many cases in which the same rules apply to investment advisers and their representatives, so mention is made of them as well.

TEST TOPIC ALERT   On your exam, always keep in mind which one of the four categories of persons is the subject of the question. Rules that apply to agents, for example, are not the same as those that apply to broker-dealers. You will be tested on your understanding of the distinctions between each class of person defined in this unit.

A **broker-dealer** is defined in the Uniform Securities Act as any person (think back to the broad definition we gave you a few pages ago) engaged in the business of effecting transactions in securities for the accounts of others or for its own account. Any person (e.g., a securities firm, even one organized as a sole proprietorship) with an established place of business (an office) in the state that is in the business of buying and selling securities for the accounts of others (customers) or for its own proprietary account is a broker-dealer and must register in the state as such.

In other words, broker-dealers are firms for which agents (registered representatives) work. They are firms that engage in securities transactions, such as sales and trading. When acting on behalf of their customers—that is, buying and selling securities for their clients' accounts—broker-dealers act in an agency capacity. When broker-dealers buy and sell securities for their own accounts, called proprietary accounts, they act in a principal capacity as dealers.

TAKE NOTE   Individuals who buy and sell securities for their own accounts are not broker-dealers because they are engaged in personal investment activity, not the business of buying and selling securities for others. They are individual investors, not securities dealers.

TEST TOPIC ALERT   One of the roles of a broker-dealer is underwriting (distributing) shares of new securities for issuers. When they do that, they generally earn a spread (the difference between the public offering price and what they pay the issuer) or receive a commission on the sales, which they then use to pay their agents who actually made the sales to the clients.

1. 2. 1   EXCLUSIONS FROM THE DEFINITION OF BROKER-DEALER

Broker-dealers are firms that buy and sell securities for others or themselves as a business. There are, however, many persons, legal and natural, who effect securities transactions but are excluded from the definition of broker-dealer for purposes of state regulation. Persons not included in the definition of broker-dealer are:

■ agents (they work for broker-dealers);

■ issuers (they issue the securities, stocks, or bonds that broker-dealers buy and sell); and

■ banks, savings institutions, and trust companies (they are not engaged in broker-dealer activities).

Domestic commercial banks and other financial institutions are generally excluded from the definition of broker-dealer. Today, most banks and other financial institutions engage in securities activities through broker-dealer subsidiaries. The broker-dealer subsidiaries of banks are, as a result, not excluded from the definition of a broker-dealer and are therefore subject to the same securities regulations as other broker-dealers. Keep in mind that formation of these subsidiaries eliminates the need for the bank holding companies to register as broker-dealers. Their broker-dealer subsidiaries must, of course, register.

TAKE NOTE   Keep in mind the distinction between a bank holding company and a wholly owned commercial bank subsidiary. Commercial banks, the subsidiaries of bank holding companies, do not have to register because they are exempt. When engaged in securities transactions with the public, broker-dealer subsidiaries are subject to securities legislation as any other broker-dealer.

TEST TOPIC ALERT   It will be safe to assume that any question mentioning securities activities by a bank will treat the bank as exempt from registration—it isn't a broker-dealer. The only exception will be if the question specifically describes the entity as a "wholly owned subsidiary."

1. 2. 1. 1   No Place of Business in the State

There is another exclusion from the definition of broker-dealer. This exclusion relates to the location of the broker-dealer's place of business. *Broker-dealer* does not include a person who has no place of business in this state if:

■ it effects transactions in this state exclusively with or through the issuers of the securities involved in the transactions (such as when underwriting a new issue), other broker-dealers, or banks, savings institutions, trust companies, insurance companies, investment companies, and pension or profit-sharing trusts; or

■ the person is licensed under the securities act of a state in which the person maintains a place of business, and the person offers and sells in this state to a person who is an existing customer of the person and whose residence is not in this state. This is sometimes referred to as the *snowbird exemption* and applies as well to agents, investment advisers, and investment adviser representatives.

In other words, the USA excludes broker-dealers with no place of business in the state from the definition of a broker-dealer in that state to allow firms that deal exclusively with other broker-dealers, issuers of the securities being traded, and financial institutions to operate in the state without registering. The reason for this exclusion is that the regulators understand that this category of investor has a high level of investment sophistication and expertise and does not need the same degree of protection as the so-called "little guy."

The USA also allows broker-dealers to do business with existing customers who are temporarily in a state to avoid unnecessary multiple registrations. In most states, when an existing client legally changes residence to another state in which the broker-dealer is not registered, the firm has 30 days during which it may continue to do business with that client without registration in the new state. Should it wish to continue to maintain that client, the broker-dealer would have to register in that state.

As long as your client has not changed state of residence, there is no time limit. For example, many "snowbirds" spend the entire winter in Florida, which is no problem for the firms they do business with up North. Or, many people, after a couple of years in the workforce, decide to get an MBA. If they go out of state to a resident program for a year or two, that does not mean they've changed their state of residence, merely that they are not commuter students. Only when official residency is changed (new driver's license or voter registration) does the 30-day rule apply.

Notice how important language is here: If persons with no place of business in the state were defined as broker-dealers, they would be subject to state registration. If such persons with no place of business in the state are not defined as broker-dealers, however, those persons are not subject to the registration requirements of that state. If a person or entity is defined as a broker-dealer, that person is covered by (subject to) the provisions of the act. If a person or entity is excluded from a definition, that person is not subject to (covered by) the act.

TAKE NOTE

Under the USA, you are a broker-dealer if:	Under the USA, you are not a broker-dealer if:
1. you have a place of business in the state; OR 2. you have even one retail client in the state.	1. you have no place of business in the state; AND 2. your only clients are other BDs, institutions, and issuers of the security involved in the transaction; and/or your only business in the state is with existing clients who are temporarily in the state.

1. 2. 1. 2   Using the Internet

Obviously, there was no internet when the Uniform Securities Act was written in 1956. As with other changes in the way we do business, NASAA has written Model Rules to update the regulatory scheme. An example that has recently been addressed by NASAA is broker-dealers and investment advisers using the internet. A firm's website, considered advertising, can be seen everywhere. Does that mean the firm has a place of business in the state? Without getting too technical, there are several requirements to ensure that the person is not deemed to be in the state.

■ The communication clearly states that the person may only do business in this state if properly registered or exempt from registration.

■ Any follow-up individualized responses with prospects in this state that involve either effecting or attempting to effect transactions in securities, or rendering personalized investment advice for compensation, as may be, will not be made without compliance with state broker-dealer, investment adviser, agent, or investment adviser representative registration requirements, or an applicable exemption or exclusion.

■ The site may only make available general information, not specific advice or recommendations.

■ In the case of an agent or IAR

— the affiliation with the broker-dealer or investment adviser of the agent or IAR is prominently disclosed within the communication,

— the broker-dealer or investment adviser with whom the agent or IAR is associated retains responsibility for reviewing and approving the content of any internet communication by an agent or IAR,

— the broker-dealer or investment adviser with whom the agent or IAR is associated first authorizes the distribution of information on the particular products and services through the internet communication, and

— in disseminating information through the internet communication, the agent or IAR acts within the scope of the authority granted by the broker-dealer or investment adviser.

What this basically means is that if a person or entity just generally advertises on the internet, it doesn't have to be registered in the state. BUT, if it follows up with advice (IAR) or offering securities (agent), it either has to register or find some kind of exemption.

TEST TOPIC ALERT

The exam focuses more on the exclusions from the definition of broker-dealer than on the definition itself. Know these exclusions well.

EXAMPLE

Exclusion from the Definition of Broker-Dealer

First Securities Corporation (FSC) is a broker-dealer registered in State A, the location of its only office. One of their agents contacts a client who is currently on vacation in State B and recommends the purchase of XYZ common stock. The client agrees and purchases 100 shares of XYZ. Neither the broker-dealer nor the agent is registered in State B. Is this a problem? What if the client enjoys being in State B to the extent that it becomes his permanent residence?

When a broker-dealer has no place of business in a state and deals with an existing client who is temporarily in that state, the USA does not define that entity as a broker-dealer in the state. Therefore, FSC would not be required to register in State B and neither would any of its agents.

Things change, however, if the client becomes a resident of State B. Once that client's residence has officially changed, the relationship can only continue for a maximum of 30 days. After that, both FSC and the agent would have to register in State B if they wanted to keep the client. Let's take the example one step further. A question might appear something like this:

First Securities Corporation (FSC) is a broker-dealer registered in State A, the location of its principal office. They have begun doing business in State B with the First Fidelity Bank and Trust Company and open a small branch office in State B to service the account. Which of the following statements is CORRECT?

A. FSC does not need to register in State B because its only client is an institution.

B. FSC needs to register in State B because it has a place of business in the state.

C. Broker-dealers are only required to register in the state where their principal office is located.

D. FSC would have to register in State B even if it didn't have a place of business there.

We learned that the USA excludes from the definition of broker-dealer, a firm with no place of business in a state whose only clients are, among others, institutions, such as banks. That exclusion only applies when there is no place of business in the state; opening a small branch in State B voids that exclusion so **B** is the correct answer. Even if there is no place of business in the state, if they have a single individual (called a retail client on the exam) who resides in the state, then registration is always required.

1. 2. 2   BROKER-DEALER REGISTRATION REQUIREMENTS

Under the Uniform Securities Act, any person included in the definition of broker-dealer must register as a broker-dealer in the states where it does business. The Uniform Securities Act is clear about broker-dealer registration. It states, "It is unlawful for any person to transact business in this state as a broker-dealer ... unless he is registered under this act."

This means every person (legal entity) that falls within the definition of a broker-dealer must register with the Administrator of the state. Again, keep in mind that if a person falls under one of the exclusions from the definition, that person does not have to register in the state.

What exactly are the registration procedures?

Unless qualifying for an exemption, any person who meets the definition of broker-dealer (or agent, investment adviser, or investment adviser representative) must register with the state. To register with the state securities Administrator, such persons must:

- submit an application;
- provide a consent to service of process;
- pay filing fees;
- post a bond (if required by the Administrator); and
- take and pass an examination (if required by the Administrator), which may be written, oral, or both.

The Administrator may require that an applicant publish a notice of the registration in one or more newspapers in the state.

TEST TOPIC ALERT   Please note that, unlike FINRA (NASD) registration requirements, fingerprints do not have to be submitted.

1. 2. 2. 1   Submitting an Application

All persons must complete and submit an initial application to the state securities Administrator. The application (Form BD for broker-dealers; Form U4 for agents) must contain whatever information the Administrator may require by rule and may include:

- form and place of business (broker-dealers);
- proposed method of doing business;
- qualifications and business history (broker-dealers must include the qualifications and history of partners, officers, directors, and other persons with controlling influence over the organization);
- disclosure if the applicant has *ever* been the subject of any court-issued injunctions and administrative orders;

- disclosure if the applicant has *ever* been the subject of any adjudications by the SEC or any securities SRO;
- disclosure of any charge, conviction, or guilty plea to a *misdemeanor* involving investments or an investment-related business or bribery, forgery, extortion, or similar offenses;
- disclosure of any charge, conviction, or guilty plea to any *felony*;
- financial condition and history (broker-dealers only, but only of the firm—no credit reports on the officers); and
- in the case of an individual registrant (agent), citizenship information.

TEST TOPIC ALERT   As stated previously, the Form U4 requires disclosing if you have ever been convicted or even just arrested (charged) with no time limit. The 10 years is for statutory disqualification (by statute, that is, generally automatic denial or revocation).

1. 2. 2. 2   Provide A Consent to Service of Process

New applicants for registration must provide the Administrator of every state in which they intend to register with a consent to service of process. The **consent to service of process** appoints the Administrator as the applicant's attorney to receive and process noncriminal securities-related complaints against the applicant. Under the consent to service of process, all legal documents (e.g., subpoenas or warrants) received by the Administrator have the same legal effect as if they had been served personally on the applicant.

TAKE NOTE   The consent to service of process is submitted with the initial application and remains in force permanently. It does not need to be supplied with each renewal of a registration.

TEST TOPIC ALERT   If a securities professional is registering in six states, the Administrator of each state must receive a consent to service of process.

1. 2. 2. 3   Payment of Initial and Renewal Filing Fees

States require filing fees for initial applications as well as for renewal applications. If an application is withdrawn or denied, the Administrator is entitled to retain a portion of the fee. Filing fees for broker-dealers, investment advisers, and their representatives need not be identical. Broker-dealers or investment advisers may file, without a fee, an application for registration of a successor firm, whether or not the successor is then in existence, for the unexpired portion of the year.

The renewal date for all registrations is December 31, and there is no proration of fees. In the case of broker-dealers and investment advisers, a successor firm (an entity that acquires or takes over the operation of the existing firm) pays no fees until the renewal date.

One of the tricks the exam likes to play is asking about a person who registers in November. When does that registration come up for renewal? Well, even if it is only a month or so later, every registration of a securities professional comes up for renewal on the next December 31, so your first year is always a short one.

1. 2. 2. 4   Financial Requirements

For the protection of investors, the Administrator may establish minimum financial standards for broker-dealers—generally, the requirement to maintain *minimum net capital*. Think of net capital as the broker-dealer's liquid net worth. Net capital requirements of the states may not exceed those required by federal law—in this case, the Securities Exchange Act of 1934. The Administrator may require broker-dealers who are registered in his state and who have custody of or discretionary authority over client funds or securities to post surety bonds in amounts that the Administrator may prescribe, subject to the limitations of the Securities Exchange Act of 1934. A deposit of cash or securities in the appropriate amount may be accepted in lieu of any bond so required. However, if the broker-dealer's net capital exceeds the amounts required by the SEC, a bond will not be required by the state.

The NSMIA of 1996 amended the Securities Exchange Act of 1934 to add section 15(h)(1), which reads as follows:

> No law, rule, regulation, or order, or other administrative action of any State or political subdivision thereof shall establish capital, custody, margin, financial responsibility, making and keeping records, bonding, or financial or operational reporting requirements for broker-dealers, that differ from, or are in addition to, the requirements in those areas established under the Exchange Act.

Simply stated, when it comes to broker-dealers, regardless of how many states in which they are registered, other than enforcing anti-fraud statutes, the Administrator has relinquished most control to the SEC.

You will have to know that broker-dealers who meet the SEC's net capital or bonding requirements *cannot* be required to meet higher ones in any state in which they do business.

In lieu of a surety bond, the Administrator will accept deposits of cash or securities.

1. 2. 2. 5   Effectiveness of Registration

Unless a legal proceeding is instituted or the applicant is notified that the application is incomplete, the license of a broker-dealer, agent, investment adviser, or investment adviser representative becomes effective at noon, 30 days after the later of the date an application for licensing is filed and is complete or the date an amendment to an application is filed and is complete. An application is complete when the applicant has furnished information responsive to each applicable item of the application. By rule or by order, the Administrator may authorize an earlier effective date of licensing. In other words, there could be an occasion where, in effect, a person was the subject of a rush order. When everything is complete, including passing the exam, the Administrator will notify the employing firm of the effectiveness of the registration. The final step is for the firm to notify the applicant that she is now legal to begin soliciting clients.

In the same manner, as a registration becomes effective on the 30th day after application, a request to withdraw registration also becomes effective on the 30th day after submission. However, should there be any legal proceedings in progress, the withdrawal will be delayed until resolution of the issue. In any event, once withdrawal has taken place, the Administrator has jurisdiction of the former registrant for a period of one year.

TEST TOPIC ALERT   Although withdrawal of registration normally takes 30 days, the Administrator has the power to shorten that period, in effect, permitting a rush order.

TEST TOPIC ALERT   While registration as an agent or IAR is pending, the individual may not take part in any activity that would require registration. Clerical work or assisting with research would be permitted.

QUICK QUIZ 1.B   True or False?

_____   1. In general, a person who effects transactions in securities for itself or for the account of others in the course of business must register in the state as a broker-dealer.

_____   2. Under the USA, a broker-dealer with no place of business in this state, who is transacting business with an established customer who is on vacation in this state, is not considered a broker-dealer in this state.

_____   3. A person not defined under the USA as a broker-dealer in the state need not register as such.

_____   4. A broker-dealer registered in several states must meet the net capital standard of the state with the most stringent requirement.

5. Under the Uniform Securities Act, a broker-dealer is defined as any person who
   A. buys securities
   B. sells securities
   C. is in the business of effecting securities transactions for its own account or for the accounts of others
   D. is registered with the SEC

1. 2. 3   POST-REGISTRATION REQUIREMENTS OF BROKER-DEALERS

Once registered, broker-dealers and investment advisers (the firms) are subject to numerous administrative requirements to keep their registrations current and in good order. The exam will deal primarily with the requirements pertaining to broker-dealers. If any material information in those documents relating to the application for registration becomes inaccurate or incomplete, the registrant must promptly file a corrected copy (*amend* their application) with the Administrator.

The USA requires registered broker-dealers to keep account records, blotters (records of original entry), correspondence (including emails), memoranda, papers, books, advertisements, and other records the Administrator requires. These records must be preserved for three years by broker-dealers unless the Administrator prescribes otherwise. All records must be readily accessible (in the principal office) for the first two years.

The Administrator may also require registered broker-dealers to file financial reports. As noted previously, for SEC-registered broker-dealers, the recordkeeping and financial reports required by the state Administrator may not exceed those required by the Securities Exchange Act of 1934.

All required documents are subject to reasonable periodic, special, or other examination as the Administrator deems appropriate, in the public interest, or for the protection of the investor.

TEST TOPIC ALERT   Although it is required to keep all records relating to customers, there are no requirements to keep copies of their **tax returns**.

1. 2. 3. 1   Maintenance and Preservation of Records

How may these records be kept and preserved by the broker-dealer? The records may be maintained and preserved for the required time by a broker-dealer on:

■ paper or hard copy form, as those records are kept in their original form;

■ micrographic media, including microfilm, microfiche, or any similar medium; or

■ electronic storage media, including any digital storage medium or system that meets the terms of this section.

The firm must:

■ arrange and index the records in a way that permits easy location, access, and retrieval of any particular record;

■ promptly provide any of the following that the Administrator may request

— a legible, true, and complete copy of the record in the medium and format in which it is stored,

— a legible, true, and complete printout of the record, and

— means to access, view, and print the records; and

■ separately store, for the time required for preservation of the original record, a duplicate copy of the record on any medium allowed by the rules.

In the case of records created or maintained on electronic storage media, the firm must establish and maintain procedures:

- to preserve the records, so as to reasonably safeguard them from loss, alteration, or destruction;
- to limit access to the records to properly authorized personnel and the Administrator; and
- to reasonably ensure that any reproduction of a non-electronic original record on electronic storage media is complete, true, and legible when retrieved.

TAKE NOTE   We will discuss data protection again in greater detail in Unit 5.

TEST TOPIC ALERT   Keeping up with current trends, the exam is likely to ask about retention requirements for electronic communications, specifically email. Email has the same requirements as any other documents: three years for broker-dealers and five years for investment advisers. Emails from a registered person that are strictly of a personal nature and not to a client ("Honey, I'll be late for dinner," or, "I'll pick up the kids after basketball practice") do not have to be retained.

TAKE NOTE   To avoid unnecessary duplication of examinations, the Administrator may cooperate with the securities Administrators of other states, the SEC, and any national securities exchange or national securities association registered under the Securities Exchange Act of 1934.

TEST TOPIC ALERT   The Administrator's authority does not stop at the state line. The Administrator, or his representative, of any state in which the person is registered may demand an inspection of any of these books and records during reasonable business hours with whatever frequency the Administrator deems necessary.

1. 2. 3. 1. 1   Website Storage

What about a broker-dealer's website? Websites are treated as any other advertisement would be. The original site design is kept for three years, and, whenever revised, the new copy is maintained and starts a new retention requirement for that copy. Therefore, you will likely have several different versions in your advertising file at the same time.

1. 2. 4   BROKER-DEALER SUPERVISION OF AGENTS

For those of you who have taken a FINRA exam, you know there is a supervisory level of registration—registered principal. No such gradations apply under NASAA rules. So, no matter how high ranking the officer of a broker-dealer (or an investment adviser), the registration status is that of an agent (or an IAR). However, that does not mean that supervisory responsibility is ignored by NASAA.

Registered broker-dealers are responsible for the supervision of individuals registered as agents of the firm. It makes no difference if the individual is an actual employee of the broker-dealer or is acting in the capacity of an independent contractor.

TAKE NOTE   Many financial planners set up their own independent financial planning business. If they wish to be able to sell securities, they affiliate with a broker-dealer (register as an agent of that BD) and indicate the relationship on their business cards with a statement to the effect of, "Securities offered through ABC Securities, member FINRA and SIPC." Although considered independent contractors for tax (and other) purposes, all securities-related activity is under the supervisory responsibility of the broker-dealer.

The Uniform Securities Act states that the Administrator shall consider that an agent who will work under the supervision of a registered broker-dealer need not have the same qualifications as a broker-dealer. That means that new agents (like you) are not expected to have the knowledge, experience, and background of the employing broker-dealer.

In a later unit, we will cover reasons for disqualifying an agent, but here is what the USA says about improper supervision: "The disqualification of any agent may not automatically be used against the broker-dealer. But, when the agent's disqualification is due to lack of reasonable supervision, the Administrator may proceed against the broker-dealer." Put into plain English, if an agent commits a violation serious enough to lead to a revocation of his license, the firm can also be disciplined if it can be shown that there was a lack of adequate supervision of the agent.

1.3   AGENT

The Series 63 exam will ask nine questions dealing with agents. The USA defines an **agent** as any **individual** who represents a broker-dealer or an issuer in effecting (or attempting to effect) transactions in securities.

As agents, they act on behalf of others and usually are compensated on a commission basis. Other than on this exam, agents are usually referred to as **registered representatives.** A partner, officer, director of a broker-dealer or issuer, or a person occupying a similar status or performing similar functions is an agent only if she otherwise comes within this definition. That is, being an agent depends upon functions performed, not the individual's title.

The use of the term *individual* here is important. Only an individual, or a natural person, can be an agent. A corporation, such as a brokerage firm, is not a natural person—it is a legal entity. The brokerage firm is the legal person (entity) that the agent (natural person) represents in securities transactions.

TAKE NOTE   Individuals representing broker-dealers in a sales capacity must register as agents whether they sell registered securities or securities exempt from registration.

1. 3. 1   EXCLUSIONS FROM DEFINITION OF AGENT FOR ADMINISTRATIVE PERSONNEL

Knowing who is **not** an agent is just as important as knowing who is an agent. In fact, it sometimes seems that the exam asks more about who isn't rather than who is. Therefore, it is critical to know the circumstances under which certain individuals are not agents.

Clerical and administrative (sometimes referred to as *ministerial*) employees of a broker-dealer are generally not included in the definition of agent and, therefore, are not required to register. The logic for this exclusion from the definition should again be obvious. Clerical and administrative employees do not effect securities transactions with the public. They attend to the administration of the broker-dealer as a business organization. Under these circumstances, they are similar to administrative or clerical employees of any other corporation. A testable point is that if the broker-dealer they work for wishes to pay its employees, including this group, a year-end bonus based on company profits (not related to any individual's sales efforts), it would be allowable and would not require registration of the clerical personnel.

The situation changes when administrative personnel take on sales-related functions. When they do so, they lose their exemption and must register as agents.

EXAMPLE   Secretaries and sales assistants are not agents if their activities are confined to administrative activities, including responding to an existing client's request for a quote or posting to client records. However, if secretaries or sales assistants accept customer transactions or take orders over the phone, they are engaging in securities transactions and are subject to registration as agents.

TEST TOPIC ALERT   *Cold callers* working for a broker-dealer would have to register as agents if they did any more than ask if clients wanted to receive information. For example, if they pre-qualified clients or suggested ways to receive more money for their stocks or bonds, they would have to register as agents.

As is customary in other industries, broker-dealers frequently hire summer interns. If these interns received any selling-related compensation, such as $10 for each existing client solicited, they would be considered agents and would have to register.

1. 3. 2   EXCLUSIONS FROM THE DEFINITION OF AGENT FOR PERSONNEL REPRESENTING ISSUERS

Although the majority of new securities issues are sold to investors through the efforts of broker-dealers acting in the capacity of investment bankers (underwriters), there are cases where the issuer itself takes on the chore of selling a stock or bond issue to the public.

When might the issuer choose not to use an underwriter? In many cases, a local company is looking to raise some additional capital—something in the range of several million dollars. Instead of going through the normal investment banking procedure (and paying all of those fees and commissions to the investment bankers), the company (known under the USA as the issuer), either uses its own employees or hires an independent sales force acting under contract with the issuer to sell the new security. Determining if these individuals are defined as agents depends on the nature of the security being sold, the way it is being sold, or to whom it is being sold.

Individuals representing an issuer are excluded from the definition of agent and, therefore, are exempt from registration in a state when representing issuers in effecting transactions:

- in certain exempt securities (listed below);
- exempt from registration (exempt transactions); and
- with existing employees, partners, or directors of the issuer, if no commission or other remuneration is paid or given directly or indirectly for soliciting any person in this state.

1. 3. 2. 1   Effecting Transactions in Exempt Securities

Securities exempt from registration are called **exempt securities**. Although there are almost a dozen different securities that qualify for exemption under the Uniform Securities Act (they will be discussed in the next unit), an individual is excluded from the term *agent* only when that individual represents an issuer in effecting transactions for the following five exempt securities:

- Any security issued or guaranteed by the United States, any state, any political subdivision of a state, or any agency of one or more of these, or any security issued or guaranteed by Canada, any Canadian province, or any political subdivision of any such province
- Any security issued or guaranteed by any foreign government with which the United States currently maintains diplomatic relations
- Any security issued or guaranteed by any bank organized under the laws of the United States, or any bank, savings institution, or trust company organized and supervised under the laws of any state
- Commercial paper rated in the top three categories by the major rating agencies with denominations of $50,000 or more and maturities of nine months or less
- Investment contracts issued in connection with an employee's stock purchase, savings, pensions, or profit-sharing plans

1. 3. 2. 2   Effecting Exempt Transactions

An employee of an issuer is not an agent when representing an issuer in exempt transactions. Transactions exempt from registration are called **exempt transactions.** Some examples are:

- unsolicited brokerage transactions (the client initiates the trade);
- transactions between issuers and underwriters;
- transactions with financial institutions, such as banks or trust companies, insurance companies, or investment companies; and
- offerings to a limited number of investors, usually referred to as private placements.

Exempt securities and exempt transactions will be covered in thorough detail in the next unit.

1. 3. 2. 3   Effecting Transactions with Employees of the Issuer

The final exclusion applies when the individual is effecting transactions with existing employees, partners, or directors of the issuer, as long as no commission or other remuneration is paid or given directly or indirectly for soliciting any person in this state. In other words, salaried employees engaged in distributing their employers' shares as part of an employee benefit plan would not be required to register as agents because they are, by definition, excluded from the definition. If such employees were compensated on the basis of the number of shares sold, they would be defined as agents and, therefore, would be subject to registration.

TAKE NOTE

An employee of an issuer is not an agent when representing an issuer if the issue is exempt from registration, as long as it is one of the five listed above.). Additionally, the employee is not an agent when representing an issuer in exempt transactions (e.g., transactions between an underwriter and issuer).

TEST TOPIC ALERT

Individuals representing *broker-dealers* in a sales capacity must register as agents whether they sell registered securities, securities exempt from registration, or in exempt transactions.

QUICK QUIZ 1.C

Here are examples of how this might be presented on the exam:

1. Under the Uniform Securities Act, the term *agent* would include an individual who represents an issuer in effecting non-exempt transactions in

   A. a city of Montreal general obligation bond
   B. common stock offered by a commercial bank
   C. a New Jersey Turnpike revenue bond
   D. commercial paper with a 19-month maturity

2. Under the Uniform Securities Act, the term *agent* would include

   A. an individual who represents an issuer in exempt transactions
   B. an individual who represents a broker-dealer in a transaction in an exempt security
   C. a receptionist for a broker-dealer who directs calls for trade information to the appropriate individual
   D. the vice president of human resources for a national brokerage firm

3. Under the Uniform Securities Act, the term *agent* would NOT include an individual who represents an issuer in effecting non-exempt transactions in any security

   A. issued or guaranteed by any federal credit union
   B. issued or guaranteed by any bank organized under the laws of the United States
   C. issued or guaranteed by a regulated public utility or public utility holding company
   D. of an issuer equal to or senior to common stock which is a federal covered security

1. 3. 3 AGENT REGISTRATION REQUIREMENTS

The registration requirements for an agent who is not exempt are similar to those covered previously for a broker-dealer. An application, generally the Form U4, must be completed. One thing, however, that is on the agent's application that does not apply to a broker-dealer is disclosing *citizenship*.

The USA states, "It is unlawful for any person to transact business in this state as an agent unless he is registered under this act." In other words, an individual may not conduct securities transactions in a state unless that person is registered or exempt from registration in that state. This is true even when receiving unsolicited orders. Agents doing business in a state must be registered in that state, even if there is only one client who resides in that state. This is not like investment advisers and their representatives who, as we will learn later in this unit, enjoy a de minimis exemption. Furthermore, the act makes it unlawful for any broker-dealer or issuer to employ an agent unless the agent is registered.

So, what can an individual who has been hired to become an agent of a broker-dealer do while registration is pending? After all, one does not fill out the Form U4 and become an agent immediately. Permitted activities would be those allowed to any other employee of the broker-dealer who is not required to be registered. That would include clerical functions, such as posting trade details to client accounts, or administrative activities, like assisting with research. As long as it does not involve customer contact relating to selling or offering securities or opening accounts, these newbies can hang around the office and try to make themselves useful. Of course, most of their time should be spent preparing to pass the exam.

An agent's registration is not effective during any period when the agent is not associated with a broker-dealer registered in the state. Therefore, if the broker-dealer's registration is terminated, the agent is no longer considered licensed. The terminology depends on the specific state. In some cases, the agent's license is placed in *suspense*. In other states, it is put *on hold*, or some similar language. Whatever the phrase, when the broker-dealer closes up shop, either voluntarily or involuntarily (think revocation of registration by the Administrator), the agent cannot function because there is no broker-dealer affiliation. This effectively cancels the agent's active registration.

EXAMPLE

It is important to understand when someone is an agent and when someone is not. The following is an example of what you might encounter on the exam:

The City of Chicago issues bonds for the maintenance of local recreational facilities. Purchasers have two choices: they can purchase the bonds directly from the city through Ms. Stith (a city of Chicago employee responsible for selling the bonds), or they can purchase them from Mr. Thompson (an employee of First Securities Corporation of Illinois). Which of the following statements is CORRECT?

A. Ms. Stith and Mr. Thompson must be registered as agents.

B. Ms. Stith must be registered as an agent, but Mr. Thompson is excluded.

C. Mr. Thompson must be registered as an agent, but Ms. Stith is excluded.

D. Mr. Thompson and Ms. Stith are excluded from the definition of agent.

Any individual selling securities while representing a registered broker-dealer is always defined as an agent, even when the securities are exempt from registration (as are these municipal bonds). When an individual represents the issuer of certain exempt securities, such as municipal bonds, that individual is excluded from the definition of agent and does not register. This means the correct answer is **C**. It is important to remember the 5 categories of exempt issuers to which this exclusion applies.

TAKE NOTE   Exemptions from registration as an agent generally apply to individuals who represent issuers, rather than to individuals who represent broker-dealers.

TEST TOPIC ALERT   When representing the issuer, the only time where compensation comes into play is when effecting transactions with existing employees, partners, or directors of the issuer. In that case, the individual is not an agent only if no commission or other remuneration is paid or given directly or indirectly for soliciting any person in this state.

1. 3. 3. 1 Agent's Financial Requirements

Unlike a broker-dealer, there are no financial requirements, or minimum net worth requirements, to register as an agent. The Administrator may, however, require an agent to be bonded, particularly if the agent has discretion over a client's account. Please note that an agent would never maintain custody of money or securities of a client.

1. 3. 3. 2 Multiple Registrations

An individual may not act at any one time as an agent for more than one broker-dealer or for more than one issuer, unless the broker-dealers or issuers for whom the agent acts are affiliated by direct or indirect common control or the Administrator grants an exception. In the event an agent does wish to affiliate with a second broker-dealer, the agent would have to go through the registration process with the second firm in the same manner as the original application (filing another Form U4).

1. 3. 3. 3 Automatic Registration of Partners, Officers, and Directors

Let's take a look at a testable rule found in the Uniform Securities Act:

Registration of a broker-dealer automatically constitutes registration of any agent who is a partner, officer, or director, or a person occupying a similar status or performing similar functions. Registration of an investment adviser automatically constitutes registration of any investment adviser representative who is a partner, officer, or director, or a person occupying a similar status or performing similar functions.

As stated previously, it isn't the title that determines your registration, it is the function performed. Note that the rule quoted states that the agent (or IAR) is a partner, officer, or director of the broker-dealer (or investment adviser). Doesn't that mean he is already registered? What is the purpose of automatic registration to someone already registered?

When a registered broker-dealer (or state-registered IA) expands its business so that registration is required in another state (or states), the application process is basically the same as its initial state registration. That is, Form BD (or Form ADV) is filed. That filing includes the names and other pertinent information about all of the partners, officers, or directors who are already acting as agents (or IARs). Therefore, when the firm's registration becomes effective in that new state, those individuals included in the filing are granted automatic registration—

they don't have to file an individual Form U4. Please note, it is not any agent (or IAR); it is only those listed or, as the rule states, those occupying a similar status who receive this treatment. Any of the firm's other existing agents or IARs who will need to be registered in the new state must file an amended Form U4 with the Administrator and wait for their supervisor to tell them that the firm has received the word that their registration is effective within that state.

It is also important to note that, unlike FINRA, there is no separate principal registration category for those in supervisory positions—they are all agents.

1. 3. 4 POST-REGISTRATION REQUIREMENTS OF AGENTS

Unlike broker-dealers, once the initial registration has been completed, there isn't much effort required to maintain an agent's license. There are no recordkeeping requirements, and the only possible financial requirement is a surety bond if the agent will be exercising discretion in client accounts. Even the renewal process, including fee payment, is generally taken care of by the broker-dealer. Of course, if the fee is not paid, the registration is not renewed and, as stated with broker-dealers, the renewal date is December 31.

TEST TOPIC ALERT   If there is a change to any material information in the Form U4 (e.g., change of permanent address or change to military status), an amendment must be filed within 30 days.

1. 3. 4. 1 Termination Procedures

If an agent terminates employment with a broker-dealer, both parties must notify the Administrator promptly. If an agent terminates employment with one broker-dealer to join another broker-dealer, all three parties must notify the Administrator. One way to remember this is that in the case of an agent, the first letter, **A**, tells us that **A**ll the parties involved must notify the Administrator.

1. 4 LIMITED REGISTRATION OF CANADIAN BROKER-DEALERS AND AGENTS

Provided the limited registration requirements enumerated below are met, a broker-dealer domiciled in Canada that has no office in this state may effect transactions in securities with or for, or attempt to induce the purchase or sale of any security by:

- a person from Canada who is temporarily resident in this state and who was already a client of the broker-dealer; or
- a person from Canada who is a resident in this state and whose transactions are in a self-directed tax-advantaged retirement plan in Canada, of which the person is the holder or contributor. Canada's equivalent of our IRA is called a Registered Retirement Savings Plan (RRSP).

An agent who will be representing a Canadian broker-dealer who registers under these provisions may effect transactions in securities in this state on the same basis as permitted for the broker-dealer.

For the Canadian broker-dealer to register in this fashion, it must:

- file an application in the form required by the jurisdiction where it has its principal office in Canada;
- file a consent to service of process;
- provide evidence that it is registered in good standing in its home jurisdiction; and
- be a member of an SRO or stock exchange in Canada.

Requirements for agents are the same, except that membership in an SRO or stock exchange is not relevant.

However, just as with domestic broker-dealers, if there is no place of business in the state, there are no registration requirements if the only securities transactions are with issuers, other broker-dealers, and institutional clients.

TAKE NOTE
Renewal applications for Canadian broker-dealers and agents who file for limited registration must be filed before December 1 each year.

QUICK QUIZ 1.D

Write **A** if the person is an agent and **B** if not.

_____   1. A person who effects transactions in municipal securities on behalf of a broker-dealer

_____   2. An agent's salaried secretary who takes buy and sell orders from clients

_____   3. An employee of a bank whose job is selling securities issued by the bank

_____   4. An individual who represents her nonexempt employer in the sale of its securities to existing employees for a commission

_____   5. A person who represents an issuer in effecting transactions with underwriters

6. When an agent's permanent residence address changes, updates must be made to the information on file with the regulatory bodies. The proper procedure is to file a
   A. Form U4 within 30 days
   B. Form U4 within 45 days
   C. Form U5 within 30 days
   D. Form U5 within 45 days

1. 5 INVESTMENT ADVISER

The registration requirements for an investment adviser are much like those for a broker-dealer. The USA states, "It is unlawful for any person to transact business in this state as an investment adviser . . . unless he is so registered under this act or is exempt from a state's registration requirements." In other words, persons included in the definition of investment adviser must register in the states in which they do business unless they are exempt from registration.

Earlier, we gave the definition of *investment adviser*. It is important to note that the definition specifies that the advice must be related to securities. Advice given on investments not defined as securities, such as rare coins, art, and real estate, is not investment advice covered by the USA or other securities legislation. As a result, persons providing such advice are not investment advisers. Again, definitions are crucial for determining whether an activity is subject to securities law.

To be an investment adviser under both state and federal securities law, a person must:

■ provide advice about securities (not about jewelry, rare coins, or real estate);

■ provide that advice as part of an ongoing business (hang a shingle and have an office for conducting business) on a regular basis; and

■ receive compensation (payment for the advice).

TAKE NOTE   In most cases, investment advisers are legal persons, such as partnerships or corporations, who provide investment advice or portfolio management services on an ongoing basis. Investment adviser representatives work for investment advisers, just as registered sales agents work for a broker-dealer. Note that an individual can be an investment adviser when the business is organized as a sole proprietorship.

1. 5. 1 SEC RELEASE IA-1092

As a result of the proliferation of persons offering investment advice, Congress directed the SEC to define the activities that would subject a person to the Investment Advisers Act of 1940. The SEC did so in SEC Release IA-1092. Because so much of the USA's interpretations dealing with investment advisers parallels the federal law, it is important to know how this release has impacted the industry.

SEC Release IA-1092 interprets the definition of investment adviser under the Investment Advisers Act of 1940 to include financial planners, pension consultants, and others who offer investment advice as part of their financial practices.

Release IA-1092, in short, identifies as an investment adviser anyone who:

■ provides investment advice, reports, or analyses with respect to securities;

■ is in the business of providing advice or analyses; and

■ receives compensation, directly or indirectly, for these services.

TAKE NOTE   If a person engages in these three activities (sometimes referred to as the *three-prong test*), that person is an investment adviser subject to the Investment Advisers Act of 1940 or the Uniform Securities Act. As an investment adviser, this person must register with either the SEC or the states.

1. 5. 1. 1   Provides Investment Advice

In Release IA-1092, the SEC (and NASAA as well) maintains that a person who gives advice, whether in written or oral form, and issues reports, analyses, and recommendations about specific securities is an investment adviser if that person is in the business of doing so and receives compensation for the advice. This definition of investment adviser includes financial planners, pension consultants, and sports and entertainment representatives.

1. 5. 1. 1. 1   Financial Planners

Financial planners who make recommendations regarding a person's financial resources or perform analyses that concern securities are investment advisers if such services are performed as part of a business and for compensation. Under this interpretation, the SEC holds that there is no such thing as a comprehensive financial plan that does not involve securities. In fact, the SEC even includes financial planners who advise clients as to the desirability of investing in securities as an alternative to other investments, such as real estate, intangibles, or other assets.

1. 5. 1. 1. 2   Pension Consultants

Consultants who advise employee benefit plans on how to fund their plans with securities are also considered investment advisers by the SEC. In addition, under Release IA-1092, the SEC considers pension consultants who advise employee benefit plans on the selection, performance, and retention of investment managers to be investment advisers. A bit later in this unit, you will learn the conditions under which pension consultants become eligible to register with the SEC rather than the states.

1. 5. 1. 1. 3   Sports and Entertainment Representatives

Persons who provide financially related services to entertainers and athletes that include advice related to investments, tax planning, budgeting, and money management are also investment advisers. As earnings for these celebrities continue to climb, more and more of them use personal managers to handle all of their finances, and those individuals or firms are generally going to be considered investment advisers.

TAKE NOTE A sports agent who secures a favorable contract for a football player and receives a commission of 10% of the player's salary is not necessarily an investment adviser. However, if the sports agent advises the football player to invest his money in specific securities, the agent is then in the business of offering investment advice and would then be subject to the Investment Advisers Act of 1940 or the Uniform Securities Act.

1. 5. 1. 2   Is in the Business of Providing Advice

A person is in the business of providing advice and is subject to regulation as an investment adviser if he:

■ gives advice on a regular basis such that it constitutes a business activity conducted with some regularity (although the frequency of the activity is a factor, it is not the only determinant in whether a person is in the business of giving advice, and providing advice does not have to be the person's principal activity); and

■ advertises investment advisory services and presents himself to the public as an investment adviser or as one who provides investment advice.

TAKE NOTE   A person is in the business of giving investment advice if he receives separate compensation that represents a charge for giving the advice.

Even when the advice doesn't mention specific securities, such as recommending an allocation of assets into highly rated bonds, technology stocks, or growth mutual funds, the person meets the definition of an investment adviser. On the other hand, a person whose business is to offer only nonspecific investment advice, through publication of a general newsletter, for example, is not covered by the act. We'll discuss this exclusion shortly.

1. 5. 1. 3   Receives Compensation

A person who receives an economic benefit as a result of providing investment advice is an investment adviser. The compensation can be direct or indirect. Compensation includes advisory fees, commissions, and other types of fees related to the service rendered. A separate fee for the advice need not be charged; the fee can be paid by a third party on behalf of the beneficiary of the advice. No matter what the source, all compensation must always be disclosed to the client.

EXAMPLE   Fees that an investment adviser receives from a corporation for advice given to the corporation's employees or retirees are considered compensation. A financial planner who designs a comprehensive financial plan for the corporation's employees without charging a fee but receives commissions on insurance policies sold as part of the plan is acting as an investment adviser. Even though that compensation is indirect, it meets the release's definition of compensation for investment advice.

1. 5. 2   EXCLUSIONS FROM THE DEFINITION OF INVESTMENT ADVISER

As is the case with broker-dealers and agents, there are exclusions from the term *investment adviser*. If a person is excluded, none of the registration requirements apply. Under the USA, the following are excluded from the definition and are not investment advisers:

■ Investment adviser representatives (the business entity is the investment adviser, not the representative)

- Banks, savings institutions, and trust companies
- Any lawyers, accountants, teachers, or engineers (L.A.T.E) whose advice is solely incidental to the practice of their profession are excluded. This exclusion is not available to any of these who have established a separate advisory business. Also, the exclusion would not be available to any of these who hold themselves out as offering investment advice.
- Any broker-dealer whose investment advisory services are incidental to their brokerage business and who receive no special or separate compensation (wrap fees) for offering advice. This exclusion also applies to agents of these broker-dealers.

TAKE NOTE
Why is that broker-dealers qualify for this exclusion? Including this exception in the law amounts to a recognition that brokers/dealers commonly give a certain amount of advice to their customers in the course of their regular business, and that it would be inappropriate to bring them within the scope of the definition of an IA merely because of this aspect of their business. On the other hand, reference to *special compensation* amounts to an equally clear recognition that a broker-dealer who is specially compensated for the rendition of advice should be considered an investment adviser and not be excluded from the purview of the act merely because he is also engaged in effecting market transactions in securities. It is well known that many broker-dealers have investment advisory departments which furnish investment advice for compensation in the same manner as an investment adviser who operates solely in an advisory capacity. The essential distinction to be borne in mind in considering borderline cases is the distinction between compensation for advice itself and compensation for services of another character, to which advice is merely incidental.

- A publisher, employee, or columnist of a newspaper, news magazine, or business or financial publication of regular and general circulation; or an owner, operator, producer, or employee of a cable, radio, or television network, station, or production facility if, in either case, the financial or business news published or disseminated is made available to the general public and the content does not consist of rendering advice on the basis of the specific investment situation of each client

---

TEST TOPIC ALERT
An investment newsletter is being published for a subscription fee. Rather than being published on a regular basis (weekly, monthly, quarterly, and so forth), issues are released in response to market events. How does the law view this publisher? In this case, the publisher would be considered an investment adviser requiring registration. The exclusion requires that the publication is published with some sort of regular schedule rather than being timed to specific market events.

- Federal covered investment advisers registered with the SEC (advisers with $110 million or more in assets under management or under contract to a registered investment company) or those excluded from the definition under the Investment Advisers Act of 1940
- Any other person the Administrator specifies

TAKE NOTE

Sometimes the exam will refer to *exceptions* rather than *exclusions*. Both terms mean the same thing for test purposes.

TAKE NOTE

For purposes of the exclusion, the term *bank* does not include a savings and loan association or a foreign bank.

TAKE NOTE

When referring to the L.A.T.E. exclusion, it is important to understand the meaning of *incidental*. A lawyer advising clients to carefully invest a settlement from a legal case is not giving investment advice unless charging a separate fee for helping set up the portfolio. An accountant is not giving investment advice when suggesting to a wealthy client that investing in tax-exempt municipal bonds might be a wise idea, unless charging a separate fee to help select the bonds.

QUICK QUIZ 1.E

1. Under the USA, the definition of investment adviser would include

    A. a bank
    B. a lawyer charging a fee to advise clients how to invest an injury settlement she just won for them
    C. an investment adviser representative
    D. none of the above

2. Which of the following is NOT considered one of the three prongs making a person an investment adviser?

    A. Giving advice on securities
    B. Being in the business of giving advice
    C. Executing trades in recommended securities
    D. Receiving compensation for the advice rendered

1. 5. 2. 1 Federal Covered Advisers

The National Securities Markets Improvement Act of 1996 (NSMIA) made major changes in the way investment advisers register. The NSMIA divided registration responsibilities between the SEC and the states' securities departments. Basically, the largest firms are required to register with the SEC, and the smaller ones are required to register with the states. Unlike broker-dealers, who almost always register with the SEC and one or more states, investment advisers are registered with one or the other, never both.

Advisers registered with the SEC are known as **federal covered investment advisers** or, sometimes on the exam, just as covered advisers (without the word *federal*). Federal covered advisers are those:

■ required to be registered or registered as an investment adviser with the SEC because they meet the minimum threshold of assets under management (currently $110 million);

- registered with the SEC because they are under contract to manage an investment company registered under the Investment Company Act of 1940, regardless of the amount of assets under management; or

- not registered with the SEC because they are excluded from the definition of an investment adviser by the Investment Advisers Act of 1940. The only testable example of a person who is excluded under this provision is one whose advice, analyses, or reports are related only to securities that are direct obligations of, or obligations guaranteed by, the United States, or by certain U.S. government-sponsored corporations designated by the Secretary of the Treasury (e.g., FNMA, GNMA).

TAKE NOTE   Because so much of this exam deals with interpreting the laws, it is sometimes necessary to review some legal concepts. For example, if a person is excluded from the definition of investment adviser under the Investment Advisers Act of 1940, the states, under the NSMIA, cannot define this person as an investment adviser because federal law excluded that person from the definition. In other words, if the separate states could define the persons who were excluded from the federal definition as investment advisers, the federal law would have no meaning.

TAKE NOTE   As a general rule, the SEC or federal rules involve bigger numbers than the state rules—large investment advisers must register with the SEC; small and mid-size investment advisers must register with the state.

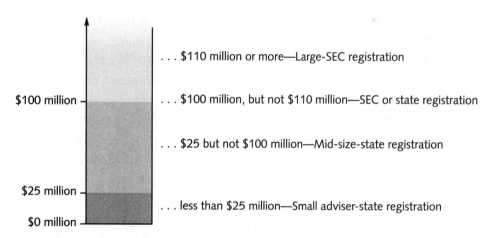

1. 5. 2. 2   Dodd-Frank and Assets Under Management

As stated previously, the NSMIA eliminated state registration requirements for federal covered advisers, largely based upon assets under management. Dodd-Frank has created three thresholds: one for the large adviser, one for the mid-size adviser, and, logically, one for the small adviser. Let's examine each of these thresholds' requirements and exceptions, if any.

1. 5. 2. 2. 1 Large Investment Advisers

Large advisers, those advisers with at least $100 million or more in assets under management (AUM), are eligible for SEC registration; once AUM reach $110 million, registration with the SEC is mandatory. Unless covered by one of the exemptions mentioned previously, all large IAs must register with the SEC. State registration is not required because the NSMIA preempts state registration.

1. 5. 2. 2. 2 Small Investment Advisers

This category includes advisers with assets under management of less than $25 million. Unless the investment adviser is an adviser to an investment company registered under the Investment Company Act of 1940, registration with the SEC is prohibited and, unless exempted under state rules, registration with the state is required. In addition, if the adviser would be required to register in 15 or more states, registration with the SEC would be permitted instead. The only other specific exception is that if the IA has its principal office in a state that does not call for registration of IAs (that exception applied to Wyoming until July 1, 2017, when the state finally adopted investment adviser regulations), then registration with the SEC would be permitted. With Wyoming's change, it is highly unlikely this exception will be tested.

1. 5. 2. 2. 3 Mid-Size Advisers

This is a new category added by Dodd-Frank. It includes those with AUM of at least $25 million but not $100 million. Generally, these advisers are prohibited from SEC registration and must register with the state. However, there are more extensive exceptions than exist with the small advisers. Just as with any other category, those who are advisers to an investment company registered under the Investment Company Act of 1940 also register with the SEC. That is true regardless of their size.

There are several other ways for a mid-size firm to qualify for SEC registration. A mid-sized adviser is not prohibited from registering with the SEC:

- if the adviser is not required to be registered as an investment adviser with the securities Administrator of the state in which it maintains its principal office and place of business;
- if registered, the adviser would not be subject to examination as an investment adviser by that securities Administrator;
- if the adviser is required to register in 15 or more states; or
- if the adviser elects to take advantage of the buffer (described below).

1. 5. 2. 2. 4 Exceptions Under Dodd-Frank

The SEC is permitted to grant exceptions to advisers from the prohibition on commission registration, including small and mid-sized advisers, if the application of the prohibition from registration would be "unfair, a burden on interstate commerce, or otherwise inconsistent with the purposes" of the act. Under this authority, they have adopted several exemptions from the prohibition on registration, including:

- pension consultants, but only those with at least $200 million under control—the SEC picked that number to ensure that, in order to register with the SEC, the consultant's activities are "significant enough to have an effect on national markets";

- those mid-size advisers with at least $100 million in AUM, but less than $110 million in AUM who elect to register with the SEC rather than the state(s) (this buffer will be described below);
- investment advisers expecting to be eligible for SEC registration within 120 days of filing Form ADV; and
- multistate investment advisers (required to register in 15 or more states).

1. 5. 2. 2. 5   The $20 Million Buffer

The SEC recognized that market conditions (or obtaining or losing clients) can cause AUM to fluctuate, so they established a buffer to keep advisers from having to switch back and forth. The numbers work like this: once a state-registered adviser has assets under management of at least $100 million (subject to the exceptions previously mentioned; everyone needs at least $100 million to initiate registration with the SEC), it may choose to remain state-registered or register with the SEC. Once the AUM reach $110 million, registration with the SEC is mandatory—it can no longer stay state-registered. Then, once registered with the SEC, an investment adviser need not withdraw its SEC registration unless it has less than $90 million of assets under management. This means that an investment adviser can register with the SEC with AUM of as little as $100 million, but *must* register once AUM reach $110 million. Having become SEC registered, the IA can remain so, as long as AUM remain at or above the $90 million level. Likewise, those investment advisers registered at the state level can choose to remain there until they reach the $110 million level. This buffer is designed to avoid the expense and hassle involved in potentially annual changes to where the investment adviser is registered.

1. 5. 2. 2. 6   Time for Measuring AUM

These numbers are based on the AUM reported on the IA's annual updating amendment. The effect of this is that a federal covered adviser's AUM could drop below $90 million during the year without triggering the need to change to state registration, just as long as the annual update showed at least the minimum $90 million required. Of course, the same would be true of a state- registered adviser whose AUM peaked above $110 million during the year but then fell at the time of the update. If, at the time of filing the annual updating amendment to the Form ADV by an SEC-registered IA, the reported AUM is less than $90 million, it is necessary for the investment adviser to withdraw its SEC registration and register with the appropriate state(s) within 180 days. On the other hand, if a state-covered adviser's reported AUM exceed $110 million, registration with the SEC must take place within 90 days.

TEST TOPIC ALERT   An investment adviser registered under state law whose assets reach $110 million under management has 90 days to register with the SEC. A federal covered investment adviser whose assets under management fall below $90 million no longer qualifies for SEC registration and has 180 days to register with the state(s).

1. 5. 2. 3   Notice Filing for Federal Covered Investment Advisers

Even though these advisers are not defined as such under the Uniform Securities Act, Administrators still have the ability to request information about those firms who are doing business in their states. This is accomplished through the process of notice filing. As part of the notice filing procedure, the Administrator can require the federal covered investment adviser to submit copies of ALL documentation filed with the SEC and, of course, pay a filing fee.

Federal covered advisers must make a notice filing with the state if they have a place of business in the state or have six or more **retail** clients in that state in a twelve-month period, regardless of place of business.

1. 5. 2. 3. 1   Exceptions to the Notice Filing Requirements

Notice filing is not required by a federal covered investment adviser if the investment adviser has no place of business in this state and the adviser's only clients in this state are

- investment companies;
- other investment advisers;
- broker-dealers;
- banks, trust companies, savings and loan associations;
- insurance companies;
- employee benefit plans with assets of not less than one million dollars ($1,000,000); and
- governmental agencies or instrumentalities.

Alternatively, if during the preceding twelve-month period, the adviser has had no more than five clients, other than those specified in in the bullet points above, notice filing would not be required.

1. 5. 3   EXEMPTION FROM REGISTRATION FOR INVESTMENT ADVISERS

The USA exempts from registration certain persons who, although included in the definition of investment adviser (unlike those we've just been discussing who are excluded from the definition), do not have to register as such in the state. There are several categories of exemptions, and we'll examine the most common ones first.

1. 5. 3. 1   No Place of Business in This State Exemption

Among the exemptions from registration are advisers who have no place of business in this state but are registered in another state. This exemption applies only when the adviser's only clients in this state are:

- broker-dealers registered under the act;
- other investment advisers;
- institutional investors, including employee benefit plans with assets of not less than $1 million;
- existing clients who are not residents but are temporarily in this state (e.g., "snowbirds"); or
- any others the Administrator exempts by rule or order.

1. 5. 3. 1. 1   De Minimis Exemption

An exemption from registration is offered to an investment adviser who does not maintain a place of business in the state and limits its business to five or fewer retail clients who are legal residents in the state during the preceding 12 months. This is called the de minimis exemption and is derived from the Latin phrase which means "the law cares not for small things." (The English word *minimum* comes from the Latin *minimis*.)

TAKE NOTE

Because these exemptions all apply when the investment adviser does not have a place of business in the state, it is relevant to understand that an investment adviser or one of its representatives who advertises to the public, in any way, its availability for meeting with prospective clients in a hotel, seminar, or any other location in the state is considered to maintain a place of business in the state. However, an investment adviser representative who contacts clients in the state and notifies them that he will be passing through their town and is available to meet with them in his hotel room is not considered to have an office in the state because the announcement is being made only to existing clients and not to the public. If the IAR asks clients to bring their friends, the exemption is lost.

TEST TOPIC ALERT

The de minimis provision applies only to IAs and IARs, not to broker-dealers or agents.

EXAMPLE

How might this point be asked on the exam?

Wealth Management Experts (WME) is an investment adviser registered in State X, the location of its only offices. During the past 12 months, WME has directed investment advice to 6 individual clients in State Y. This means that WME

A.   is required to register in State Y because it has exceeded the de minimis limit

B.   is not required to register in State Y because it is within the de minimis limit

C.   does not need to register in State Y if that state has a reciprocal licensing arrangement with State X

D.   would be required to register in State Y as soon as advice was directed to a single retail client

What is the de minimis exemption? It is available to an investment adviser who does not maintain a place of business in the state and limits its business to 5 or fewer retail clients who are legal residents in the state during the preceding 12 months. That would make **A** the correct answer because 6 is above the limit of 5. There is no such thing as a reciprocal licensing arrangement between states.

How would things change if the question was worded to say that there were 6 clients, 3 of whom were retail and the other 3 insurance companies? In that case, no registration would be required because the retail clients are within the de minimis limit, and there is no limit on the number of institutional clients an investment adviser can have in a state without the need to register (as long as there is no place of business in the state).

Completing our example, suppose you had a question like this on your exam:

A state-registered investment adviser would NOT qualify for the de minimis exemption if, over a 12-month period, it had

A.   5 retail clients

B.   5 or fewer retail clients

C.   fewer than 6 retail clients

D.   6 or fewer retail clients

Because the maximum is 5 retail clients in a 12-month period, choice **D** with 6 clients is over the limit. Notice that, "fewer than 6" and "5 or fewer" mean the same thing.

1. 5. 3. 2   Exemption for Private Fund Advisers

December 2011 saw the adoption of the NASAA Registration Exemption for Investment Advisers to Private Funds Model Rule. The rule set out the conditions under which these advisers could qualify for the exemption. First, the adviser had to be one who provides advice solely and exclusively to one or more qualifying private funds.

1. 5. 3. 2. 1   Definition of a Private Fund

Although it is highly unlikely you will be tested on the technical definition, a private fund is defined as "an issuer that would be an investment company, as defined in section 3 of the Investment Company Act of 1940, but for section 3(c)(1) or 3(c)(7) of that Act."

In more straightforward terms, a 3(c)(1) issuer is one whose outstanding securities are beneficially owned by not more than 100 persons and which is not making and does not presently propose to make a public offering of its securities. With no more than 100 shareholders and no public offering, the term *private fund* seems quite logical. It gets a bit more complicated because there is a special condition that must be met:

■ All investors must be qualified. That is, they must have either at least $1 million in assets managed by the investment adviser, or a net worth (excluding the value of the primary residence) of at least $2.1 million. Remember, *value of primary residence* means the fair market value of a person's primary residence, minus the amount of debt secured by the property up to its fair market value (net equity).

A 3(c)(7) issuer is one whose outstanding securities are owned exclusively by persons who, at the time of acquisition of such securities, are qualified purchasers (a federal term referring to those with at least $5 million in investments for individuals and generally $25 million in investments for business entities), and which is not making and does not at that time propose to make a public offering of such securities. In this case, the lack of a public offering is logically private, and the fact that the invested wealth requirement limits the potential universe of investors is a factor as well.

Regardless of which classification the issuer of the private fund has, there are two final conditions that must be met:

■ Neither the private fund adviser nor any of its advisory affiliates are subject to an event that would disqualify an issuer under Rule 506(d)(1) of SEC Regulation D, (the "bad actor" provisions).

■ The private fund adviser files with the state the reports specified by the Securities and Exchange Commission for an exempt reporting adviser (ERA reports). These are reports that the SEC determines are "necessary or appropriate in the public interest or for the protection of investors."

The point is, regardless of how it's defined, if one is an adviser solely to private funds, it is possible to qualify for an exemption from registration with the Administrator.

TAKE NOTE   Please note that these exemptions are granted on the basis of who you advise, not on which types of securities are the subject of your advice. Note also that *exclusion* means exclusion from a definition, whereas *exemption* means not subject to registration. All of the cases mentioned here involve investment advisers; it's just that they qualify for an exemption from registration under state law.

1. 5. 4 REGISTERING WITH THE FORM ADV

The application for registration as an investment adviser is on the Form ADV. There are four parts to this form: Parts 1A and 1B and Parts 2A and 2B.

Part 1A contains information about the IA, including:

- location of the principal office;
- location of books and records (if not at the principal office);
- form of business organization (sole proprietorship, partnership, corporation);
- advisory activities (portfolio management for individuals, portfolio management for investment companies, financial planning services);
- other business activities (broker-dealer, agent of a broker-dealer);
- maintaining custody of customer assets or exercising discretion;
- details relating to all control persons (officers, directors, partners, etc.);
- disciplinary history; and
- states in which the IA intends to or is already registered.

Part 1B asks additional questions required by state securities authorities. Federal covered advisers do not complete Part 1B.

Part 2A is known as the investment adviser's brochure and tends to focus on customer-related information, such as:

- compensation arrangements (fees, commissions, hourly charges);
- types of clients (individuals, institutions, pension plans);
- type of investments recommended (equities, corporate debt, municipal securities, U.S. Treasuries, investment companies);
- types of strategies employed (buy and hold, value, growth);
- methods of analysis used (technical, fundamental);
- educational and business background of those who formulate investment advice for a client and have direct client contact, as well as those who have discretionary authority over a client's assets; and
- an audited balance sheet if the investment adviser requires or solicits substantial prepayment of fees or maintains custody.

The brochure is arranged in a narrative form using plain English. Part 2B requires advisers to create brochure supplements containing information about certain supervised persons. Together, Part 2A and Part 2B are delivered to the client as described later at 4.5.4

State registered advisers file both Part 1 and Part 2 with the Administrator of each state in which they are registering. Similar to the case with broker-dealers, anytime there is a material change to the information on the Form ADV, an amended copy must be filed with the Administrator.

TAKE NOTE

Although there are no minimum educational or experience requirements, there is a specific area on the Form ADV Part 2 where state-registered advisers must identify each of the principal executive officers and management persons, and describe their formal education and business background. If this information has been supplied elsewhere in the Form ADV, it is not necessary to repeat it in response to this question.

TEST TOPIC ALERT

Under the USA, if a federal covered investment adviser has an office in the state, the Administrator may require, by rule or by order, that the IA submit any documents that have been filed with the SEC. A federal covered IA submits only Part 1A of the Form ADV. Therefore, if the Administrator requests the Form ADV, all that will be sent is Part 1A. If it is a state-registered adviser, the investment adviser has already filed Parts 1A and 1B.

TAKE NOTE

Because it is important that clients and prospective clients understand that the state, or the SEC if appropriate, is not approving the adviser's information or the adviser's methods of business, it is required that the cover page of Part 2A contain the following statement:

This brochure provides information about the qualifications and business practices of (name of the IA). If you have any questions about the contents of this brochure, please contact us at (phone number and/or email address). The information in this brochure has not been approved or verified by the SEC or by any state securities authority.

1. 5. 5 FINANCIAL REQUIREMENTS FOR INVESTMENT ADVISERS

Under the USA, the Administrator may, by rule or order, establish minimum financial requirements for an investment adviser registered in the state. The Administrator may require an adviser who has custody of client funds or securities or has discretion over a client's account to post a surety bond or maintain a minimum net worth. Usually, the requirement is higher for custody than for discretion. Typically, the net worth required of investment advisers with discretionary authority is $10,000 and that for those taking custody is $35,000.

TAKE NOTE

Because the USA is only a template, some states have higher net worth or bonding requirements. The exam may want you to know that if an IA meets the net worth or surety bonding requirements of the state where its principal office is located, that is sufficient in any other state in which it may be registered.

QUICK QUIZ 1.F

Write **A** if the phrase describes an investment adviser that must register under the USA and **B** if it does not.

_____ 1. Publisher of a newspaper that renders general financial advice

_____ 2. Broker-dealer that charges a fee for providing investment advice over and above commissions from securities transactions

_____ 3. Investment adviser that manages $10 million in assets

_____ 4. Publisher of a monthly investment newsletter with an annual subscription fee that does not render specific advice based on the needs of any subscriber

5. If a prospective client wanted to know what type of investment strategies are used by an investment adviser, that information would be found in the adviser's
    A. Form ADV Part 1A
    B. Form ADV Part 1B
    C. Form ADV Part 2A
    D. Form ADV Part 2B

6. Mammon Money Managers (MMM) has its principal office in State A and is also registered in States B, C, and D. MMM exercises discretion in client accounts. As a result, MMM would have to meet the net worth or bonding requirements of
    A. the SEC
    B. State A
    C. the state with the highest requirement
    D. each state

7. Thomas Hobson is the founder and principal owner of Hobson Investment Strategies (HIS). HIS has its principal office in State A and also has branches in States B, C, and D. On its last annual updating amendment, HIS reported AUM of $300 million. HIS maintains custody of client assets. As a result, when it comes to meeting financial requirements, Hobson's choice would be adhering to those of
    A. the SEC
    B. State A
    C. the state with the highest requirements
    D. the state where the custody is maintained

1. 6   INVESTMENT ADVISER REPRESENTATIVE

Investment adviser representative (IAR) means any partner, officer, director (or an individual occupying a similar status or performing similar functions), or other individual employed by or associated with an investment adviser that is registered or required to be registered under the Uniform Securities Act (state-registered IA). If employed by or associated with a federal covered adviser, this individual only comes under the registration requirements by having a place of business in the state. In both cases (state or federal), the individual meets the definition of an IAR by doing any of the following:

- Making any recommendations or otherwise rendering advice regarding securities
- Managing accounts or portfolios of clients
- Determining which recommendation or advice regarding securities should be given
- Soliciting, offering or negotiating for the sale of, or selling investment advisory services
- Supervising employees who perform any of the foregoing

TAKE NOTE   The use of the term *individual* here is important. Only an individual, or a natural person, can be an investment adviser representative. The investment advisory firm is the legal person (entity) that the IAR (natural person) represents in performing the above listed functions.

1. 6. 1   REGISTRATION REQUIREMENTS FOR INVESTMENT ADVISER REPRESENTATIVES

It is unlawful for any state-registered investment adviser to employ an investment adviser representative unless the investment adviser representative is registered under this act. However, the registration of an investment adviser representative is not effective during any period when she is not employed by an investment adviser registered under this act. The same holds true for a federal covered adviser to employ, supervise, or associate with an investment adviser representative having a place of business located in this state, unless such investment adviser representative is registered under this act or is exempt from registration.

TEST TOPIC ALERT   The effect of the previous statement (found in Section 203A of the Investment Advisers Act of 1940), is that for those performing as IARs for federal covered advisers, state registration is required only in those states where that individual has a place of business. Place of business of an investment adviser representative means:

(1) an office at which the investment adviser representative regularly provides investment advisory services, solicits, meets with, or otherwise communicates with clients; and

(2) any other location that is held out to the general public as a location at which the investment adviser representative provides investment advisory services, solicits, meets with, or otherwise communicates with clients.

Just as was the case described earlier with a broker-dealer, registration of an investment adviser also leads to automatic investment adviser representative registration of partners, officers, or directors active in the business, and anyone else performing a similar function.

Many independent financial planners operate as independent contractors, not employees of investment advisory firms or broker-dealers. Regardless, they are required to be registered as investment adviser representatives of the firm and must be placed under the same level of supervisory scrutiny as employees. Their business cards may contain the name of their separate planning entity but must also disclose the name of the entity registered as the investment adviser.

TEST TOPIC ALERT   Registered investment advisers are responsible for the supervision of individuals registered as investment adviser representatives, but acting in the capacity of independent contractors, to the same extent that they supervise those who are actual employees of the firm.

TEST TOPIC ALERT   Registration as an IAR is done solely on a state basis. IARs never register with the SEC, even when they are representing a federal covered adviser. That is why it is NASAA who has the responsibility for this exam, rather than FINRA or the SEC.

TAKE NOTE   An individual may act as both an investment adviser and an investment adviser representative. This is typically the case when the business is organized as a sole proprietorship. However, an individual who acts solely as an investment adviser representative is excluded from the definition of investment adviser.

1. 6. 1. 1 Financial Requirements of IARs

Unlike an investment adviser, there are no financial requirements, or net worth requirements, to register as an investment adviser representative. However, as with the other securities professionals, insolvency (bankruptcy) is a cause for denial or revocation of registration.

In our many years of preparing applicants for this exam, one thing we have observed is that many students do not have a clear idea of the difference between a broker-dealer and an investment adviser and, similarly, between an agent and an investment adviser representative. Perhaps the following will help:

Broker-Dealer	Investment Adviser
■ Primary business function is executing transactions in securities	■ Primary business function is giving advice
■ Compensation is earned in the form of commissions and markups (markdowns)	■ Compensation is earned in the form of fees or other charges, generally based on the amount of assets managed

Agents	IARs
■ Individuals employed by broker-dealers to handle their customer orders to buy or sell securities	■ Individuals employed by investment advisers to give advice to their clients
■ Separate function from an IAR (although many in large firms wear both hats)	■ After an IAR advises a client about a specific security, the next step is to contact the broker-dealer where that client maintains a brokerage account to give the buy/sell order to an agent

1.6.2 EXCLUSIONS FROM THE DEFINITION OF INVESTMENT ADVISER REPRESENTATIVE

Certain employees of investment advisory firms are excluded from the term *investment adviser representative*, provided their activities are confined to clerical duties or those activities that are solely incidental to the investment advisory services offered, such as mailing out a research report to an advisory client when directed by an IAR. Should the investment advisory employee *step over the line*, as the saying goes, and perform any activity that makes one an IAR, the employee would then have to register as an investment adviser representative. Exclusion criteria for administrative employees of investment advisers are much the same as those for administrative personnel of broker-dealers.

TAKE NOTE   Although not specifically tested, you should know that to become an investment adviser representative, one must pass either the NASAA Series 65 or Series 66 exam. In some jurisdictions, a FINRA exam, such as the Series 6 or Series 7, must also be completed.

QUICK QUIZ 1.G   True or False?

_____   1. An investment adviser representative must register with the SEC if she has clients with assets of $110 million or more under management.

_____   2. An employee of an investment advisory firm is an investment adviser representative if his duties are limited to clerical activities.

_____   3. An administrative employee who receives specific compensation for offering investment advisory services is not an investment adviser representative.

_____   4. An employee of an investment advisory firm is an investment adviser representative if his duties involve making investment recommendations.

5. Under the USA, the term *investment adviser representative* would NOT include
   A. an officer of a registered investment advisory firm whose responsibility includes supervision of solicitors
   B. an associated person of the firm who, from time to time, makes specific recommendations to clients
   C. a payroll clerk employed by an advisory firm whose responsibilities include computing the earnings of investment adviser representatives
   D. a new employee of an advisory firm who has only been able to sign up 2 clients in his first 4 months

6. Risible Research and Recommendations, Inc. (RRR) is an investment adviser registered in State P. Last year's updating amendment to its Form ADV showed AUM of $85 million. Business has been very good this year and it is anticipated that the next updating amendment will show AUM of about $125 million. The effect of this would be

   A. RRR would continue its registration in State P
   B. RRR would continue its registration in State P while also registering with the SEC
   C. RRR would have the choice of registering with the SEC or remaining registered in State P
   D. RRR would have 90 days to register with the SEC and withdraw its registration from State P

7. Wilson Erving works for Broad Street Limited (BSL) a registered investment adviser. Wilson limits his advice exclusively to equity securities traded on the Nasdaq Stock Market. Under the USA, Wilson

   A. must register as an IAR
   B. does not need to register as an IAR
   C. would need registration as a federal covered IAR
   D. is not covered by the anti-fraud rules because these are federal covered securities

1. 7   SUMMARY OF THE FOUR SECURITIES PROFESSIONALS

Now that we have defined the four categories of securities professionals, here is an explanatory summary. Many students, particularly those without any securities background, seem to have a problem sorting out who is who. Perhaps the following will help.

A **broker-dealer** is a business entity. From a legal standpoint, this entity may be organized as a sole proprietorship, but, in the real world, there are less than a handful of FINRA members who are. Virtually every BD is a corporation, partnership, or LLC. The primary business function of all broker-dealers is the **execution of securities transactions**, either for their clients or for their own accounts. These firms hire individuals, known on this exam as agents, to work for them. You may have heard the term stockbroker, registered rep, account executive, and so forth, but on this exam, they are only called agents.

The role of an **agent** is to represent her employer (the broker-dealer) in working with clients or supervising those who do. Upon completing the registration requirements, including passing this exam, a person will be an agent.

An **investment adviser**, like a broker-dealer, is a business entity. Unlike broker-dealers, there are a number of IAs who are organized as sole proprietorships. There is a reason for this, but it is totally unrelated to anything you will ever have to know for the exam. Still, most investment advisers are structured as corporations, partnerships, or LLCs. The primary function of every investment adviser is, as the name implies, to give **investment advice**. They do *not* engage in securities transactions—that is the role of a BD.

Just as broker-dealers hire individuals (agents) to work for them, investment advisers hire individuals, known as **investment adviser representatives**, to represent them in the rendering of investment advice. Once again, we have an employer/employee relationship.

There are many firms that are registered as both broker-dealers and investment advisers. Therefore, there are many individuals who are agents as well as IARs. These are two different roles that perform different functions. Hopefully, this summary makes it clear what these are.

QUICK QUIZ 1.H

1. Under the USA, which of the following automatically becomes registered as an agent when a broker-dealer registration becomes effective?
   A. Only the designated supervisory principal
   B. Any partner, officer, or person of similar status or similar function whose activities fall under the definition of an agent
   C. All agents currently registered with FINRA through that broker-dealer
   D. No one

2. Under the USA, which of the following statements regarding the registration of a successor firm is(are) TRUE?
   A. The appropriate filing fee must be included with the application.
   B. The successor firm must be in existence before the filing of the application.
   C. The registration of the successor firm will be effective until the December 31 renewal date.
   D. All of the above.

True or False?

_____ 3. A consent to service of process must be submitted with each renewal application.

_____ 4. An Administrator may establish net capital requirements for agents of broker-dealers.

_____ 5. When a securities professional registers in a state, he must provide the state Administrator with a list of all states in which he intends to register.

_____ 6. A Canadian broker-dealer, properly registered with the Administrator of the province in which he is headquartered and with no office in the state, may do business with his customers who are on a skiing vacation in Vail without registering with the Colorado Administrator.

U N I T   T E S T

1. Which of the following would be an agent under the terms of the USA?

    I. A sales representative of a licensed broker-dealer who sells securities in the secondary markets to the general public
    II. An assistant to the president of a broker-dealer who, for administrative purposes, accepts orders on behalf of the senior partners
    III. A subsidiary of a major commercial bank registered as a broker-dealer that sells securities to the public
    IV. An issuer of nonexempt securities registered in the state and sold to the general public

    A. I and II
    B. I, II, and III
    C. III and IV
    D. I, II, III, and IV

2. A publicly traded corporation offers its employees an opportunity to purchase shares of the company's common stock directly from the issuer. A specific employee of the company is designated to process orders for that stock. Under the Uniform Securities Act, the employee

    A. must register as an agent of the issuer
    B. need not register as an agent of the issuer under any circumstances
    C. may receive commissions without registration
    D. must register as an agent if he will receive commissions or remuneration either directly or indirectly

3. Registration as an investment adviser would be required for any firm in the business of giving advice on the purchase of

    A. convertible bonds
    B. gold coins
    C. rare convertible automobiles
    D. apartments undergoing a conversion to condominiums

4. Under the Uniform Securities Act, which of the following requires registration as an investment adviser representative?

    A. An employee, highly skilled in evaluating securities, who performs administrative or clerical functions for an investment adviser
    B. An individual who renders fee-based advice on precious metals
    C. A solicitor for an investment advisory firm who is paid a fee for his services
    D. An agent of a broker-dealer who offers incidental advice on securities as part of his sales commissions

5. Under the Uniform Securities Act, all of the following may provide investment advice incidental to their normal business without having to register as an investment adviser EXCEPT

    A. a teacher
    B. an economist
    C. a lawyer
    D. an engineer

6. Which of the following persons is defined as an agent by the Uniform Securities Act?

    A. Silent partner of a broker-dealer
    B. Secretary of a branch office sales manager
    C. Clerk at a broker-dealer who is authorized to take orders
    D. An officer of a broker-dealer who does not solicit or transact securities business

7. Under the Uniform Securities Act, any partner, officer, or director of a registered investment adviser is an investment adviser representative if he

    I. offers advice concerning securities
    II. manages client accounts or portfolios
    III. determines securities recommendations for representatives to disseminate
    IV. supervises personnel engaged in the above activities but does not sell these services to the public

    A. I only
    B. I and II
    C. I, II, and III
    D. I, II, III, and IV

8. Under the Uniform Securities Act, an agent is
   A. a broker-dealer who sells registered securities to the general public
   B. an individual who represents an investment adviser
   C. an individual representing a broker-dealer who sells securities exempt from registration under the act
   D. an individual who represents an issuer in an exempt transaction

9. For purposes of the definition found in Rule 501 of Regulation D of the Securities Act of 1933, the term accredited investor would not apply to
   A. an investment adviser representative
   B. an investment company registered under the Investment Company Act of 1940
   C. an officer of the company involved in the underwriting
   D. a large employee benefit plan

10. Under the Uniform Securities Act, an investment adviser is all of the following EXCEPT
   I. a broker-dealer who charges for investment advice
   II. a publisher of a financial newspaper
   III. a person who sells security analysis
   IV. a CPA who, as an incidental part of her practice, suggests tax-sheltered investments to her affluent clients

   A. I and II
   B. II and III
   C. II and IV
   D. III and IV

11. Under the Uniform Securities Act, the term person would include all of the following EXCEPT
   A. an unincorporated association
   B. a child prodigy, gifted in math, in the custody of his parents, for whom his parents opened an account at a major securities firm
   C. a political subdivision
   D. an individual

12. Under the USA, which of the following is considered a broker-dealer in a state?
   A. First Federal Company Trust
   B. XYZ broker-dealer with an office in the state whose only clients are insurance companies
   C. An agent effecting transactions for a broker-dealer
   D. A broker-dealer with no place of business in the state who only does business with other broker-dealers

13. Which of the following must register as an agent?
   A. An individual representing a broker-dealer who sells commercial paper
   B. An individual who sells commercial paper for ABC National Bank
   C. An employee of the Fed whose job is selling Treasury bonds to the public
   D. An individual who is paid a commission to sell certificates of deposit for ABC National Bank

14. A broker-dealer hires two individuals to solicit and prequalify new customers for the firm's newest branch office. Under the USA,
   A. they may begin soliciting as soon as they have passed their licensing examinations
   B. soliciting is generally prohibited
   C. each of them would have to register as an investment adviser
   D. registration as agents is required

15. All of the following would meet the definition of investment adviser under the Uniform Securities Act EXCEPT
   A. a broker-dealer charging separately for investment advice
   B. the publisher of a weekly magazine, sold on newsstands, that contains at least 5 stock recommendations per issue
   C. a civil damages attorney who advertises that he is available to assist clients by suggesting appropriate investments for their successful claims
   D. a finance teacher at a local community college who offers weekend seminars on comprehensive financial planning at a very reasonable price

16. The term *agent* would include
    A. an employee of a broker-dealer whose sole responsibility is filing paid bills and similar documents
    B. a receptionist operating the switchboard at the office of a broker-dealer
    C. a minority stockholder whose only activity is soliciting new clients
    D. the operator of the word processing equipment used as a desktop publishing system to prepare the broker-dealer's weekly list of recommendations

17. With regard to state-registered investment advisers, all of the following statements regarding the powers of the Administrator are true EXCEPT
    A. the Administrator may request submission of literature used by the adviser to solicit new business
    B. the Administrator must be provided with a detailed description of the adviser's proposed method of selecting investments
    C. an investment adviser's registration must be renewed each December 31
    D. the Administrator may rule that custody of client funds is not permissible

18. A broker-dealer, having no place of business in the state, would be exempt from registration under the Uniform Securities Act if its only clients were
    I. banks or other financial institutions
    II. investment companies
    III. accredited investors

    A. I and II
    B. I and III
    C. II and III
    D. I, II, and III

19. Which of the following statements regarding a broker-dealer's withdrawal of registration under the Uniform Securities Act are TRUE?
    I. Unless a proceeding is involved, withdrawal will become effective 30 days after application unless the Administrator elects to shorten the period.
    II. Unless a proceeding is involved, withdrawal will become effective 30 days after application unless the Administrator elects to lengthen the period.
    III. Once withdrawal becomes effective, the Administrator can no longer commence an action against the former broker-dealer.
    IV. If an action is commenced against the broker-dealer after application for withdrawal is filed, but before the 30th day, effectiveness of the withdrawal is withheld until resolution of the action.

    A. I and III
    B. I and IV
    C. II and III
    D. II and IV

20. Under the USA, an investment adviser with no place of business in the state would be required to register if its only clients in the state are
    A. banks
    B. insurance companies
    C. 6 or fewer individual clients
    D. closed-end investment companies

21. An investment adviser would be exempt from registration under the Uniform Securities Act if it had no place of business in the state and
    I. it offered their services to no more than 5 individuals in that state during any consecutive 12-month period
    II. it offered their services to fewer than 15 individuals in that state during any consecutive 12-month period
    III. its only clients were registered investment companies
    IV. its only clients were broker-dealers and other investment advisers

    A. I and III
    B. I, III, and IV
    C. II and III
    D. II and IV

22. During the application process for registration as an agent, the Administrator may NOT request information about the applicant's

    A. annual income
    B. citizenship
    C. record involving a securities-related misdemeanor conviction 5 years ago
    D. permanent residence address

23. A broker-dealer is registered in state X. It has no offices in state Y, although it does do business in that state. Under the Uniform Securities Act, registration in Y is required if the client is

    A. a bank
    B. a broker-dealer
    C. an insurance company
    D. an investment adviser representative

24. In the absence of any other possible exemption, registration with the SEC would be prohibited for which of the following investment advisers?

    A. A pension consultant managing $150 million
    B. An adviser to an open-end investment company with $18 million in assets
    C. An adviser whose assets under management are $103 million
    D. An adviser who would be required to register in 17 states

25. Records that must be kept by a broker-dealer include all of the following EXCEPT

    A. copies of emails sent to customers
    B. blotters
    C. customer tax returns
    D. customer ledgers

ANSWERS AND RATIONALES

1. **A.** Under the USA, only individuals can be agents. A person who sells securities for a broker-dealer is an agent. An administrative person, such as the assistant to the president of a broker-dealer, is considered an agent if he takes securities orders from the public. Corporate entities are excluded from the definition of agent. Broker-dealers and issuers are not agents.

2. **D.** Under the USA, an individual is an agent when effecting transactions with an issuer's existing employees if commissions are paid. Therefore, there are cases where the employee would have to register as an agent.

3. **A.** Only persons in the business of giving advice on securities are required to register as investment advisers. Only the convertible bonds are securities.

4. **C.** A solicitor is considered an investment adviser representative under the Uniform Securities Act. An employee who performs only clerical or administrative functions is not an investment adviser representative. Precious metals are not securities; therefore, a person advising on them is not considered an investment adviser representative. An agent is a representative of a broker-dealer, and, as long as the only form of compensation is sales commissions, registration as an investment adviser representative is not required.

5. **B.** The Uniform Securities Act does not exclude economists from the definition of investment adviser as it does lawyers, accountants, teachers, and engineers who give advice that is incidental to the practice of their professions. Remember the acronym *LATE*—lawyers, accountants, teachers, and engineers. Test takers often mistake the *E* in LATE for economist.

6. **C.** Anyone who solicits or receives an order while representing a broker-dealer is an agent. Silent partners and administrative personnel are not agents under the terms of the USA if they do not solicit or receive orders. As long as the officer has no supervisory role, or other active participation in the securities business of the broker-dealer, the USA does not consider this position to require registration as an agent. An example might be the vice-president of human resources. Remember, broker-dealers are not agents; agents represent broker-dealers. If, however, any of these individuals were authorized to accept orders, registration as an agent would be required.

7. **D.** The Uniform Securities Act defines persons associated with an investment adviser as investment adviser representatives, including any partner, officer, or director who offers advice concerning securities. Persons who manage client accounts or portfolios, determine securities recommendations, or supervise personnel engaged in the above activities are investment adviser representatives.

8. **C.** An individual employed by a broker-dealer who sells securities to the public is an agent under the Uniform Securities Act. The USA defines an agent as "any individual other than a broker-dealer who represents a broker-dealer or issuer in effecting or attempting to effect purchases or sales of securities." The law excludes from the definition of agent individuals who represent an issuer in exempt transactions, the sale of exempt securities, and transactions with issuers' employees when no commission is paid. There is virtually no case in which a salesperson representing a broker-dealer is not an agent.

9. **A.** An individual is not an accredited investor solely by virtue of being an IAR. If that person has the net worth or income specified in the rule, then they meet the qualifications of such, but just being in the business does not qualify someone.

10. **C.** A publisher of a financial newspaper and a CPA who, as an incidental part of her practice, suggests tax-sheltered investments are not investment advisers.

11. **B.** The term *person* is extremely broad. Excluded from the term would be a minor, a deceased individual, and one who has legally been determined incompetent.

12. **B.** Any broker-dealer with an office in the state, regardless of the nature of its clients, is defined as a broker-dealer under the USA. If the firm did not have an office in the state and its only clients were institutions (such as insurance companies) or other broker-dealers, it would be excluded from the definition. Banks or trust companies and agents are never broker-dealers.

13. **A.** An individual who represents a broker-dealer and sells any security must register under the USA. The securities (commercial paper) are exempt; nevertheless, the representative must be registered as an agent of the broker-dealer. An individual who sells commercial paper for ABC National Bank would not have to register because the bank is excluded from the definition of broker-dealer. An employee of the federal government need not register with the state because he represents an exempt issuer. An individual who is paid a commission to sell certificates of deposit for a commercial bank does not have to register as an agent because he is not selling a security.

14. **D.** The definition of agents includes individuals who solicit and prequalify clients for the firm's business, whether for a new branch office or an existing one.

15. **B.** Publishers of general circulation newspapers and magazines are excluded from the definition of investment adviser, even if the entire publication is devoted to investment advice. A broker-dealer loses its exclusion the moment it offers advice for a separate charge, as does an attorney who holds himself out as offering investment advice. Normally, a teacher is excluded, but not when charging for advice, as would appear to be the case here. On this examination, the term *comprehensive financial planning* always includes securities advice.

16. **C.** Clerical and administrative employees are not considered to be agents. Minority stockholder or not, someone involved in soliciting accounts would be an agent.

17. **B.** It is not required that an investment adviser disclose to the Administrator the methods he uses to select investments.

18. **A.** Do not be misled by the term *accredited investor*. It has absolutely no meaning other than when referring to a private placement of securities under the Securities Act of 1933. This term will appear frequently on the exam out of context (i.e., unrelated to private placements). Whenever it does, you can make the question easier by replacing the term with the phrase *ordinary public investor who needs all of the protection available under the law*. As long as the broker-dealer has no place of business in the state, it is exempt from registration if its only clients are institutional investors such as banks, insurance companies, investment companies, other investment advisers, broker-dealers, $1 million or larger employee benefit plans, college endowment funds, and governmental units.

19. **B.** Withdrawal of registration normally becomes effective 30 days after application. The Administrator may shorten that period but may not lengthen it unless an action against the BD is commenced. Once an action is commenced, withdrawal may not take effect until resolution of the case. The Administrator may take action against any registrant for up to one year after withdrawal.

20. **C.** Under the Uniform Securities Act, an investment adviser with no place of business in the state is exempt if its clients are institutional (banks, insurance companies, investment companies, and so forth). But, when the advice is given to more than 5 non-institutional clients who are residents of the state, registration is required.

21. **B.** To enable an investment adviser to service a small number of clients in neighboring states without the hassles of registration, the de minimis requirements allow offers to up to 5 persons, other than institutional accounts, during any 12-month period. There is no limit to the number of institutional clients (e.g., investment companies and broker-dealers) an out-of-state adviser can have and still be exempt from registration in that state.

22. **A.** The earnings of an agent are not within the purview of the Administrator and are not pertinent to an applicant for registration. The Administrator asks all registrants about their address—in the case of individuals, their home address. Individual registrants may be asked about their citizenship. Being charged with or convicted of any securities-related misdemeanor must be reported, although denial is generally reserved for convictions within the past 10 years.

23. **D.** Broker-dealers must always register in a state if they do business with noninstitutional clients, regardless of the nature of the individual's employer.

24. **A.** In order for a pension consultant to be eligible for SEC registration, it must manage at least $200 million. An investment adviser to an investment company always registers with the SEC, regardless of the size of the fund. Advisers who would otherwise be required to register in 15 or more states qualify for an exception, and once an investment adviser has reached the $100 million threshold, SEC registration is permitted (not required until reaching $110 million).

25. **C.** It is not required that any securities professional maintain copies of customers' tax returns. Copies of all customer-related correspondence, including that by electronic means, must be kept for a period of 3 years.

QUICK QUIZ ANSWERS

Quick Quiz 1.A

1. **T.** Governments and political subdivisions are considered persons under the act. Remember there are only three choices that are not a person—minors, persons since deceased, and those judged mentally incompetent.

2. **F.** In order for an employee benefit plan to be included in the definition of institution, it must have assets of not less than $1 million.

3. **A.** The USA specifies that a state's securities Administrator has the authority to enforce the act in that state. A transfer agent is the person or corporation responsible for recording the names and holdings of registered security owners.

Quick Quiz 1.B

1. **T.** A person who effects transactions in securities for itself or for the account of others must register in the state as a broker-dealer unless specifically excluded from the definition.

2. **T.** A firm with an out-of-state registration is not considered a broker-dealer in that state if transacting business with a customer who is passing through the state on vacation.

3. **T.** If a person is excluded from the definition, that person need not register as a broker-dealer; however, if not excluded, the person must register.

4. **F.** Any broker-dealer registered in several states is also going to be registered with the SEC. Under the NSMIA, federal law always trumps state law, so the only requirement to be met is that of the SEC.

5. **C.** A broker-dealer is any person, partner, officer, director, or securities firm engaged in the business of effecting securities transactions for the accounts of others (broker) or for its own account (dealer).

Quick Quiz 1.C

1. **D.** As long as the individual represents the issuer in a transaction involving exempted securities, he is not included in the definition of agent, even when the transaction is non-exempt. But, when the securities themselves are non-exempt and the transactions are non-exempt, the individual is defined as an agent. And, yes, you may see this many negatives in a single question. Notice that a 19-month commercial paper is not exempt, but the other choices are.

2. **B.** There is almost no case where an individual performing a sales function for a broker-dealer is not an agent. Clerical persons are not agents, nor are officers with no apparent sales function. Anytime an individual represents the *issuer* in an *exempt transaction*, that individual is not defined as an *agent* under the USA.

3. **B.** Although each of these choices is an exempt security under the USA, only those issued by banks, savings institutions, and trust companies are in the group of 5 that exempt the individual representing the issuer from being defined as an agent.

Quick Quiz 1.D

1. **A.** Persons must be registered as agents when they effect transactions on behalf of broker-dealers, whether the securities are exempt or not.

2. **A.** Any individual taking orders on behalf of a broker-dealer must be registered, regardless of whether or not they receive a commission.

3. **B.** An employee who represents an issuer of exempt securities (a bank) in selling its securities does not register as an agent because such an individual is not an agent under the USA.

4. **A.** A person who represents an employer in selling securities to employees must register as an agent if the person receives a commission. If no commission is paid, registration is not necessary.

5. **B.** Persons who represent issuers in securities transactions with underwriters need not register as agents because this is an exempt transaction.

6. **A.** It is Form U4 that is most commonly used when registering as an agent of a broker-dealer. Changes to material information, such as home address or a bankruptcy filing, are accomplished by filing an amended Form U4 within 30 days. Form U5 is used for terminations.

Quick Quiz 1.E

1. **B.** Although lawyers are generally excluded from the definition of investment adviser, that exclusion holds true only if the advice given is solely incidental to the practice of the profession and no separate fees are charged. The separate billing here is what loses the exclusion. Remember, investment adviser representatives are not investment advisers, just as agents are not broker-dealers.

2. **C.** Execution of trades is the role of the broker-dealer, not an investment adviser.

Quick Quiz 1.F

1. **B.** Publishers of newspapers and magazines of general circulation that offer general financial advice need not register.

2. **A.** Broker-dealers must register as investment advisers if they receive special or separate compensation for giving investment advice.

3. **A.** Unless qualifying for an exception (don't assume such—it would have to be stated in the question), an investment adviser that manages less than $100 million in assets must register as an investment adviser under the USA. If the client is an investment company registered under the Investment Company Act of 1940, registration with the SEC is mandatory, regardless of the amount under management.

4. **B.** The exclusion pertaining to securities advisory publishers includes newsletter publishers who do not give advice to subscribers on the subscriber's specific investment situation and who publish on a regular basis.

5. **C.** The Form ADV Part 2A contains the most useful information to clients, such as the type of strategies used by the adviser. Part 1A contains information needed by the regulators; Part 1B is only for state-registered IAs; and Part 2B contains information dealing with individuals in the firm who manage accounts.

6. **B.** A state-registered investment adviser only needs to meet the financial requirements of the state in which its principal office is located. SEC requirements are meaningless here because this is a state-registered firm.

7. **A.** With AUM of $300 million, Hobson Investment Strategies is a federal covered adviser. Therefore, no state may impose financial or recordkeeping requirements; it is only those of the SEC that must be followed.

Quick Quiz 1.G

1. **F.** An investment adviser (not the investment adviser representative) must register with the SEC if the firm manages assets of $110 million or more. The individual would have to be registered as an investment adviser representative in the state(s) in which she does business with retail clients.

2. **F.** An employee of an investment advisory firm is not an investment adviser representative if his duties are confined to clerical activities.

3. **F.** Any employee who receives specific compensation for offering investment advisory services is considered an investment adviser representative.

4. **T.** Any employee of an investment advisory firm is an investment adviser representative if his duties involve making investment recommendations.

5. **C.** Clerical and administrative personnel are excluded from the definition of investment adviser representative. Remember, the definition includes anyone who makes recommendations (even if only upon occasion), manages accounts, solicits accounts, or supervises any of the above.

6. **D.** Once a state-registered investment adviser's annual amendment to its Form ADV shows AUM of $110 million or more, the IA has 90 days to register with the SEC and withdraw from state registration. An investment adviser has the option of state or SEC registration only when AUM is at least $100 million, but not $110 million.

7. **A.** If an individual works for an investment adviser and dispenses advice, he must register as an IAR, regardless of the nature of the securities that are the subject of his advice. There is no such thing as a federal covered IAR, only a federal covered IA. If the advice relates to securities, no one is exempt from the anti-fraud rules. Note that the question did not specify if BSL was federal covered or state-registered because it doesn't make a difference. An individual giving advice while working for an investment adviser would have to be registered in at least one state as an IAR.

Quick Quiz 1.H

1. **B.** Registration of a broker-dealer automatically constitutes registration of any individual meeting the definition of an agent who is a partner, officer, or director, or a person occupying a similar status or performing similar functions.

2. **C.** No filing fee is necessary, nor is it required that the successor firm even be in existence at the time of filing. The registration is effective for the unexpired portion of the year and then must be renewed (with a renewal fee) each December 31.

3. **F.** A consent to service of process is filed with the initial application and permanently remains on file with the Administrator.

4. **F.** There are no financial requirements for an agent (other than perhaps the need to post a bond if exercising discretion in clients' accounts. It is the broker-dealer who has a minimum net capital requirement.

5. **F.** A list of other states in which a securities professional intends to register is not required on a state application for registration.

6. **F.** In order to do business with their Canadian customers who are temporarily in any state(s), Canadian broker-dealers (and their agents) must obtain a form of limited registration.

2

Regulations of Securities and Issuers

State securities Administrators regulate securities transactions that occur in their states similarly to the way they regulate persons engaged in those transactions. This unit discusses the procedures for the registration of securities as well as their exemptions from registration. For a securities transaction to be lawful under the USA, the security itself must be registered unless it or the transaction is exempt from registration requirements.

The Series 63 exam will include 3 questions on the material presented in this unit. ■

Please Note: There is a great deal of material covered in this unit, considering that only 3 questions will appear on the exam. It is necessary to include all of this because those few questions will be drawn from the breadth of the topic.

When you have completed this unit, you should be able to:

- **recognize** what is and is not a security;

- **determine** who is and is not a security issuer;

- **compare** and contrast the different methods of securities registration;

- **identify** instruments that are securities;

- **list** the categories of exempt securities;

- **define** an exempt transaction and provide examples; and

- **describe** the requirements for exemption from registration for private placements.

2. 1   WHAT IS A SECURITY UNDER THE UNIFORM SECURITIES ACT?

Perhaps the most important term in the Uniform Securities Act is the term *security*. Why is it so important? The reason is simple: the USA applies only to those financial instruments that are securities. The purchase, sale, or issuance of anything that is not a security is not covered by the act. The definition of a security, however, is complex. Over the years, courts have determined case by case what constitutes a security. The U.S. Supreme Court, in the Howey decision, defined the primary characteristics of what constitutes a security. Howey is still the leading case on the definition of an *investment contract* (a security). For an instrument to be a security, the court held, it must constitute (1) an investment of money, (2) in a common enterprise, (3) with the expectation of profits, (4) to be derived primarily from the efforts of a person other than the investor. A **common enterprise** means an enterprise in which the fortunes of the investor are interwoven with those of either the person offering the investment, a third party, or other investors.

EXAMPLE   Let's show how common stock in a corporation meets the Howey definition. If you purchase shares, you have invested money (1), as have a number of other investors (2), hoping to make money by receiving dividends or selling the stock at a profit (3), and your success depends not on your efforts, but on the skill of the management of that corporation (4).

2. 1. 1   LIST OF SECURITIES UNDER THE UNIFORM SECURITIES ACT

The USA does not define the term *securities* but provides a comprehensive list of financial instruments that are securities under the act and, therefore, are covered by its provisions. Under the Uniform Securities Act, *security* means any:

- note;
- stock;
- treasury stock;
- bond;
- debenture;
- evidence of indebtedness;
- certificate of interest or participation in a profit-sharing agreement;
- collateral trust certificate;
- preorganization certificate or subscription;
- transferable share;
- investment contract;
- voting trust certificate;
- certificate of deposit for a security (ADRs, not a bank CD);
- certificate of interest or participation in an oil, gas, or mining title or lease, or in payments out of production under such a title or lease;
- puts, calls, straddles, options, or privileges on a security;

- any interest or instrument commonly known as a security; or
- certificate of interest or participation in, receipts of, guarantees of, or warrants or rights to subscribe to or purchase any of the above.

The following six items are not securities under the act:

- An insurance or endowment policy or annuity contract under which an insurance company promises to pay a fixed sum of money either in a lump sum or periodically (this is basically any product from a life insurance company that does not use the word *variable*)
- Interest in a retirement plan, such as an IRA or Keogh plan
- Collectibles
- Commodities such as precious metals and grains or futures contracts for commodities
- Condominiums used as personal residences
- Currency

TEST TOPIC ALERT   The exam will want you to know what is and what is not a security. We suggest that you concentrate on learning the six that are not securities because they are much easier to remember, and you will still be able to answer the questions correctly. You might also have to know that a confirmation of a securities trade is not a security; it is just a document evidencing that a transaction took place.

2. 1. 1. 1 Nonsecurity Investments

Although collectibles, fixed annuities, precious metals, grains, futures, real estate, and currencies can be attractive investments, they are not securities. Because these items are not securities, their sale is not regulated by state securities law. Furthermore, if a registered agent commits fraud in the sale of any of these items, he has not committed a violation of state securities law. He has violated the antifraud provisions of another act prohibiting fraudulent commercial transactions.

An individual's direct ownership of an automobile is not a security—it is just ownership of a car. However, if that individual makes an investment of money in the stock of an automobile manufacturer with the expectation of making money due to the efforts of the company's management skill, he has purchased a security. In the same manner, if a condominium is purchased in a resort area with the goal of placing it into a rental pool and renting it out most of the year, and it is used only for personal vacation time, the condo is considered a security because there is a profit motive, typically reliant on the efforts of a third party—the rental agent. On the other hand, if the individual has chosen to live in the condominium as a personal residence, it is a home, not a security.

EXAMPLE   Annuities with fixed payouts are not securities, but variable annuities are because they are dependent on the investment performance of securities within the annuity.

2. 1. 2   NONEXEMPT SECURITY

A nonexempt security is a security subject to the registration provisions mandated by the USA. **Exempt** means not subject to registration. Therefore, unless the nonexempt security is registered, it may not be sold in a state unless it is sold in an exempt transaction (more about that in just a bit). As you will learn, unless in an exempt transaction, the sale of an unregistered nonexempt security is a prohibited practice under the USA and may subject an agent to both civil and criminal penalties.

TAKE NOTE   The methods of registration discussed in this unit refer to nonexempt securities because if they were exempt, they would not have to register. For example, a registered nonexempt security is most likely a common stock properly registered for sale in a state.

2. 1. 3   ISSUER

An **issuer** is any person who issues (distributes) or proposes to issue a security. The most common issuers of securities are companies or governments (federal, state, and municipal governments and their agencies and subdivisions).

If an issuer is nonexempt, it must register its securities in the states where they will be sold under one of the registration methods described in the unit.

EXAMPLE   ABC Shoe Co. (a retail chain store) issues shares to the public. Mr. Bixby (an investor) buys the shares through his agent, Mr. Thompson, at First Securities Corporation. ABC Shoe Co. is the issuer, Mr. Bixby is the investor, First Securities is the broker-dealer, and Mr. Thompson is the agent.

TEST TOPIC ALERT   You might need to know this legal fact: under the USA, with respect to certificates of interest, participation in oil, gas, or mining titles or leases, or in payments out of production under such titles or leases, there is not considered to be any issuer.

2. 1. 3. 1   Issuer Transaction

An **issuer transaction** is one in which the proceeds of the sale go to the issuer. All newly issued securities are issuer transactions. In other words, when a company raises money by selling (issuing) securities to investors, the proceeds from the sale go to the company itself.

2. 1. 3. 1. 1   Primary Offering

An issuer transaction involving new securities is called a **primary offering**. If it is the first time an issuer distributes securities to the public, it is called an **initial public offering (IPO)**. Any offering of new securities, whether initial or an offering of additional securities at a later time, is an issuer transaction because the issuer (the company) receives the proceeds from the investor investing in the company.

2. 1. 3. 2   Nonissuer Transaction

A **nonissuer transaction** is one in which the proceeds of the sale do not go, either directly or indirectly, to the entity that originally offered the securities to the public. The most common example is everyday trading in the secondary markets such as the New York Stock Exchange or Nasdaq. In a nonissuer transaction, the proceeds of the sale go to the investor who sold the shares. Because the shares are not "new," we refer to this as secondary trading.

EXAMPLE

The first time that ABC Shoe Co. issued shares to the public, ABC Shoe engaged in an IPO, or a primary offering, because it received the proceeds from distributing its shares to the public. After ABC Shoe went public, transactions between its investors executed on exchanges through brokerage agents were secondary transactions in nonissuer securities.

If Mr. Bixby, an investor, sells 100 shares of stock he owns in ABC Shoe Co. (the issuer of the security) on the New York Stock Exchange (NYSE), Mr. Bixby receives the proceeds from the sale, not ABC Shoes. This is a nonissuer transaction.

QUICK QUIZ 2.A

1. Which list of instruments below is NOT composed of securities?

    A. Stock, treasury stock, rights, warrants, transferable shares
    B. Voting trust certificates, interests in oil and gas drilling programs
    C. Commodity futures contracts, fixed-payment life insurance contracts
    D. Options on stock, debentures

2. In the Howey Case, the U.S. Supreme Court defined an investment contract as having 4 components. Which of the following is NOT part of the 4-part test for an investment contract?

    A. An investment of money
    B. An expectation of profit
    C. Management activity by owner
    D. Solely from the efforts of others

3. A nonissuer transaction is a transaction

    A. between two corporations, in which one is issuing the stock and the other is purchasing_
    B. in which the issuing corporation will not receive the proceeds from the transaction
    C. in which a mutual fund purchases a Treasury bond directly from the government
    D. in which the security must be registered

Quick Quiz answers can be found at the end of the unit.

2. 2   REGISTRATION OF SECURITIES UNDER THE UNIFORM SECURITIES ACT

It is unlawful for any person to offer or sell any security in this state unless:

- it is registered under the act;
- the security or transaction is exempted from registration under the act; or
- it is a federal covered security.

If the security or transaction is not exempt or is not a federal covered security as defined by the NSMIA, it must be registered in the state, or it cannot be lawfully sold in the state.

2. 2. 1   NATIONAL SECURITIES MARKETS IMPROVEMENT ACT OF 1996 (NSMIA)

We introduced you to the NSMIA in the previous unit. This law effectively divided the responsibility for regulating investment advisers between the states and the SEC by bifur-cating (splitting in two) the regulation of investment advisers and creating the category of registration known as a federal covered adviser. Of importance to this unit, the NSMIA also created the term **federal covered security**, a security that was exempt from registration on the state level.

State securities registration requirements were preempted with respect to federal covered securities. However, states may require notice filings, consisting of filing fees and copies of documents filed with the Securities and Exchange Commission (SEC), primarily in the case of registered investment companies such as mutual funds.

2. 2. 1. 1   Categories of Federal Covered Securities

The major categories of federal covered securities (securities covered by federal securities laws) that cannot be regulated by state securities Administrators (except for violating anti-fraud provisions), include:

- securities listed on the New York Stock Exchange, the NYSE American, LLC (formerly known as the American Stock Exchange [AMEX]), the Nasdaq Stock Market, and (not tested) several other U.S. exchanges. In addition, any security equal in seniority (rights or warrants) or senior to these securities (bonds and preferred stock) is also considered federal covered;

- investment company securities registered under the Investment Company Act of 1940, such as

    — open-end management investment companies (mutual funds),

    — closed-end management investment companies,

    — unit investment trusts, and

    — face-amount certificates; and

- offers and sales of certain exempt securities, such as

    — any security issued or guaranteed by the United States or any bank regulated by the Federal Reserve Board;

— securities offered by a municipal issuer, unless the issuer is located in the state in which the municipal securities are being offered; and

— offers and sales of securities sold through certain exempt transactions, such as securities offered to qualified purchasers under Regulation D of the Securities Act of 1933 (private placements).

✓ **TAKE NOTE**   Although investment company securities are federal covered securities, the USA allows states to impose filing fees on them under a process called notice filing, which is described below. Other federal covered securities are generally not required to notice file, but the Administrator reserves the right to request a filing from listed and Nasdaq securities.

Bonds issued by municipalities—for example, those issued by states or cities—are federal covered securities exempt from registration requirements in the states. However, there is an exception to the rule. States may impose certain requirements on municipal securities issued within their own states, but they may not require registration of municipal securities issued by other states. Why? Municipal securities of other states are federal covered securities exempt from state registration. Municipal securities issued in an Administrator's state are not federal covered securities; they are not covered by the exemption (states retain authority over the issue of the municipal securities by their own municipalities). Even though these municipal bonds are exempt securities under the USA, they are not included in the NSMIA definition of federal covered security. Yes, this is confusing, but just try to keep it simple as in the following example:

❋ **EXAMPLE**   A bond issued by the city of Columbus, OH, is a federal covered security everywhere *except* in the state of Ohio. The effect of this is that no state regulators can enforce any of their rules against the bond. But, in the state of Ohio, even though the security is exempt under Ohio's securities laws, the Administrator *could* request that the issuer (the city) furnish certain details about the issue.

✓ **TAKE NOTE**   It is important to note that registering a security with the SEC does not automatically make it federal covered. Yes, that is true of investment companies and those securities listed on the exchanges and Nasdaq, but there are thousands of stocks registered with the SEC that trade on the OTC Bulletin Board or the OTC Link of the OTC Markets Group, formerly known as the Pink Sheets, that are not federal covered and, as we will shortly explain, generally have to register with both the SEC and the state(s). Furthermore, a security does not have to be registered with the SEC to be included in the definition of federal covered security. For example, U.S. government and municipal securities are federal covered securities and are exempt from registration with the SEC.

2. 2. 2   METHODS OF STATE REGISTRATION OF SECURITIES

The USA provides two methods for securities issuers to register their securities in a state, plus a special method for certain federal covered securities. They are:

■ notice filing;

■ coordination; and

■ qualification.

2. 2. 2. 1   Notice Filing

As previously mentioned, the National Securities Markets Improvement Act of 1996 (NSMIA) designated certain securities as federal covered and, therefore, removed from the jurisdiction of the state regulatory authorities. Although the states are preempted from requiring registration for federal covered securities, status as a federal covered security is not a preemption of the licensing or antifraud laws. Any person who sells a federal covered security must be licensed as a broker-dealer or agent (unless otherwise exempted) and must also comply with the antifraud provisions of state laws.

The Uniform Securities Act gives the Administrator the authority to require notice filings with respect to federal covered securities (generally, investment companies registered with the SEC under the Investment Company Act of 1940). So, what is this notice filing? Primarily, it is an opportunity for the states to collect revenue in the form of filing fees because, unlike with the two actual methods of registration we are going to discuss, the Administrator has limited powers to review any documentation filed with his department.

The fees for notice filing are generally lower than for the two forms of state registration.

Under the notice filing procedure, state Administrators may require the issuer to file the following documents as a condition for sale of their securities in the state:

■ Documents filed along with their registration statements filed with the SEC

■ Documents filed as amendments to the initial federal registration statement

■ A report on the value of such securities offered in the state

■ Consent to service of process

TEST TOPIC ALERT   Before the initial offer of any federal covered security in this state, the Administrator may, by rule or order, require the filing of all documents that are part of a federal registration statement filed with the U.S. Securities and Exchange Commission under the Securities Act of 1933, together with a consent to service of process signed by the issuer. However, unless there is an appearance of fraud, the Administrator does not have the power (because of lack of jurisdiction) to prevent the sale of a federal covered security in his state.

TEST TOPIC ALERT   Even though an issuer of a federal covered security (think about a Fortune 500 company listed on the NYSE) may not have to notice file, that does not mean that the company can make misrepresentations during an offer made in any state. Doing so would violate the antifraud provisions of the USA.

2. 2. 2. 2   Registration by Coordination

The most common form of registration for those securities that are not federal covered (typically securities traded on the OTC Bulletin Board or the OTC Link) is coordination. A security may be registered by coordination if a registration statement has been filed under the Securities Act of 1933 in connection with the same offering.

In coordinating a federal registration with state registration, issuers must supply the following records in addition to the consent to service of process:

- Copies of the latest form of prospectus filed under the Securities Act of 1933 if the Administrator requires
- Copy of articles of incorporation and bylaws
- Copy of the underwriting agreement
- Copies of any other information filed by the issuer under the Securities Act of 1933, if the Administrator requests
- Each amendment to the federal prospectus promptly after it is filed with the SEC

2. 2. 2. 2. 1   Effective Date

Registration by coordination becomes effective at the same time the federal registration becomes effective, provided that:

- no stop orders have been issued by the Administrator and no proceedings are pending against the issuer;
- the registration has been on file for at least the minimum number of days specified by the Administrator, a number that currently ranges from 10 to 20 days, depending on the state; and
- a statement of the maximum and minimum proposed offering prices and maximum underwriting discounts and commissions have been on file for two full business days.

Registration by coordination is by far the most frequently used method and, from a practical standpoint, is the only sensible way to register a multistate offering.

2. 2. 2. 3   Registration by Qualification

Any security can be registered by qualification, but this method is almost exclusively used for intrastate (single state) offerings, which are not registered with the SEC. Registration by qualification requires a registrant to supply any information required by the state securities Administrator. Securities not eligible for registration by another method must be registered by qualification.

To register by qualification, an issuer must supply a consent to service of process and the following information:

- Name, address, and form of organization; description of property; and nature of business
- Information on directors, officers, and every owner of 10% or more of the issuer's securities, and the remuneration paid to owners in the last 12 months
- Description of the issuer's capitalization and long-term debt
- Estimated proceeds and the use to which the proceeds will be put
- Type and amount of securities offered, offering price, and selling and underwriting costs
- Stock options to be created in connection with the offering

- Copy of any prospectus, pamphlet, circular, or sales literature to be used in the offering
- Specimen copy of the security, along with opinion of counsel as to the legality of the security being offered
- Audited balance sheet current within four months of the offering, with an income statement for three years before the balance sheet date

The Administrator may require additional information by rule or order. The Administrator may require that a prospectus be sent to purchasers before the sale and that newly established companies register their securities for the first time in a state by qualification.

TAKE NOTE

As we've noted previously, in order to register, even by notice filing, there must be a consent to service of process filed with the Administrator. However, a person (remember the broad definition) who has filed such a consent in connection with a previous registration or notice filing need not file another. A practical effect of this is if a company decides to raise additional capital by issuing more stock, a new consent is not required.

2. 2. 2. 3. 1 Effective Date

Unlike coordination, in which the effective date is triggered by SEC acceptance of the registration, a registration by qualification becomes effective whenever the state Administrator so orders.

Regardless of the method used, every registration statement is effective for one year from its effective date. Unlike agent and broker-dealer registrations, the date December 31 is of no consequence. One interesting facet of the law is that the registration may remain in effect past the first anniversary if there are still some unsold shares remaining, as long as they are still being offered at the original public offering price by either the issuer or the underwriter.

Although the previous rule applies to all methods of registration, as a practical matter, it would rarely apply other than in a security registered by qualification. Those registered by coordination are also obviously registered with the SEC and, therefore, are sold by the major investment banking houses. Unless the issue is a real dog, it will sell out rather quickly. Even those that are not popular are usually completely subscribed to in a week or two.

On the other hand, what if the issue, regardless of the method of registration, is in very high demand? Is it possible to increase the number of shares in the offering without having to file a new registration statement? Yes. A registration statement may be amended after its effective date so as to increase the securities specified to be offered and sold if two conditions are met.

- The public offering price is not changed from the amount stated in the original registration statement.
- The underwriters' discounts and commissions are not changed from the respective amounts stated in the original registration statement.

The amendment becomes effective when the Administrator so orders. Every person filing such an amendment shall pay a late registration fee and a filing fee, calculated in the same manner as the original quantity, levied against the additional securities proposed to be offered.

TEST TOPIC ALERT   A registration statement may be amended after its effective date to change the number of shares to be offered and sold, as long as the public offering price and underwriter's discounts and commissions are unchanged.

QUICK QUIZ 2.B   True or False?

_____ 1. ABC Shoe Company, a new retail shoe store chain, has applied for the registration of its securities with the SEC as required by the Securities Act of 1933 and wants to register its securities in the state of Illinois. ABC Shoe Company would most likely register by coordination.

_____ 2. Any company may register by qualification, whether or not it files a statement with the SEC.

2. 3   EXEMPTIONS FROM REGISTRATION

One of the most important statements found in the USA is the following.

It is unlawful for any person to offer or sell any security in this state unless:
- it is registered under the act;
- the security or transaction is exempted under the act; or
- it is a federal covered security.

In certain situations, the USA exempts both securities and transactions from registration and filing requirements of sales literature. A security, a transaction, or both, can be exempt.

An **exempt security** retains its exemption when initially issued and in subsequent trading. However, justification as an **exempt transaction** must be established before each transaction.

The USA provides for a number of categories of exempt securities and even more categories of exempt transactions. Those securities that are **nonexempt** must register unless sold in exempt transactions. Federal covered securities do not register with the Administrator but may, especially in the case of investment companies, have to notice file with the Administrator. As mentioned above, an **exempt security** retains its exemption at its initial issue and in subsequent trading.

An exemption for a transaction, on the other hand, must be established with each transaction. Provided it is in the public interest, the state Administrator can deny, suspend, or revoke any securities transaction exemption other than that of a federal covered security. This action may be taken with or without prior notice (summarily).

TAKE NOTE   A security is exempt because of the nature of the issuer, not the purchaser.

An **exempt transaction** is exempt from the regulatory control of the state Administrator because of the manner in which a sale is made or because of the person to whom the sale is made. A transaction is an action and must be judged by the merits of each instance.

For example, an agent can sell a security that is not exempt from registration in the state if the purchaser of the security is a bank or other institutional buyer. Why is that so? Because the sale of securities to certain financial institutions is an exempt transaction (as will be enumerated shortly), the sale can be made without registration. This means that the securities sold in exempt transactions do not have to be registered in the state. If such securities were not sold in exempt transactions, such as to an individual investor, they would have to be registered in the state.

2. 3. 1   EXEMPT SECURITIES

Securities exempt from state registration are also exempt from state filing of sales literature. Exempt securities include the following:

- **U.S. and Canadian government and municipal securities**. These include securities issued, insured, or guaranteed by the United States or Canada, by a state or province, or by their political subdivisions.*

- **Foreign government securities**. These include securities issued, insured, or guaranteed by a foreign government with which the United States maintains diplomatic relations. However, unlike U.S. or Canadian issues, political subdivisions are not included (unless guaranteed by the sovereign government).*

- **Depository institutions**. These include securities that are issued, guaranteed by, or are a direct obligation of a depository institution. The USA divides them into the following categories: (1) any security issued by and representing an interest in or a debt of, or guaranteed by, any bank organized under the laws of the United States, or any bank, savings institution, or trust company organized and supervised under the laws of any state;* (2) any security issued by and representing an interest in or a debt of, or guaranteed by, any federal savings and loan association, or any building and loan or similar association organized under the laws of any state and authorized to do business in this state; and (3) any security issued or guaranteed by any federal credit union or any credit union, industrial loan association, or similar association organized and supervised under the laws of this state. Please note that for categories (2) and (3), if the institution is not federally chartered, then it must be authorized to do business in the state (under the supervision of a regulator in that state).

- **Insurance company securities**. These include securities issued, insured, or guaranteed by an insurance company authorized to do business in the state. Insurance company securities refer to the stocks or bonds issued by insurance companies, not the variable policies sold by the companies. Fixed insurance and annuity policies are not securities.

- **Public utility securities**. These include any security issued or guaranteed by a public utility or public utility holding company, or an equipment trust certificate issued by a railroad or other common carrier, regulated in respect to rates by federal or state authority, or regulated in respect to issuance or guarantee of the security by a governmental authority of the United States, any state, Canada, or any Canadian province.

- **Federal covered securities**. These include any security of an issuer equal to or senior to the common stock, such as rights, warrants, preferred stock, and any debt security.

- **Securities issued by nonprofit organizations**. These include securities issued by religious, educational, fraternal, charitable, social, athletic, reformatory, or trade associations and which are not for pecuniary profit. *Nonprofit* is the key word.

- **Securities issued by cooperatives**. These include securities issued by a nonprofit membership cooperative to members of that cooperative.

- **Securities of employee benefit plans**. These include any investment contract issued by an employee stock purchase, saving, pension, or profit-sharing plan.*

- **Certain money market instruments**. Commercial paper and banker's acceptances are the two most common examples.*

TAKE NOTE

The five above items listed with an asterisk (*) are the only cases where an individual representing the issuer in the sale of its securities is excluded from the definition of an agent. (This was described previously at 1.3.2.1.)

The distinction between exemptions and exceptions (or exclusions) from definitions is important in view of the fact that an exempt security is not exempt from the antifraud provisions of the Uniform Securities Act.

For example, as we covered earlier in this unit, the typical life insurance policy or fixed annuity is not a security, and the blue-sky law has no impact on it. On the other hand, we have just seen that securities issued by insurance companies are exempted from registration under the conditions of the act. Even though these securities are exempt from registration and the filing of advertising and sales literature with the Administrator, they are still subject to the antifraud provisions. Therefore, an individual cannot be charged with violating the USA in the sale of a fixed annuity but could be in the sale of stock in an insurance company (or any other exempt security).

TAKE NOTE

The USA also grants an exemption for certain short-term debt securities. Examples are a promissory note (commercial paper), draft, bill of exchange, or banker's acceptance if it

- matures in nine months or less;

- is issued in minimum denominations of $50,000; and

- receives one of the three highest ratings from a nationally recognized rating agency.

Please note that this is the only case where a security's rating is part of the registration or exemption under the Uniform Securities Act.

QUICK QUIZ 2.C

1. Which of the following securities is(are) exempt from the registration and advertising filing requirements under the USA?

   I. Shares of investment companies registered under the Investment Company Act of 1940
   II. Shares sold on the Nasdaq Stock Market
   III. AAA rated promissory notes of $100,000 that mature in 30 days
   IV. Shares sold on the New York Stock Exchange

   A. I only
   B. II, III, and IV
   C. II and IV
   D. I, II, III, and IV

2. Which of the following securities is NOT exempt from the registration and advertising requirements of the USA?

    A. Shares of Commonwealth Edison, a regulated public utility holding company
    B. Securities issued by the Carnegie Endowment for Peace
    C. Securities issued by a bank that is a member of the Federal Reserve System
    D. Variable annuity contract issued by Metrodential Insurance Co.

2. 3. 2   EXEMPT TRANSACTIONS

Before a security can be sold in a state, it must be registered unless exempt from registration or traded in an exempt transaction. This section covers exemptions for transactions that take place in a state.

There are many different types of exempt transactions. We begin by focusing on those most likely to be on your exam and finish with several others.

- **Isolated nonissuer transactions.** Isolated nonissuer transactions include secondary (nonissuer) transactions, whether effected through a broker-dealer or not, that occur infrequently (very few transactions per agent per year; the exact number varies by state). However, these usually do not involve securities professionals. In the same manner that individuals placing a "for sale by owner" sign on their front lawns do not need a real estate license, one individual selling stock to another in a one-on-one transaction is engaging in a transaction exempt from the oversight of the Administrator because the issuer is not receiving any of the proceeds and the parties involved are not trading as part of a regular practice.

- **Unsolicited brokerage transactions.** These are transactions initiated by the client, not the agent. They are the most common of the exempt transactions. If a client calls a registered agent and requests that the agent buy or sell a security, the transaction is an unsolicited brokerage transaction exempt from state registration. But, the Administrator may by rule require that the customer acknowledge upon a specified form that the sale was unsolicited and that a signed copy of the form be kept by the broker-dealer for a specified period.

- **Underwriter transactions.** These include transactions between the issuer (or any other person on whose behalf the offering is made) and broker-dealers performing in the capacity of an underwriter (such as a firm commitment underwriting), as well as those between underwriters themselves (as when functioning as members of a selling syndicate).

- **Bankruptcy, guardian, or conservator transactions.** Transactions by an executor, administrator, marshal, sheriff, trustee in bankruptcy, or other fiduciary are exempt transactions.

TEST TOPIC ALERT   Note that a custodian under UTMA or UGMA is not included in this list and that the only trustee who is included is one in a bankruptcy case.

- **Institutional investor transactions.** These are primarily transactions with financial institutions and would include any offer or sale to a bank, savings institution, trust company, insurance company, or investment company as defined in the Investment Company Act of 1940. Employee benefit plans with assets of at least $1 million are also included, as are transactions with a broker-dealer, whether acting for itself or in some fiduciary capacity. There is no minimum order size used to determine these trades.

- **Limited offering transactions.** These include any offering, called a private placement, directed at not more than 10 persons (called **offerees**) other than institutional investors during the previous 12 consecutive months, provided that:

  — the seller reasonably believes that all of the noninstitutional buyers are purchasing for investment purposes only;

  — no commissions or other remuneration is paid for soliciting noninstitutional investors; and

  — no general solicitation or advertising is used.

TEST TOPIC ALERT   The USA does not require a written representation by each retail buyer that she is purchasing for investment; all that is required is that the seller *reasonably* believes that the buyer is purchasing for investment only.

The number 10 is the figure that will be tested. But, for example, an Administrator may want to reduce it for uranium stocks or oil royalties, or increase it for a closely held corporation that wants to solicit 20 or 30 friends and relatives of the owners for additional capital. As we continue to learn, the Administrator has a great deal of power.

- **Preorganization certificates.** An offer or sale of a preorganization certificate or subscription is exempt if:

  — no commission or other remuneration is paid or given directly or indirectly for soliciting any subscriber;

  — the number of subscribers does not exceed 10; and

  — no payment is made by any subscriber.

  You have probably never heard of a preorganization certificate or subscription, so a little explanation is in order. A new corporation cannot receive a charter unless their documents of incorporation provide evidence that minimum funding is assured. Since the purpose of these preorganization certificates is to enable a new enterprise to obtain the minimum number of subscriptions required by the corporation law, the USA places a limitation on the number of *subscribers* rather than the number of *offerees* (as in the private placement exemption above). Hence, there may be a publicly advertised offering of preorganization subscriptions. But there may be *no payment* until effective registration, unless another exemption is available. This tool itself simply postpones registration; it does not excuse registration altogether.

- **Transactions with existing security holders.** A transaction made under an offer to existing security holders of the issuer (including persons who are holders of convertible securities, rights, or warrants) is exempt as long as no commission or other form of remuneration is paid directly or indirectly for soliciting that security holder.

- **Nonissuer transactions by pledgees.** A nonissuer transaction executed by a bona fide pledgee (i.e., the one who received the security as collateral for a loan), as long as it was not for the purpose of evading the act, is an exempt transaction. For example, imagine that you pledged stock as collateral for a loan and defaulted on your obligation. The lender will sell your stock to try to recoup his loss and, under the USA, this is considered an exempt transaction.

Some students find it helpful to remember that an exempt security is a noun, while an exempt transaction is a verb (hence the word *action*).

Remember the distinction between an accredited investor and institutional investor. An **accredited investor** is an investor who meets the accredited investor standards of Regulation D. Rule 501 of Regulation D considers an individual with net worth greater than $1 million on the date of purchase, individually or with a spouse, excluding the net equity in the primary residence, to meet the definition of accredited investor. Alternatively, one may qualify with earnings greater than $200,000 per year ($300,000 if including spouse) in each of the previous two years and a reasonable expectation of reaching that level in the current year. This term only applies to federal law, not the USA, and probably will never be the correct answer to a USA question.

An **institutional investor** is an investor that manages large amounts of money, such as a mutual fund, an insurance company, a bank, or a pension fund.

2. 3. 3   ADMINISTRATOR'S POWER OVER EXEMPTIONS

The USA grants the Administrator the authority, by rule or order, to exempt a security, transaction, or offer from the USA's registration and filing requirements. In addition, the Administrator may waive a requirement for an exemption of a transaction or security.

Try to follow this next point because it is a bit tricky. The Administrator may, by rule or order, deny or revoke the registration exemption of:

■ any security issued by any person organized and operated not for private profit but exclusively for religious, educational, benevolent, charitable, fraternal, social, athletic, or reformatory purposes, or as a chamber of commerce or trade or professional association (your basic nonprofit exemption); and

■ any investment contract issued in connection with an employees' stock purchase, savings, pension, profit sharing, or similar benefit plan.

Please note that a few pages ago, we gave you a list of 10 different exempt securities, from U.S. and Canadian government issues through certain money market instruments. However, the Administrator can only deny exemption to the two specified above. On the other hand, with the exception of those involving federal covered securities qualifying for the designation due to being listed on an exchange or Nasdaq, the Administrator may deny any exempt transaction. That means that, for example, if an agent solicited a securities transaction with an insurance company, the Administrator has the power, if he feels it is justified, to consider that transaction nonexempt even though it is a transaction with an institutional client.

Under the USA, the burden of providing an exemption or an exception from a definition falls upon the person claiming it.

There are only two securities exemptions that the Administrator may revoke, whereas all exempt transactions, other than in federal covered securities, may be revoked.

2. 3. 4 SUMMARY OF EXEMPTIONS FROM REGISTRATION

Let's start our summary with the key statement from the USA:

It is unlawful for any person to offer or sell any security in this state unless (1) it is registered under this act or (2) the security or transaction is exempted under this act; or (3) it is a federal covered security.

We must point out that these exemptions apply to the security or transaction only, not to the securities professional. So if a security is exempt, such as a government security, it can be sold in this state without any registration. But, the person who sells it must be properly registered in this state (unless that person qualifies for an exemption). Are you confused? Remember, we learned in Unit 1 that broker-dealers with no place of business in the state, dealing exclusively with other broker-dealers or institutional clients, are not considered to be BDs in the state (as long as they are properly registered in at least one state—the location of their principal office). Let's apply that to the following examples.

EXAMPLE   ABC Securities is a broker-dealer registered in state A. They have no place of business in state B, but they do effect transactions on behalf of a number of banks and insurance companies located in state B. Therefore, they are not considered BDs in state B and are exempt from registering. Should ABC Securities sell some government securities to these clients, neither ABC nor the agents making the sale are required to be registered. This is not because the government securities are exempt (that just means that they don't have to register with the Administrator), but because, under the USA, ABC does not meet the definition of a broker-dealer in state B.

However, should ABC decide to have any of their agents sell these government bonds to individual (sometimes referred to as *retail*) clients in state B, then, even though the bonds are exempt securities, both ABC and the selling agents must register in that state.

The same applies to exempt transactions. One of the most common cases is when a client calls an agent to purchase a security that is not exempt and not registered in your state. But, because the transaction has been initiated by the client, as an unsolicited trade, it is an exempt transaction and, therefore, the trade may be made even though the security is not registered.

One way the exam will try to trick you is by asking about an individual calling an agent from a state in which the agent is not registered. The broker-dealer is registered in that state, and the individual is a client of the firm, but not that particular agent. The individual wishes to enter an unsolicited order—can the agent accept it? No! Although the transaction is exempt (which only means that the security does not have to be registered in that state), an agent can only do business with a resident of a state if the agent is properly licensed in that state. In this case, the agent would have to turn the order over to an agent who is licensed in that other state.

TAKE NOTE   As we have mentioned several times, regardless of whether the security or the transaction is exempt, as long as it is a security, it is not exempt from the antifraud provisions of the Uniform Securities Act.

QUICK QUIZ 2.D

Indicate an exempt transaction with **Y** and a nonexempt transaction with **N**.

_____ 1. Mr. Thompson, an agent with First Securities, Inc., (a broker-dealer), receives an unsolicited request to purchase a security for Mary Gordon, a high net worth individual

_____ 2. The sale of an unregistered security in a private, nonpublicly advertised transaction offered to 10 or fewer retail investors over the last 12 months

_____ 3. The sale of unclaimed securities by the sheriff of Santa Fe, New Mexico

_____ 4. Sale of stock of a privately owned company to the public in an initial public offering

5. Which of the following are exempt transactions?
   I. An agent sells a security issued by a foreign government with which the United States has diplomatic relations to an individual client
   II. An unsolicited request from an existing client to purchase a nonexempt security
   III. The sale of an unregistered security in a private, nonpublicly advertised transaction to 14 noninstitutional investors over a period not exceeding 12 months
   IV. The sale of unlisted securities by a trustee in bankruptcy

   A. I and II
   B. I and III
   C. II and IV
   D. III and IV

6. All of the following describe exempt transactions EXCEPT
   A. ABC, a broker-dealer, purchases securities from XYZ Corporation as part of an underwriting commitment
   B. First National Bank sells its entire publicly traded bond portfolio to Amalgamated National Bank
   C. Amalgamated National Bank sells its publicly traded bond portfolio to ABC Insurance Company
   D. Joe Smith, an employee of Amalgamated National Bank, buys securities from ABC Brokerage Corporation

7. Under the USA, all of the following are exempt securities EXCEPT
   I. U.S. government securities
   II. unsolicited transactions
   III. transactions between issuers and underwriters
   IV. securities of federally chartered credit unions

   A. I, II, and IV
   B. I and IV
   C. II and III
   D. IV only

8. Nonexempt securities

A. need not be registered in the state in which they are sold
B. always must be registered in the state in which they are sold
C. need not be registered if sold in an exempt transaction
D. need not be registered if sold in a nonexempt transaction

2. 4   STATE SECURITIES REGISTRATION PROCEDURES

The first step in the registration procedure is for the issuer or its representative to complete a registration application and file it with the state securities Administrator. The person registering the securities is known as the **registrant**. There are some provisions applicable to all registrations regardless of the method used. The exam will want you to know these well.

2. 4. 1   FILING THE REGISTRATION STATEMENT

State Administrators require every issuer to supply the following information on their applications:

■ Amount of securities to be issued in the state

■ States in which the security is to be offered, but not the amounts offered in those other states

■ Any adverse order or judgment concerning the offering by regulatory authorities, court, or the SEC

■ Anticipated effective date

■ Anticipated use of the proceeds (why are we raising this money?)

TEST TOPIC ALERT   One item that will not be found in the registration statement is the rating of the security.

TEST TOPIC ALERT   Although most registration statements are filed by the issuer, the exam may require you to know that they may also be filed by any other person, such as a stockholder making a large block sale, or by a broker-dealer.

2. 4. 2   FILING FEE

The issuer (or any other person on whose behalf the offering is to be made) must pay a filing fee as determined by the Administrator when filing the registration. The filing fees are often based on a percentage of the total offering price.

2. 4. 3   ONGOING REPORTS

The Administrator may require the person who filed the registration statement to file reports to keep the information contained in the registration statement current and to inform the Administrator of the progress of the offering.

TAKE NOTE   These reports cannot be required more often than quarterly.

---

2. 4. 4   ESCROW

As a condition of registration under coordination or qualification, the Administrator may require that a security be placed in **escrow** if the security is issued:

■ within the past three years;

■ to a promoter at a price substantially different than the offering price; or

■ to any person for a consideration other than cash.

In addition, the Administrator may require that the proceeds from the sale of the registered security in this state be impounded until the issuer receives a specified amount from the sale of the security either in this state or elsewhere. There have been many instances where companies were unable to raise their targeted goal and just took the money and ran. This impound, or escrow, lessens the likelihood that this will happen.

2. 4. 5   SPECIAL SUBSCRIPTION FORM

The Administrator may also require, as a condition of registration, that the issue be sold only on a form specified by the Administrator and that a copy of the form or subscription contract be filed with the Administrator or preserved for up to three years.

QUICK QUIZ 2.E

1. With regard to the registration requirements of the Uniform Securities Act, which of the following statements are TRUE?

    I.   Only the issuer itself can file a registration statement with the Administrator.

    II. An application for registration must indicate the amount of securities to be issued in the state.

    III. The Administrator may require registrants to file quarterly reports.

    A. I and II
    B. I and III
    C. II and III
    D. I, II, and III

2. 4. 6 PROSPECTUS DELIVERY REQUIREMENTS

As previously mentioned, the Administrator may require that, in the case of a security registered by qualification, the prospectus be delivered prior to or concurrent with the sale. For registrants using the other methods, the USA follows the rules of the Securities Act of 1933, requiring that delivery be no later than the mailing of the trade confirmation or actual delivery of the security.

TAKE NOTE

In the next unit, we will learn what the Administrator can do to deny a registration so that it does not become effective or, when it has already become effective, to suspend or revoke the registration.

UNIT TEST

1. Which of the following is defined as a security under the Uniform Securities Act?

   A. A guaranteed, lump-sum payment to a beneficiary
   B. Fixed, guaranteed payments made for life or for a specified period
   C. Commodity futures contracts
   D. An investment contract

2. Under the Uniform Securities Act, which of the following persons is responsible for proving that a securities issue is exempt from registration?

   A. Underwriter
   B. Issuer
   C. State Administrator
   D. There is no need to prove eligibility for an exemption

3. Registration is effective when ordered by the Administrator in the case of registration by

   A. coordination
   B. integration
   C. notice filing
   D. qualification

4. Under the Uniform Securities Act, which of the following would be considered an exempt transaction?

   I. The call from an existing client to purchase 1,000 shares of a common stock that is not registered in this state
   II. The sale of shares that are part of a registered secondary of a NYSE-listed company to an individual client
   III. The sale of shares of a bank's IPO to an institutional client
   IV. The sale of shares of an insurance company's IPO to an individual client

   A. I and III
   B. I, III, and IV
   C. II and IV
   D. I, II, III, and IV

5. Which of the following securities is NOT exempt from the registration provisions of the USA?

   A. Common stock issued by a savings and loan association authorized to do business in the state
   B. General obligation municipal bond
   C. Bond issued by a company that has common stock listed on the New York Stock Exchange
   D. Variable annuities sold by a life insurance company authorized to do business in the state

6. A primary transaction is

   A. the first transaction between two parties in the over-the-counter market
   B. a sale between investors of securities traded on the New York Stock Exchange
   C. a new offering of an issuer sold to investors
   D. a secondary market transaction in a security recently offered to the public

7. All of the following describe exempt transactions EXCEPT

   A. ABC, a broker-dealer, purchases securities from XYZ Corporation
   B. First National Bank sells its entire publicly traded bond portfolio to Amalgamated National Bank
   C. Amalgamated National Bank sells its publicly traded bond portfolio to ABC Insurance Company
   D. Joe Smith, an employee of Amalgamated Bank, buys securities from ABC Brokerage Corporation

8. Under the USA, all of the following are exempt securities EXCEPT

   A. U.S. government securities
   B. unsolicited transactions
   C. bonds issued by Saskatoon, Saskatchewan
   D. securities of federal credit unions

9. Registration statements for securities under the Uniform Securities Act are effective for

   A. a period determined by the Administrator for each issue
   B. 1 year from the effective date
   C. 1 year from the date of issue
   D. 1 year from the previous January 1

10. As defined in the Uniform Securities Act, each of the following would be considered an exempt transaction EXCEPT

    A. a trustee of a corporation in bankruptcy liquidates securities to satisfy debt holders
    B. an offer of a securities investment is directed to 10 individuals in the state during a period of 12 consecutive months
    C. an agent solicits insurance companies to purchase shares of non-exempt securities
    D. preorganization certificates are subscribed to by 9 investors in the state earning the agent a modest commission

11. XYZ Corporation has been in business for over 20 years. It needs additional capital for expansion and determines that a public offering in its home state and neighboring states is appropriate. Which method of securities registration most likely would be used to register this initial public offering?

    A. Coordination
    B. Notice filing
    C. Qualification
    D. Any of the above

12. Each of the following meet the USA's definition of an exempt transaction EXCEPT

    A. transactions by an executor of an estate
    B. transactions with an investment company registered under the Investment Company Act of 1940
    C. an unsolicited sale of an OTC Bulletin Board stock
    D. sale of a new issue of a federal covered security to an individual customer

13. Which of the following are exempt securities?

    I. Securities guaranteed by domestic banks
    II. Securities issued by the government of Canada
    III. Securities issued exclusively for religious purposes
    IV. Federal covered securities
    A. I, II, and III
    B. II only
    C. II and IV
    D. I, II, III, and IV

14. Which of the following would NOT be included in the definition of federal covered security?

    A. Unit investment trusts registered under the Investment Company Act of 1940
    B. Stock issued by a life insurance company authorized to do business in the state
    C. Bonds listed on the NYSE
    D. Securities sold under Regulation D of the Securities Act of 1933

15. Under the Uniform Securities Act, if a security is registered by qualification, the Administrator may require an agent to present the prospectus for a new issue to the offeree

    A. prior to making the offer
    B. prior to making the sale
    C. prior to the effective date of the issue
    D. once payment has been made

ANSWERS AND RATIONALES

1. **D.** Investment contracts are defined as securities under the Uniform Securities Act. In fact, the term is often used as a synonym for a security. A guaranteed, lump-sum payment to a beneficiary is an endowment policy excluded from the definition of a security. Fixed, guaranteed payments made for life or for a specified period are fixed annuity contracts not defined as securities. Commodity futures contracts and the commodities themselves are not securities. Remember, it is much easier to remember what is not a security than what is.

2. **B.** The burden of proof for claiming eligibility for an exemption falls to the person claiming the exemption. In the event the registration statement was filed by someone other than the issuer (such as a selling stockholder or broker-dealer), that person must prove the claim.

3. **D.** Registration by qualification is the only registration method in which the Administrator sets the effective date. The effective date under registration by coordination is set by the SEC, and notice filing is merely the filing of certain documents enabling the registrant to offer securities in that state.

4. **A.** A client calling to purchase stock is an unsolicited transaction, probably the most common of the exempt transactions. Any sale to an institutional client is an exempt transaction while those to individuals, unless unsolicited, generally are not. Please note that even though the NYSE-listed stock (a federal covered security) is exempt, the transaction is not.

5. **D.** Securities issued by a life insurance company authorized to do business in the state (their stock and bonds) are exempt, but the variable policies (variable annuities and variable life insurance) are not. The USA exempts from registration a number of different issues, including securities issued by a bank or anything that resembles a bank (i.e., a savings and loan or credit union). Securities issued by a governmental unit are always exempt. Securities listed on the New York Stock Exchange are part of a group known as federal covered securities that also includes securities listed on the Nasdaq Stock Market.

6. **C.** A primary transaction is a new offering of securities by an issuer sold to investors. Transactions between two investors in the over-the-counter market are called secondary transactions (the market between investors). A sale between investors of securities traded on the New York Stock Exchange is another example of a secondary transaction.

7. **D.** The purchase of securities from a broker-dealer by an employee of a bank is a nonexempt transaction—it is a sale of a security by a broker-dealer to a member of the public and is therefore not exempt. Transactions between brokers and issuers, transactions between banks, and transactions between banks and insurance companies are all exempt because they are transactions between financial institutions. Exempt transactions are most often identified by whom the transaction is with, rather than by what type of security is involved.

8. **B.** Unsolicited transactions are *exempt transactions*, not exempt securities. U.S. government securities, Canadian provincial and municipal securities, and securities of federal credit unions are exempt securities, not exempt transactions.

9. **B.** Securities registration statements are effective for 1 year from the effective date.

10. **D.** The 9 investors are within the required 10 but, in order for a preorganization certificate to be an exempt transaction, there can be no payment of funds or commissions. Transactions by fiduciaries, such as a trustee in bankruptcy (the only trustee who qualifies) and transactions with institutions, such as insurance companies, are exempt. The private placement exemption applies as long as there are no more than 10 offers to individual (retail) purchasers within 12 consecutive months.

11. **A.** Because this offering is being made in more than one state, SEC registration is necessary; the state registration method would be coordination, which is the simultaneous registration of a security with both the SEC and the states.

12. **D.** Sale of stock to an individual client (the term *sale* always indicates an active role by the agent so we know this is not unsolicited), new issue or not, would not be an exempt transaction, even if the security is exempt. Transactions by a fiduciary, such as the executor of an estate, are included in the definition of exempt transaction, as are transactions with certain institutional clients, such as investment companies and insurance companies. *The OTC Bulletin Board* is an electronic medium for the trading of highly speculative, thinly capitalized issues. Because the order is an unsolicited one, the transaction is exempt.

13. **D.** Among the exempt securities under the Uniform Securities Act (meaning exempt from the registration requirements) are securities issued by banks, securities issued by a recognized foreign government (particularly Canadian securities), securities issued by religious and other nonprofit organizations, and federal covered securities.

14. **B.** The term *federal covered security* includes securities listed on the NYSE (and other major exchanges), investment companies registered under the Investment Company Act of 1940, and securities that are the subject of the private placement exemption of Regulation D of the Securities Act of 1933. The fact that the insurance company is authorized to do business in the state would make it exempt from registration in that state, but that does not make it a federal covered security.

15. **B.** Under Section 305(l) of the Uniform Securities Act, the Administrator may require that a prospectus be sent or given to each person to whom an offer is made before the sale of the security.

QUICK QUIZ ANSWERS

Quick Quiz 2.A

1. **C.** Commodity futures contracts and fixed payment life insurance contracts are included in our list of 6 items that are not securities.

2. **C.** Management activity on the part of the owner is not part of the Howey, or 4-part, test for an instrument to be a security. The 4 parts are as follows: (1) an investment of money in (2) a common enterprise with (3) an expectation of profit (4) solely from the effort of others.

3. **B.** A nonissuer transaction is one in which the company that is the issuer of the security does not receive the proceeds from the transaction. A nonissuer transaction is a transaction between two investors and may or may not require the security to be registered. Whenever the proceeds go to the issuer, it is an issuer transaction.

Quick Quiz 2.B

1. **T.** Registration by coordination involves coordinating a state registration with that of a federal registration.

2. **T.** Any company may register by qualification. Companies that are not established or that intend to offer their securities in 1 state register by qualification.

Quick Quiz 2.C

1. **D.** All of the securities are federal covered securities and, therefore, are not subject to the registration and advertising filing requirements of the USA.

2. **D.** Variable annuities (whose performance depends on the securities in a segregated fund) are nonexempt, which means they are covered by the act and have to be registered. Securities issued by regulated public utilities, charitable organizations, and banks that are members of the Federal Reserve System are exempt under the USA.

Quick Quiz 2.D

1. **Y.** Mr. Thompson's receipt of an unsolicited order from Ms. Gordon is an exempt transaction.

2. **Y.** The sale of an unregistered security in a private, nonpublicly advertised transaction to 10 or fewer offerees over the last 12 months is an exempt transaction (a private placement).

3. **Y.** The sale of unclaimed securities by certain persons, such as a sheriff or marshal, is an exempt transaction.

4. **N.** The sale of stock of a privately owned company to the public in an initial public offering is not an exempt transaction.

5. **C.** The private placement exemption is limited to 10 noninstitutional offerees, so 14 purchasers would certainly be over the limit. While a security issued by a foreign government with which we have diplomatic relations is an exempt security, a solicited sale by an agent to an individual client is not an exempt transaction.

6. **D.** The purchase of securities from a broker-dealer by an employee of a bank is a nonexempt transaction—it is a sale of a security by a broker-dealer to a member of the public and is therefore not exempt. Transactions between broker-dealers and issuers as part of an underwriting commitment; transactions between banks; and transactions between banks and insurance companies are exempt because they are transactions between financial institutions. Exempt transactions are most often identified by who the transaction is with rather than what type of security is involved.

7. **C.** Both unsolicited transactions and transactions between issuers and underwriters are exempt transactions, not exempt securities. U.S. government securities and securities of credit unions are exempt securities, not exempt transactions.

8. **C.** Nonexempt securities usually are required to be registered, but not always. If the nonexempt security is sold in an exempt transaction, registration is not required.

Quick Quiz 2.E

1. **C.** The USA requires that any application for registration include the amount of securities to be sold in that state. The Administrator has the power to request regular filings of reports, but no more frequently than quarterly. Although the issuer is most commonly the registrant, selling stockholders and broker-dealers may also file an application.

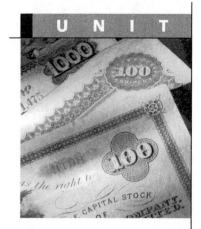

3

Remedies and Administrative Provisions

T he USA is model legislation for the states to use in writing their own securities laws. On your exam, you will not be tested on the specifics of your state's securities laws but on the principles of state regulation laid out in the USA.

This unit addresses the administrative provisions of the act and the remedies available to the Administrator. Under the USA, the state Administrator has jurisdiction over securities transactions that originate in, are directed into, or are accepted in the Administrator's state.

When a securities transaction falls within the Administrator's jurisdiction, the Administrator has power to make rules and orders; conduct investigations and issue subpoenas; issue cease and desist orders; and deny, suspend, or revoke registrations.

Both civil liabilities and criminal penalties exist for violating the act.

The Series 63 exam will include six questions on the material presented in this unit. ■

When you have completed this unit, you should be able to:

■ **describe** the relationship between state and national securities laws;

■ **recognize** the jurisdiction of the state securities Administrator;

■ **list** the powers of the Administrator within his jurisdiction;

■ **recognize** the difference between a cease and desist order and a stop order;

■ **describe** the rights of recovery for a security's sale or for investment advice purchased in violation of the USA; and

■ **contrast** civil and criminal penalties for violation of the act.

3. 1 AUTHORITY OF THE ADMINISTRATOR

The primary role of the Administrator is to administer the securities laws of the state as well as make rules and issue orders in the public interest to ensure a well-functioning investment climate in the state.

As we have already covered, the Administrator deals with registration of securities professionals and securities. In this unit, we will concentrate on the scope of his authority, frequently referred to as his **jurisdiction** on the exam, and the penalties for those who run afoul of the law.

3. 1. 1 OFFER OR OFFER TO SELL AND SALE OR SELL

We previously defined these terms in Unit 1, but we need to go into further detail here because the Administrator's authority revolves around offers and sales of securities.

3. 1. 1. 1 Offer or Offer to Sell

The USA defines **offer** or **offer to sell** as every attempt or offer to dispose of, or solicitation of an offer to buy, a security or interest in a security for value. For test purposes, you should know that:

- any security given or delivered with, or as a bonus on account of, a purchase of securities or anything else (a car, jewelry, and so forth) is considered to constitute part of the subject of the purchase and to have been offered and sold for value;

- a purported gift of assessable stock is considered to involve an offer and a sale (assessable stock is stock issued below par for which the issuer or creditors have the right to assess shareholders for the balance of unpaid par); or

- a sale or offer of a warrant or right to purchase or subscribe to another security of the same or another issuer, as well as every sale or offer of a security which gives the holder a present or future right or privilege to convert into another security of the same or another issuer, is considered to include an offer of the other security.

3. 1. 1. 2 Sale or Sell

The USA defines **sale** or **sell** as every contract of sale, contract to sell, and disposition of a security or interest in a security for value. This means that any transfer of a security in which money or some other valuable consideration is involved is covered by this definition and subject to the act.

TAKE NOTE   You must be able to distinguish between a sale and an offer to sell. The offer is the attempt; a transaction has not taken place. In a sale, there has been an actual transaction involving money or another form of consideration for value. One must be properly registered to both make a sale and make the offer.

EXAMPLE   If a car dealer, as an essential part of a sale, offers $1,000 in corporate bonds as an incentive, this would be considered a bonus under the act; therefore, this sale falls under the jurisdiction of the state securities Administrator. As a result, to do this, the car dealer, believe it or not, would have to register with the state as a broker-dealer.

3. 1. 1. 3 Gifts of Assessable Stock

When **assessable** stock is given as a gift, the Administrator has jurisdiction over the transaction because there is a potential future obligation in that either the issuer or, more likely, creditors can demand payment for the balance of the par value. For example, if an individual owned assessable stock and felt that the issuer was on the verge of bankruptcy, that person could give the stock as a present. If the bankruptcy occurred, the new owner would then be subject to the assessment. That, at least in the eyes of the law, means that this is an offer and sale rather than a gift.

TEST TOPIC ALERT   Assessable stock no longer exists, but the exam may ask about it. Look for this direct quote from the Uniform Securities Act: "A purported gift of assessable stock is considered to involve an offer and sale."

3. 1. 1. 4 Exclusions From the Terms Offer, Offer to Sell, Sale, or Sell

The terms *offer* and *offer to sell*, and *sell* or *sale* do not include any:
- bona fide pledge or loan (pledging stock as collateral for a loan, such as for a loan at the bank, is not a sale; you expect to get your stock back when the loan is paid off—you haven't sold it);
- gift of non-assessable stock (this is the way all stocks are today);
- stock dividend, if nothing of value is given by stockholders for the dividend (and this would include stock splits);
- class vote by stockholders, pursuant to the certificate of incorporation or the applicable corporation statute, or a merger, consolidation, reclassification of securities, or sale of corporate assets in consideration of the issuance of securities of another corporation; or
- act incidental to a judicially approved reorganization with which a security is issued in exchange for one or more outstanding securities.

TEST TOPIC ALERT   Because you have just learned that the gift of nonassessable stock is not considered a sale, you have to be careful not to be tricked by a question on the exam in which shares of nonassessable stock are given free as a bonus with the purchase of something else (e.g., a security, a car, a house). This would not be a gift and would, in fact, be an offer or a sale.

3. 1. 2   LEGAL JURISDICTION OF THE ADMINISTRATOR

Under law, for any agent of a state (e.g., the Administrator) to have authority over an activity such as a sale or offer of securities, he must have legal jurisdiction to act. **Jurisdiction** under the USA specifically means the legal authority to regulate securities activities that take place in the state.

The USA describes activities considered to have taken place in the state as any offer to buy or sell a security, as well as any acceptance of the offer, if the offer:

- originated in the Administrator's state;
- is directed to the Administrator's state; or
- is accepted in the Administrator's state.

TAKE NOTE

Because securities transactions often involve several states, more than one Administrator may have jurisdiction over a security or a transaction.

EXAMPLE

Let's work through some examples to see how this might appear on your exam.

Jane is an agent registered in States A and B. While sitting in her office in State A, she contacts a client who lives in State B with a recommendation to buy ABC stock. The client agrees to make the purchase. Jurisdiction here would belong to

A.   the State A Administrator

B.   the State B Administrator

C.   both the State A and State B Administrators

D.   neither Administrator because this is an existing client

In this case, it would be the Administrators of both States A and B (choice C). Why is that? Remember that the Administrator has jurisdiction over any offer that originated in his state and clearly this offer originated from Jane in State A. Recall that the Administrator has jurisdiction over any offer that was accepted in his state and this client who accepted the offer lives in State B. The status of the client, existing or prospective, does not affect the Administrator's jurisdiction.

Let's take a look at another possible question:

Jane has another State A-based client, Sally, who spends the winters in State C, a state where neither Jane nor her broker-dealer have a place of business or any retail clients. Jane sends Sally a research report with a strong buy recommendation for XYZ stock. Sally calls Jane with an order to purchase 100 shares of XYZ. Jurisdiction over this transaction belongs to

A.   the State A Administrator

B.   the State C Administrator

C.   both the State A and State B Administrators

D.   both the State A and State C Administrators

Just as with the previous question, we have an offer being made from State A resulting in that Administrator having jurisdiction. Although the client lives in State A, the offer was accepted while she was in State C, so the State C Administrator has jurisdiction. Had the client waited until she returned home to buy, then we would have had all three with jurisdiction because the offer was directed to State C and accepted in State B.

Although not related to the issue of jurisdiction, for review purposes, we should ask ourselves, "Can this transaction legally take place?" Jane is not registered in State C—how can she make the offer to a client who is there and how can she (and her broker-dealer) accept a retail order when neither of them are registered in State C? As noted in Unit 1, a broker-dealer with no place of business in a state who deals with existing clients (such as Sally) who are temporarily in the state (as Sally is), is not defined as a broker-dealer in that state and, therefore, does not register (nor do their agents).

3. 1. 2. 1   Publishing and Broadcast Exceptions to Jurisdiction

There are special rules regarding the Administrator's jurisdiction over offers made through a TV or radio broadcast or a bona fide newspaper.

The Administrator would not have jurisdiction if the offer were made under any of the following circumstances:

- Television or radio broadcast that originated outside of the state
- Bona fide newspaper or periodical published outside of the state
- Newspaper or periodical published inside the state but with more than two-thirds (66%) of its circulation outside the state in the last year

---

TAKE NOTE

A bona fide newspaper is a newspaper of general interest and circulation, such as *The New York Times*. Private investment advisory newsletters, usually distributed by subscription, are not bona fide newspapers and therefore are not included in the publishing exception.

TEST TOPIC ALERT

A radio or television program is considered to originate in the state where the microphone or television camera is located.

EXAMPLE

Publishing and Broadcast Exemptions

Let's take a look at how this publishing exemption might appear on the exam:

Wayne and Grayson, LTD., is a broker-dealer with offices in Gotham, New Jersey. They place an ad for a new securities issue in the Gotham Gazette. Approximately 55% of the Gazette's readership is in Delaware. Under the Uniform Securities Act, jurisdiction over this ad would lie with

    A. the Administrator of New Jersey
    B. the Administrator of Delaware
    C. the Administrator of both New Jersey and Delaware
    D. the Administrator of neither New Jersey and Delaware

The correct choice is **A**. Although more than half the readers of the Gazette live in Delaware, under the terms of the publishing and broadcasting exemption of the

USA, the offer is not made in Delaware because the paper is not published there. Therefore, the Administrator of New Jersey has sole jurisdiction over the offering. No dual or multiple jurisdiction applies in this case, unless the offer is actually accepted in Delaware. What would the answer be if the question stated that more than ⅔ of the circulation was outside of New Jersey? Once that happens, believe it or not, no state has jurisdiction.

QUICK QUIZ 3.A

1. A state's securities Administrator has jurisdiction over a securities offering if it

    A. was directed to residents of that state
    B. originated in that state
    C. was accepted in that state
    D. any of the above

2. An Administrator has jurisdiction over an offer to sell securities if it was made in a newspaper published within the state with no more than

    A. one-third of its circulation outside the state
    B. one-half of its circulation outside the state
    C. two-thirds of its circulation outside the state
    D. 90% of its circulation outside the state

    Quick Quiz answers can be found at the end of the unit.

3. 2 ACTIONS TO BE TAKEN BY THE ADMINISTRATOR

The USA not only establishes the jurisdiction of the Administrator but also outlines the powers or the actions that the Administrator can take within its jurisdiction.

The four broad powers the Administrator has to enforce and administer the act in his state are to:

- make, amend, or rescind rules and orders and require the use of specific forms;
- conduct investigations and issue subpoenas;
- issue cease and desist orders and seek injunctions; and
- deny, suspend, cancel, or revoke registrations and licenses.

Because the Administrator has the power to enforce the act for the benefit of the public, the Administrator, as well as his employees, have an obligation not to use the office for personal gain. Administrators are, as a result, prohibited from using, for their own benefit, any information derived from their official duties that has not been made public.

3. 2. 1 RULES, ORDERS, AND FORMS

To enforce the USA, the Administrator has the authority to make, amend, or rescind rules, forms, and orders necessary to administer the act. A rule or order of the Administrator has the same authority as a provision of the act itself, but these rules and orders are not part of the USA itself. The difference between a rule and an order is that a rule applies to everyone, whereas an order applies to a specific instance.

E X A M P L E   The Administrator may decide to issue a rule requiring all agents to pay an annual registration fee of $250. This *rule* applies to everyone. Or, the Administrator may find that a specific agent has violated a provision of the law and orders a 30-day suspension. This *order* applies only to that particular agent.

A person may appeal an order of the Administrator in court within 60 days of order issuance.

Although the Administrator has the power to make and amend rules for compliance with his state's blue-sky law, he does not have the power to alter the law itself.

The composition or content of state securities law is the responsibility of the state legislature, not of administrative agencies. Rules for administration and compliance with the law are the responsibility of the securities Administrator.

C A S E   S T U D Y   **Rules and Orders of the Administrator**

Situation: The Iowa state securities Administrator requires, by rule, that all companies registering their securities in Iowa must supply financial statements in a specific form and with content prescribed by the Administrator. However, the Administrator does not publish the rule because the rule is too long and complex.

Analysis: The USA allows state Administrators to issue rules and orders in carrying out their regulatory functions, and the Iowa Administrator acted properly in designing the form and content for financial reports. However, the USA requires that Administrators publish all rules and orders. The Administrator, despite the latitude he has in administering the USA, cannot suspend any provision of the USA itself. The Iowa Administrator acted within his authority in designing the forms but acted without authority (i.e., he violated the USA) in suspending the requirement that all rules and orders be published.

3. 2. 2   CONDUCT INVESTIGATIONS AND ISSUE SUBPOENAS

The Administrator has broad discretionary authority to conduct investigations and issue subpoenas. These investigations may be made in public or in private and may occur within or outside of the Administrator's state. Normally, these investigations are open to the public, but when, in the opinion of the Administrator and with the consent of all parties, it is felt that a private investigation is more appropriate, that investigation will be conducted without public scrutiny.

In conducting an investigation, the Administrator, or any officer designated by him, has the power to:

- require statements in writing, under oath, regarding all matters relating to the issue under investigation;
- publish and make public the facts and circumstances concerning the issue to be investigated;
- subpoena witnesses and compel their attendance and testimony; and
- take evidence and require the production of books, papers, correspondence, and any other documents deemed relevant.

3. 2. 2. 1   Contumacy

So, what happens if a person who is the subject of an investigation refuses to furnish the required evidence or just ignores the subpoena? After all, the Administrator is not a police officer—he doesn't wear a badge and cannot arrest anyone. There is a legal term that describes this type of disobedience. That term is **contumacy**. This means that the Administrator may apply to the appropriate court in his state and ask for help. Upon application by the Administrator, the court can issue an order to the person requiring compliance with the request. Failure to obey the order of the court may be punished by the court as a contempt of court. Contempt of court can, of course, lead to jail time.

In addition to having the power to conduct investigations, the Administrator may enforce subpoenas issued by Administrators in other states on the same basis as if the alleged offense took place in the Administrator's state. However, the Administrator may issue and apply to enforce subpoenas in his state at the request of a securities agency or Administrator of another state only if the activities constituting an alleged violation for which the information is sought would be a violation of the USA if the activities had occurred in his state.

3. 2. 3   ISSUE CEASE AND DESIST ORDERS

If an Administrator determines that a person is about to engage in an activity that constitutes a violation of the USA or her rules, the Administrator may issue a cease and desist order with or without a hearing. The Administrator is granted this power to prevent potential violations before they occur. It is sometimes said that the Administrator can act when she "smells the smoke, even without seeing the fire." Sometimes a tipster or whistleblower will divulge information to the Administrator that might be relevant to a serious infraction. To prevent any further damage to investors, a cease and desist order can be entered.

Although the Administrator has the power to issue cease and desist orders, she does not have the legal power to compel compliance with the order. To compel compliance in the face of a person's resistance, the Administrator must apply to a court of competent jurisdiction for an injunction. Only the courts can compel compliance by issuing injunctions and imposing penalties for violation of them. You will need to know that **enjoined** is the legal term that is used to refer to a person who is the subject of an injunction. If a temporary or permanent injunction is issued, upon request of the Administrator, a receiver or conservator may be appointed over the defendant's assets.

3. 2. 4   DENY, SUSPEND, CANCEL, OR REVOKE REGISTRATIONS

The Administrator also has the power to deny, suspend, cancel, or revoke the registration of broker-dealers, investment advisers, and their representatives, as well as the registration of securities issues.

3. 2. 4. 1   Broker-Dealers, Advisers, and Their Representatives

To justify a denial, revocation, or suspension of the license of a **securities professional**, the Administrator must find that the order is in the public interest and also find that the applicant or registrant, or in the case of a broker-dealer or investment adviser, any partner, officer, or director, or any person occupying a similar status or performing similar functions:

- has filed an incomplete, false, or misleading registration application;
- has willfully violated the USA;
- has been convicted of a securities-related misdemeanor as a result of an action brought by any securities or commodities regulatory body within the last 10 years;
- has been convicted of any felony within the last 10 years;
- has been enjoined by law from engaging in the securities business;
- is subject to any other Administrator's denial, revocation, or suspension;
- is engaged in dishonest or unethical securities practices;
- is insolvent;
- has, in the case of a broker-dealer or investment adviser, been found guilty on the charge of failure to supervise;
- has failed to pay application filing fees; and
- is not qualified because of lack of training, experience, or knowledge of the securities business.

In the USA, it states that the Administrator may not enter an order solely on the basis of lack of experience if the applicant or registrant is qualified by training, knowledge, or both.

Finally, the Administrator may not suspend or revoke a registration on the basis of facts that were known to the Administrator at the time the registration became effective.

TEST TOPIC ALERT   Because of a lack of uniformity in state criminal laws, it can happen that one is convicted of a misdemeanor in one state and then moves to a state where that same crime is a felony. If the person were to then apply for registration, the Administrator must consider the crime under the statutes of the state where it occurred, not his own. In other words, the Administrator may only consider what is on the person's record.

TEST TOPIC ALERT   If a person is subject to a disqualification by any SRO, even the NASD (before it became FINRA), for something that was *not* a violation of the Uniform Securities Act, that would still be a possible cause for denial.

TEST TOPIC ALERT   Denial is generally limited to convictions for any felony or investment-related misdemeanors within the past **10 years**. However, as pointed out in Unit 1, these convictions (and even just being charged) must always be disclosed on the application for registration—there is no time limit.

TAKE NOTE   The public's best interest is not reason enough for the denial, suspension, or revocation of a registration. There must be an additional reason, as described previously.

Other than when acting summarily, no order to deny, suspend, or revoke may be entered without:

■ appropriate prior notice to the applicant or registrant (as well as the employer or prospective employer if the applicant or registrant is an agent or investment adviser representative);

■ an opportunity for a hearing; and

■ written findings of fact and conclusions of law.

In addition, if the registrant is an agent or an IAR, the employing broker-dealer or IA, respectively, will receive notice of the final order from the Administrator.

3. 2. 4. 1. 1   Summary Powers

One of the powers of the Administrator is known as acting **summarily**. This means that he may order, without going through the hearing process, a postponement or suspension of a registration pending final determination of any proceeding based upon actions described above. Once the summary order is entered, the Administrator will promptly notify the applicant or registrant, as well as the employer or prospective employer if the applicant or registrant is an agent or investment adviser representative, that it has been entered and of the reasons for it. If the applicant wishes a hearing, written request must be made and, within 15 days after the receipt of the written request, the matter will be set down for hearing. If no hearing is requested and none is ordered by the Administrator, the order will remain in effect until it is modified or vacated by the Administrator.

As stated previously (and repeated because it is likely to be on the exam), other than when the Administrator has acted summarily as described above, no final order may be issued without the Administrator:

■ giving appropriate prior notice to the affected persons;

■ granting an opportunity for a hearing; and

■ providing findings of fact and conclusions of law.

3. 2. 4. 1. 2   Lack of Qualification

An Administrator may not base a denial of a person's registration solely on his lack of experience. However, the Administrator may consider that registration as a broker-dealer does not necessarily qualify one for a license as an investment adviser and may restrict that applicant's registration as a broker-dealer conditional upon its not functioning as an investment adviser.

To better understand these two points, let's look at the wording in the act itself:

1. The Administrator may not enter an order denying registration solely on the basis of lack of experience if the applicant or registrant is qualified by training or knowledge or both.

Obviously, a new applicant for registration as an agent is not going to have any experience selling securities. So, the act says that this lack of experience by itself is not enough to deny the registration, as long as the Administrator feels assured that the individual will receive adequate training or has the requisite knowledge. One could suppose that passing this exam demonstrates the necessary knowledge.

2. The Administrator may consider that an investment adviser is not necessarily qualified solely on the basis of experience as a broker-dealer or agent. When he finds that an applicant for initial or renewal registration as a broker-dealer is not qualified as an investment adviser, he may, by order, condition the applicant's registration as a broker-dealer upon his not transacting business in this state as an investment adviser.

In this case, the act is dealing with a person who has experience, albeit not necessarily in the giving of advice. Just because a person has been a broker-dealer, or an agent for a broker-dealer, that does not mean the person is qualified to be an investment adviser. So, the registration will be limited to acting only in its stated capacity as long as it does not cross over the line and give investment advice.

3. 2. 4. 2 Securities Issues

As is the case with a securities professional, a securities Administrator may deny, suspend, cancel, or revoke a security's registration if the order is in the public's interest and the securities registrant:

- files a misleading or incomplete registration statement;
- is engaged in an offering that is fraudulent or made on unfair, unjust, or inequitable terms;
- charges offering fees that are excessive or unreasonable;
- has a control person convicted of a securities-related crime;
- is subject to a court injunction;
- is engaged in a method of business that is illegal; or
- is subject to an administrative stop order of any other state.

In addition, the Administrator may deny a registration if the applicant fails to pay the filing fee. When the fee is paid, the denial order will be removed, provided the applicant is in compliance with all registration procedures.

TEST TOPIC ALERT   When the conditions that led to the issuance of the stop order have changed for the better, the legal term (remember, this is a law exam) used to describe the lifting of the stop order is **vacated** (e.g., "The order has been vacated.").

EXAMPLE

It is important that you be able to recognize the difference between a cease and desist order and a stop order. Look at the following examples:

An agent of a broker-dealer solicits clients to purchase unregistered promissory notes. The agent claims that promissory notes are not securities and, therefore, do not need to be registered. The Administrator disagrees with that position and would issue

A. a cease and desist order against the agent
B. a cease and desist order against the issuer of the note
C. a stop order against the agent
D. a stop order against the issuer

Unless we had reason to believe that the issuer was the one claiming that its notes were not securities, the only person guilty here is the agent. Stopping the agent from continuing to solicit the purchase of unregistered securities is done by issuing a cease and desist order, choice **A**.

Alternatively, if the question went like this:

Palterer Products, Inc. (PPI), headquartered in State J, has sent an announcement to a number of broker-dealers in the state promoting their 8% promissory notes as a high interest non-security alternative to a bank CD. The compliance officer of your firm forwards this to the State J Administrator. What action would the Administrator likely take?

A. Issue a cease and desist order against the compliance officer with or without a hearing
B. Issue a cease and desist order against PPI with or without a hearing
C. Issue a stop order against the compliance officer after giving opportunity for a hearing
D. Issue a stop order against PPI after giving opportunity for a hearing

Promissory notes are securities and, therefore, PPI must stop soliciting the sale of them as non-securities. The method of doing so is through the issue of a stop order, choice **D**. No order would be forthcoming against the compliance officer; she was only doing her job correctly. Remember, cease and desist orders are against registered securities professionals and stop orders against issuers. Finally, the cease and desist order can be issued with or without a hearing and the stop order only after a hearing.

QUICK QUIZ 3.B

True or False?

_____ 1. A final order may be entered only after opportunity for a hearing has been granted.

_____ 2. If an Administrator determines that a registration statement for a security is incomplete, he may issue a cease and desist order.

3. With regard to the powers of the Administrator, which of the following statements are NOT true?

   I. The Administrator must seek an injunction to issue a cease and desist order.
   II. The USA requires an Administrator to conduct a full hearing, public or private, before issuing a cease and desist order.
   III. The USA grants the Administrator the power to issue injunctions to force compliance with the provisions of the act.

   A. I and II
   B. I and III
   C. II and III
   D. I, II, and III

4. Although the Administrator has great power, the USA does place some limitations on the office. Which of the following statements regarding those powers are TRUE?

   I. In conducting an investigation, an Administrator can compel the testimony of witnesses.
   II. Investigations of serious violations must be open to the public.
   III. An Administrator in Illinois may enforce subpoenas from South Carolina only if the violation originally occurred in Illinois.
   IV. An Administrator may deny the registration of a securities professional who has been convicted of a felony within the past 10 years but must provide, if requested in writing, a hearing within 15 days.

   A. I, II, and IV
   B. I, III, and IV
   C. I and IV
   D. II and III

3. 2. 5 NONPUNITIVE TERMINATIONS OF REGISTRATION

A registration can be terminated even if there has not been a violation of the USA. A request for withdrawal and lack of qualification are both reasons for cancellation.

3. 2. 5. 1 Withdrawal

A person may request, on his own initiative, a withdrawal of a registration. The withdrawal is effective 30 days after the Administrator receives it, provided no revocation or suspension proceedings are in process against the person making the request. In that event, the Administrator may institute a revocation or suspension proceeding within one year after a withdrawal becomes effective.

TEST TOPIC ALERT   Once your registration has been withdrawn, the Administrator still retains jurisdiction over you for a period of one year.

3. 2. 5. 2   Cancellation

If an Administrator finds that an applicant or a registrant no longer exists or has ceased to transact business, the Administrator may cancel the registration.

TEST TOPIC ALERT

You may encounter this type of question regarding cancellation: "What would the Administrator do if mailings to a registrant were returned with no forwarding address?" The answer is, "Cancel the registration."

The Administrator may also cancel a registration if a person is declared mentally incompetent.

TAKE NOTE

Be familiar with the distinction between cancellation and denial, suspension, or revocation. Cancellation does not result from violations or a failure to follow the provisions of the act. Cancellation occurs as the result of death, dissolution, or mental incompetency and, unlike the others, is not a form of punishment.

TEST TOPIC ALERT

Because an agent's (or IAR's) registration is dependent on being associated with a broker-dealer (or IA), when the employer's registration is suspended or revoked, that of the registered individual is placed into suspense or some other term with essentially the same effect. When the period of suspension of the firm is over, registration of the individuals is reactivated. If the firm's registration has been revoked, the individual's registration will be placed in suspense until finding a new affiliation. If a period of more than two years should transpire without re-registering, retaking the exam will be necessary.

QUICK QUIZ 3.C

1. Which of the following statements relating to termination of registration is TRUE?
   A. A registration, once in effect, may never be voluntarily withdrawn.
   B. An Administrator may not cancel a registration of a securities professional who is declared mentally incompetent.
   C. An Administrator may revoke the registration of a securities professional who is declared mentally incompetent.
   D. An Administrator may cancel the registration of a registrant no longer in business.

3. 3   PENALTIES AND LIABILITIES

The USA provides both civil liabilities and criminal penalties for persons who violate the USA. In addition, the act provides for recovery by a client of financial loss that results from any action constituting a violation of any provision of the USA or any rule or order thereunder. In many cases, when an agent or IAR is found civilly liable for improper behavior, officers or other supervisory personnel of the firm may be liable as well if failure to supervise can be proven.

3. 3. 1   CIVIL LIABILITIES

Persons who sell securities or offer investment advice in violation of the USA are subject to civil liabilities (as well as possible criminal penalties).

The purchaser of securities sold in violation of the act may sue the seller to recover financial loss.

The purchaser can sue for recovery if the:

- securities were sold in violation of the registration provisions of the USA;
- sale was of an unregistered nonexempt security in violation of the registration provisions of USA;
- the securities professional omitted or made an untrue statement of material fact during a sales presentation;
- the agent was named along with the broker-dealer for a civil infraction;
- the securities were sold by an agent who should have been but was not registered under the act; or
- the securities were sold in violation of a rule or order of the securities Administrator.

Although most civil suits are brought by the purchaser, the Administrator may bring a civil enforcement action in a court, particularly to prevent publication, circulation, or use of any materials required by the Administrator to be filed under the act that have not been filed.

TEST TOPIC ALERT   Unlike some federal laws, there is no provision for receiving treble damages. That is, in addition to receiving back your investment, you receive payment equal to three times what you lost. That is primarily found in the federal laws regarding insider trading, but that is not relevant to this exam.

3. 3. 1. 1   Statute of Limitations

The time limit, or **statute of limitations,** for violations of the civil provisions of the USA is three years from the date of sale (or rendering of investment advice) or two years after discovering the violation, whichever occurred first.

TEST TOPIC ALERT   The USA provides that every cause of action under this statute survives the death of any person who might have been a plaintiff or defendant. Therefore, any bond required must provide that suit may be brought for the specified statute of limitations, even though the person who is bonded dies before the expiration of that period.

3. 3. 1. 2   Rights of Recovery from Improper Sale of Securities

If the purchaser of securities feels that the sale has been made in violation of the USA, that purchaser may file a complaint with the Administrator. If the Administrator investigates the claim and finds it has merit, then a case will be opened against the offending broker-dealer, agent, or both.

If the client's case is proven, at the direction of the Administrator, the client may recover:

- the original purchase price of the securities ("made whole");
- plus interest at a rate determined by the Administrator (generally referred to as the state's *legal rate*);
- plus all reasonable attorney's fees and court costs;
- minus any income received while the securities were held.

TAKE NOTE   The exam may refer to the interest paid to the client as being at the state's legal rate.

3. 3. 1. 3   Right of Rescission for Securities Sales

If the seller of securities discovers that he has made a sale in violation of the USA, the seller may offer to repurchase the securities from the buyer. In this case, the seller is offering the buyer the **right of rescission**. To satisfy the buyer's right of rescission, the amount paid back to the buyer must include the original purchase price and interest at a rate determined by the Administrator.

By offering to buy back the securities that were sold in violation of the act, the seller can avoid a lawsuit (and the payment of court costs and legal fees) through a **letter of rescission**. The buyer has 30 days after receiving the letter of rescission to respond. If the buyer does not accept or reject the rescission offer within 30 days, the buyer forfeits the right to pursue a lawsuit at a later date.

If the buyer accepts the rescission offer, he may recover:

- the original purchase price ("made whole") of the securities;
- plus interest at a rate determined by the Administrator (generally referred to as the state's legal rate);
- plus all reasonable attorney's fees and court costs;
- minus income received during the period in which the securities were held.

TAKE NOTE   A client **rejecting** the offer of rescission within the 30-day period retains the right to take the matter to court (sue). But, if the offer is not accepted or rejected within that 30-day period, it becomes null and void.

3. 3. 1. 4   Rights of Recovery from Improper Investment Advice

A person who buys a security as the result of investment advice received in violation of the USA also has the right to sue. In the case of securities purchased as a result of improper investment advice, the buyer may recover:

- the cost of the advice;

- plus losses resulting from the advice;
- plus all interest costs from the date of fee payment at a rate determined by the Administrator;
- plus any reasonable attorney's fees;
- less the amount of any income received from such advice.

3. 3. 1. 5   Right of Rescission for Investment Advice

Similar to the right of rescission described above for securities sales, an investment adviser who realizes that he has given advice that will subject him to civil action may avoid legal expenses by offering the client the same package as he would receive if he had sued—that is, refunding the cost of the advice, losses from the advice, and interest at the state's predetermined rate, less any income received on recommended securities.

3. 3. 1. 6   Scope of Liability

Under the USA, the actual seller of the securities or the advice is not the only person liable for the violation of the act. Every person who directly or indirectly controls the person who sold the securities or the advice, or is a material aid to the transaction, is also liable to the same extent as the person who conducted the transaction.

The effect of this is that if an agent makes a sale in violation (or IAR gives improper advice), but it can be shown that officers or partners of the broker-dealer or IA were irresponsible, action can be taken against them as well, and they can be found civilly liable.

TAKE NOTE   When securities are sold improperly, the buyer can recover the original purchase price in addition to reasonable income plus, if suit is necessary, legal costs. When improper investment advice is offered, the purchaser of the advice is entitled to recover the cost of the advice, losses incurred, and legal costs, but is not entitled to recover the original purchase price from the adviser.

3. 3. 1. 7   Surety Bond

In Unit 1, we discussed the need for securities professionals to post a surety bond under certain conditions. The USA states, "Every bond shall provide for suit thereon by any person who has a cause of action under this Act and, if the Administrator by rule or order requires, by any person who has a cause of action not arising under this act. Every bond shall provide that no suit may be maintained to enforce any liability on the bond unless brought within the time limitations of the Act."

TEST TOPIC ALERT   In other words, in order for a surety bond to meet the requirements of the USA, it must provide that any customer who can prove a violation (and does so within the statute of limitations) is entitled to collect against the bond.

EXAMPLE

How might this play out on the exam? Let's take a look at a sample question:

Martha is an agent with Rapid Execution Services (RES), a broker-dealer registered in all 50 states. Martha offers an IPO of a non-exempt security to a client without realizing that the security has not been registered in the client's state. The client purchases 500 shares of the new issue and, six months later, sells the stock at price 70% below the original purchase price. Because the stock was not registered in the client's state, the client could claim

 I. payment of the difference between the proceeds and the purchase price
 II. interest at the state's legal rate, minus any income received from the security
 III. court costs and lawyer's fees if the client has to go to court
 IV. punitive damages equal to the amount of the loss
 A. I and II
 B. I, II, and III
 C. IV only
 D. I, II, III, and IV

The correct choice is **B**. When a security is sold in violation of the USA (a non-exempt security must be registered under this scenario), the client can claim to be "made whole" plus interest, plus the expenses of going to court and paying for legal representation. There are no punitive damages; under rescission, the client recovers the entire loss. In general, to avoid the legal costs (and publicity), when a case like this is uncovered, the broker-dealer will present an offer of rescission, which gives the client all of this except the court and legal fees (because it is not necessary to go to court).

3. 3. 2   CRIMINAL PENALTIES

Persons found guilty of a fraudulent securities transaction are subject to criminal penalties (as well as possible civil liabilities). Upon conviction, the court (not the Administrator) may levy a fine against the person, impose a prison sentence, or do both. The maximum penalty is a fine of $5,000, a jail sentence of three years, or both. It is important to note that no person may be imprisoned for the violation of any rule or order if he proves that he had no knowledge of the rule or order. In other words, you have to know that you are willingly in violation in order to get jail time. It is also important to note that while the Administrator does not have the power to arrest anyone, he may apply to the appropriate authorities in his state for the issuance of an arrest warrant. The appropriate state prosecutor, usually the state attorney general, may decide whether to bring a criminal action under the USA, another statute, or, when applicable, common law. It is up to the court to determine prison time. In certain states, the Administrator has full or limited criminal enforcement powers. To be convicted of fraud, the violation must be willful and the registrant must know that the activity is fraudulent.

TAKE NOTE

Fraud is the deliberate or willful concealment, misrepresentation, or omission of material information or the truth to deceive or manipulate another person for unlawful or unfair gain. Under the USA, fraud is not limited to common-law deceit.

3. 3. 2. 1   Statute of Limitations

The statute of limitations for criminal offenses under the USA is five years from the date of the offense.

TAKE NOTE   Remember the sequence 5-5-3 for the application of criminal penalties: 5-year statute of limitations, $5,000 maximum fine, and imprisonment of no more than 3 years.

Under the civil provisions, the statute of limitations is 2 years from the discovery of the offense or 3 years after the act occurred, whichever occurs first.

3. 3. 3   JUDICIAL REVIEW OF ORDERS (APPEAL)

Any person affected by an order of the Administrator may obtain a review of the order in an appropriate court by filing a written petition within 60 days. In general, filing an appeal does not automatically act as a stay of the penalty. The order will go into effect as issued unless the court rules otherwise.

QUICK QUIZ 3.D

1. Which of the following statements relating to penalties under the USA is TRUE?

    A. Unknowing violation of the USA by an agent is cause for imprisonment under the criminal liability provisions of the act.

    B. If a violation has occurred in the sale of a security, the purchaser of the security may recover the original purchase price, legal costs, and interest, less any earnings already received.

    C. A seller who notices that a sale was made in violation of the act may offer a right of rescission to the purchaser; the purchaser must accept this right within the earlier of two years after notice of the violation or three years after the sale.

    D. Any person aggrieved by an order of the Administrator may request an appeal of the order within 15 days which, in effect, functions as a stay of the order during the appeal period.

2. When making an offer of a new issue that is in registration to a prospective client, an agent claims that his registration with the Administrator is proof of his qualifications. Under the USA,

    A. claiming his registration is approved by the Administrator while making an offer of a security undergoing registration subjects this agent to a civil liability claim

    B. claiming his registration is approved by the Administrator while making an offer of a security does not subject this agent to a civil liability claim until the registration becomes effective

    C. claiming his registration is approved by the Administrator subjects this agent only to civil liability if a sale results

    D. regardless of whether a sale takes place, an agent making a misleading statement of this type subjects himself to possible civil liability

3. 4   OTHER PROVISIONS

In addition to the items previously mentioned, there are several miscellaneous provisions under the Administrator's authority.

3. 4. 1   FILING OF SALES AND ADVERTISING LITERATURE

The Administrator may, by rule or order (remember, there is a difference between those two terms), require the filing of any prospectus, pamphlet, circular, form letter, advertisement, or other sales literature or advertising communication addressed or intended for distribution to prospective investors, including clients or prospective clients of an investment adviser, unless the security is exempt, the transaction is exempt, or it is a federal covered security.

3. 4. 2   ADMINISTRATIVE FILES AND OPINIONS

A document is considered to be filed when it is received by the Administrator.

3. 4. 2. 1   Maintenance of Records

The Administrator maintains a record of all applications for registration of securities and registration statements and all applications for broker-dealer, agent, investment adviser, or investment adviser representative registration which are or have ever been effective in his state; all written notices of claim of exemption from registration requirements; all orders entered under this act; and all interpretative opinions or no-action determinations issued. All records may be maintained in computer or microfilm format or any other form of data storage. The record is available for public inspection. The information contained in or filed with any registration statement, application, or report may be made available to the public under such rules as the Administrator prescribes.

3. 4. 2. 2   Availability of Copies

Upon request and at such reasonable charges as he prescribes, the Administrator shall furnish to any person photostatic or other copies (certified under his seal of office if requested) of any entry in the register or any document which is a matter of public record. In any proceeding or prosecution under this act, any copy so certified is prima facie evidence of the contents of the entry or document certified.

3. 4. 2. 3   Interpretive Opinions

The Administrator, in his discretion, may honor requests from interested persons for interpretative opinions or may issue determinations that the Administrator will not institute enforcement proceedings against certain specified persons for engaging in certain specified activities where the determination is consistent with the purposes fairly intended by the policy and provisions of this act. The Administrator may charge a fee for interpretative opinions and no-action determinations. This is similar to the same procedure used for "letter rulings" from the IRS.

UNIT TEST

1. If convicted of a willful violation of the Uniform Securities Act, an agent is subject to

   A. imprisonment for 5 years
   B. a fine of $5,000 and/or imprisonment for 3 years
   C. a fine of $10,000
   D. disbarment

2. To protect the public, the Administrator may

   I. deny a registration if the registrant does not have sufficient experience to function as an agent
   II. limit a registrant's functions to those of a broker-dealer if, in the initial application for registration as an investment adviser, the registrant is not qualified to act as an adviser
   III. consider approving a registration that the registrant will work under the supervision of a registered investment adviser or broker-dealer
   IV. deny a registration, although denial is not in the public's interest, if it is prudent in view of a change in the state's political composition

   A. I and II
   B. II and III
   C. III and IV
   D. I, II, III, and IV

3. Aaron is a client of XYZ Financial Services. Over the past several years, Aaron has been suspicious of possible churning of his account but has taken no action because account performance has been outstanding. After reviewing his most recent statement, Aaron suspects that excessive transactions have occurred. He consults his attorney, who informs him that under the USA, any lawsuit for recovery of damages under the USA must be started within

   A. 1 year of occurrence
   B. 2 years of occurrence
   C. 3 years of occurrence or 2 years of discovery, whichever occurs first
   D. 2 years of occurrence or 3 years of discovery, whichever occurs last

4. Which of the following accurately describes a cease and desist order as authorized by the USA?

   A. An order that a federal agency issued to a brokerage firm to stop an advertising campaign
   B. An Administrator's order to refrain from a practice of business he believes to be unfair
   C. A court-issued order requiring a business to stop an unfair practice
   D. An order from one brokerage firm to another to refrain from unfair business practices

5. A customer living in one state receives a phone call from an agent in another state. A transaction between the two occurs in yet another state. According to the Uniform Securities Act, under whose jurisdiction does the transaction fall?

   A. Administrator of the state in which the customer lives
   B. Administrator of the state from which the agent made the call
   C. Administrator of the state in which the transaction took place
   D. Administrators of all 3 states involved

6. By rule, the Administrator may

   A. forbid an adviser from taking custody of client funds
   B. allow an agent to waive provisions of the USA
   C. suspend federal law if he believes it to be in the public interest
   D. suspend the registration of a federal covered adviser because the contract did not meet the requirements for a state-sanctioned investment advisory contract

7. If it is in the public interest, the Uniform Securities Act provides that the state Administrator may deny the registration of a broker-dealer for all of the following reasons EXCEPT

   A. the applicant is not qualified because of lack of experience
   B. a willful violation of the Uniform Securities Act has taken place
   C. the applicant is financially insolvent
   D. the applicant is enjoined temporarily from engaging in the securities business

8. If an agent chooses to appeal an Administrator's order, when must the agent file for review of the order with the appropriate court?

   A. Immediately
   B. Within 30 days after the entry of the order
   C. Within 60 days after the entry of the order
   D. Within 180 days after the entry of the order

9. An Administrator may summarily suspend a registration pending final determination of proceedings under the USA. However, the Administrator may not enter a final order without each of the following EXCEPT

   A. appropriate prior notice to the applicant as well as the employer or prospective employer of the applicant
   B. an opportunity for a hearing
   C. findings of fact and conclusions of law
   D. prior written acknowledgment of the applicant

10. The Administrator has authority to

   A. issue a cease and desist order without a hearing
   B. issue a cease and desist order only after a hearing
   C. suspend a securities registration upon discovering that an officer of the registrant has been convicted of a nonsecurities-related crime that is listed on the officer's police record as a misdemeanor
   D. sentence violators of the USA to 3 years in prison

11. Which of the following statements regarding NASAA Guidelines is NOT true?

   A. The Administrator's rules apply to general situations.
   B. The Administrator's orders apply to specific situations.
   C. The Administrator may work in concert with the SEC in developing rules and regulations.
   D. At least once every 5 years, the Administrator's rules are subject to a relevancy review.

12. An agent lives in Montana and is registered in Montana and Idaho. His broker-dealer is registered in every state west of the Mississippi River. The agent's client, who lives in Montana, decides to enroll in a 1-year resident MBA program in Philadelphia. During the 1-year period when the client is in Philadelphia, the agent may

   A. conduct business with the client as usual
   B. only accept unsolicited orders
   C. not conduct business with the client
   D. not deal with the client until the broker-dealer registers in Pennsylvania

13. An Administrator may deny a person's application for registration as an agent for all of the following reasons EXCEPT

   A. lack of experience
   B. failure to post a surety bond
   C. failure to pass a written exam
   D. not meeting minimum financial standards

14. The Administrator may cancel the registration of an adviser if

   A. mail is returned with a notice that the forwarding notice has expired
   B. the adviser is not in the business any longer
   C. a court has declared the adviser to be mentally incompetent
   D. any of the above

15. An agent of a broker-dealer has been found civilly liable for making untrue statements in connection with a public offering. The officers of the firm purchased a compliance program from a third-party software developer that was designed to be able to protect against the untrue statements reaching clients. Unfortunately, the program was never used because they could not figure out how it worked. What is the nature of the civil liability of the officers?

   A. They are liable because they did not act responsibly.
   B. They are only liable if they willingly ignored the untrue statements.
   C. The liability is that of the agent's supervisor, not the officers.
   D. Officers are never liable for actions of their agents.

ANSWERS AND RATIONALES

1. **B.** Under the USA, the maximum penalty is a fine of $5,000 and/or 3 years in jail.

2. **B.** The Administrator may determine that an applicant, in his initial application for registration as an investment adviser, is not qualified to act as an adviser and thus may limit the registration to that of a broker-dealer. The Administrator can also take into consideration whether the registrant will work under the supervision of a registered investment adviser or broker-dealer when approving an application. The Administrator can deny, suspend, or revoke a registration for many reasons, but they must be in the interest of the public. The Administrator may not deny the registration simply because it is prudent. Lack of experience in itself is insufficient reason for denial.

3. **C.** Under the USA, the lawsuit for recovery of damages must commence within the earlier of 3 years after occurrence of the offense or 2 years after its discovery.

4. **B.** A cease and desist order is a directive from an administrative agency to immediately stop a particular action. Administrators may issue cease and desist orders with or without a prior hearing. Brokerage houses cannot issue cease and desist orders to each other.

5. **D.** Under the scope of the Uniform Securities Act, if any part of a transaction occurs in a state, the transaction falls under the jurisdiction of the state Administrator. The transaction is under the control of the Administrator of the state in which the customer lives (because the offer was received there), the Administrator of the state in which the agent is calling (because the offer was made from that state), and the Administrator of the state in which the transaction took place.

6. **A.** The Administrator has considerable discretion to make rules or issue orders. Specifically, the USA allows the Administrator to prohibit custody by rule. However, the USA does not allow the Administrator to waive provisions of the USA, nor can the Administrator suspend federal law.

7. **A.** If the broker-dealer qualifies by virtue of training or knowledge, registration cannot be denied for lack of experience only. Registration may be denied if the applicant willfully violates the Uniform Securities Act, is financially insolvent, or has been enjoined (is the subject of a court-issued injunction) from engaging in the securities business.

8. **C.** Under the USA, a registered person has up to 60 days to appeal any order issued against him by the state Administrator.

9. **D.** With the exception of proceedings awaiting final determination, the Administrator must provide appropriate prior notice to the applicant as well as the employer or prospective employer of the applicant and provide the opportunity for a hearing. In addition, the Administrator may issue a final order only after findings of fact and conclusions of law. An applicant is not required to provide written acknowledgment before an order is issued.

10. **A.** The Administrator may issue a cease and desist order without a hearing but does not have the authority to sentence violators of the USA. The Administrator may not suspend a security's registration upon discovering, in subsequent years, that an officer of the firm has been convicted of a nonsecurities-related crime, as long as it is a misdemeanor. Had it been any felony, then suspension of the issue's registration is a possibility.

11. **D.** Relevancy review is not part of the act.

12. **A.** Even though the college program is referred to as a resident program, that does not mean the client has changed his state of residence. Although neither the firm nor the agent is registered, the agent may continue to conduct business with the client because both the agent and his firm are properly registered in the client's state of permanent residence.

13. **A.** Lack of experience, by itself, is not cause for registration denial.

14. **D.** You must know the difference between cancellation of a registration (which requires no hearing) and revocation (which does).

15. **A.** As President Harry Truman famously said, "The buck stops here." Officers carry liability on behalf of the broker-dealer. Had they taken the initiative to learn how to use the compliance program, the agent would have been stopped in his tracks.

QUICK QUIZ ANSWERS

Quick Quiz 3.A

1. **D.** The Administrator has jurisdiction over a security offering if it was directed to, originated in, or was accepted in that state.

2. **C.** A state Administrator has jurisdiction over a securities offering made in a bona fide newspaper published within the state with no more than two-thirds of its circulation outside the state.

Quick Quiz 3.B

1. **T.** A final order, such as a suspension or revocation, may only be entered after the opportunity for a hearing has been granted.

2. **F.** Cease and desist orders are directed at securities professionals. Stop orders are used for securities offerings.

3. **D.** The Administrator need not seek an injunction to issue a cease and desist order. The USA does not require that an Administrator conduct a public or private hearing before issuing a cease and desist order. When time does not permit, the Administrator may issue a cease and desist order before a hearing to prevent a pending violation. The USA does not grant the Administrator the power to issue injunctions to force compliance with the act. The act permits the Administrator to issue cease and desist orders, and, if they do not work, the Administrator may seek an injunction from a court of competent jurisdiction. A cease and desist order is an administrative order, whereas an injunction is a judicial order.

4. **C.** An Administrator can compel the testimony of witnesses when conducting an investigation. Investigation of serious violations need not be held in public. An Administrator in Illinois may enforce subpoenas from South Carolina whether the violation occurred in Illinois or not. Conviction for any felony within the past 10 years is one of a number of reasons the Administrator has for denying a license. However, upon notice of the denial, a written request may be made for a hearing. That request must be honored within 15 days.

Quick Quiz 3.C

1. **D.** An Administrator does not revoke the registration of a person who is declared mentally incompetent but cancels such registration; cancellation is a non-punitive administrative action. An administrator may cancel the registration of a registrant that is no longer in existence. A person may request a withdrawal of a registration. Withdrawals become effective after 30 days if there are no revocation or denial proceedings in process.

Quick Quiz 3.D

1. **B.** A client who purchased a security in violation of the USA may recover the original purchase price plus costs involved in filing a lawsuit. In addition, the purchaser is entitled to interest at a rate stated by the Administrator, less any earnings already received on the investment. To be subject to time in prison, a sales agent must knowingly have violated the USA. The right of rescission must be accepted or rejected within 30 days of receipt of the letter of rescission. Although any person aggrieved by an order of the Administrator may request an appeal of the order within 60 days, such appeal does not function as a stay order during the appeal process. The person who is the subject of the order must comply with the order during the period unless a stay is granted by the court.

2. **C.** For an agent to have civil liability, a sale must take place. If the offer is made using a statement like the one in this question and a sale subsequently occurs, a client suffering a loss would be able to sue. Even though one may never claim approval by the Administrator, there is no civil liability unless the client has some kind of a claim. However, even though the client cannot bring a case, the Administrator could bring a disciplinary action against the agent for making this claim. On a law exam, you must be careful to understand who has a claim and when they do.

Communications With Customers and Prospects

Before a person can become a customer, the person is first a prospect. Knowing what can and what cannot be said at all stages of the relationship is critical to not only the protection of the client, but to the securities professional as well. Failure to abide by the required practices can lead to suspension or a more severe penalty such as a revocation or bar from the industry.

The Series 63 exam will contain 12 questions on the material presented in this unit. ∎

When you have completed this unit, you should be able to:

■ **discuss** the different disclosures that must be made both before and after the client relationship is established;

■ **recognize** those representations concerning registrations that are unlawful;

■ **identify** the restrictions against performance guarantees;

■ **discuss** the various types of customer agreements; and

■ **describe** the role that social media is playing in today's environment.

4. 1 REQUIRED DISCLOSURES

When asked about the three most important factors affecting the value of real estate, invariably, the response is Location, Location, Location. In this industry, the three most important factors involved in avoiding disciplinary actions are Disclosure, Disclosure, Disclosure. There is very little that a securities professional cannot do as long as proper disclosure is made.

4. 1. 1 DISCLOSURE OF CAPACITY

As stated in Unit 1, broker-dealers can operate either in a principal or agency capacity when executing transactions for their clients. When acting in a principal capacity, the BD is the contra party to the trade. That is, they are on the other side of the trade of the client. When the client is buying a security, the broker-dealer is selling it out of inventory. In this case, the firm's profit comes from a markup. If the client is selling a security and the broker-dealer purchases it for its inventory, once again, the firm is acting as a principal (every trade has two principals—the buyer and the seller) and, in this case, the profit comes from a markdown.

When acting in an agency capacity, the firm is acting like any other broker or agent (real estate broker, insurance agent, employment agent) in that they are simply putting the buyer and seller together. And, like all agents or brokers, they earn a commission.

For the exam, it is important to know that broker-dealers must always indicate their capacity on the trade confirmation, sent no later than completion of the trade (settlement date). They will indicate if they acted as a broker (and always disclose the amount of commission) or if they acted as a principal (and, depending on the circumstances—not tested—may have to indicate the markup or markdown).

4. 1. 1. 1 Disclosure of Capacity by Investment Advisers

It is unlikely that the Series 63 will cover this, but let's take a few lines to make sure we have it, just in case. As stated in Unit 1, the business of an investment adviser is giving advice. That is why they get compensated; they're not in the business of executing securities transactions—that is the role of the broker-dealer.

However, on rare occasions, an investment adviser might buy from or sell to an advisory client in the capacity of a principal. Or, the adviser might put together a buyer and seller acting in the capacity of an agent. This would be permitted with the following two requirements.

- The client receives full written disclosure as to the capacity in which the adviser proposes to act.
- Client consent is obtained.

Both of these must be done prior to completion of the transaction. This is unlike a broker-dealer who, when acting as a principal in a trade with a customer or as the customer's agent, need only indicate that capacity on the trade confirmation; consent is not required.

4. 1. 2 DISCLOSURE OF CONFLICTS OF INTEREST

What is a conflict of interest? One legal definition goes something like this: "A term used to describe the situation in which a person in a position of trust, contrary to the obligation and absolute duty to act for the benefit of a designated individual, exploits the relationship for personal benefit, typically pecuniary."

Clients of securities professionals expect them to do what is best for them, not for the person they're trusting with their money. The best way to avoid these conflicts of interest is to disclose them so that the customer can decide what to do. Some examples of potential conflicts of interest are:

- offering a proprietary product, such as a house fund (a mutual fund where the underwriter or adviser is affiliated with the broker-dealer);

- offering a limited partnership offering (DPP) where the sponsor is an affiliate of the broker-dealer;

- program sponsors, such as investment companies or insurance companies, providing incentives or rewards to agents for selling the sponsors' products;

- a securities professional having a financial interest in any security being recommended;

- a broker-dealer going public and placing shares of its own stock into discretionary accounts; and

- a broker-dealer publishing a favorable research report after underwriting the issuer's stock offering.

This is just a sample. The key point is, if there is any doubt about the transparency of the recommendation or transaction, be sure to make full disclosure.

TEST TOPIC ALERT   Suppose you were selling shares of a company where your sister was a control person? Do you think you'd have to disclose that potential conflict to your clients? Yes!

4.1.2.1 Fiduciary Responsibility of Investment Advisers

Unlike broker-dealers and their agents, investment advisers and their IARs have a fiduciary responsibility to their customers. That obligates these advisers and their representatives to put their clients' interests ahead of their own. That is the primary reason why advisers need their clients' consent when acting as agents or principals in trades with them (as covered above). As fiduciaries, investment advisers must identify and address all material conflicts of interest by eliminating or disclosing such conflicts. Clients rely on the advice of their advisers and must feel confident that those advisers are working in the clients' best interests. If the adviser also engages in non-securities related activities, such as selling auto insurance or real estate, these represent potential conflicts of interest (time taken away from "watching the market") and must be disclosed.

In a famous Supreme Court case, SEC v. Capital Gains Research Bureau, Inc., 375 U.S. 180 (1963), the Court stated that investors "must be permitted to evaluate overlapping motivations, through appropriate disclosure, in deciding whether an adviser is serving 'two masters' or only one, 'especially if one of the masters happens to be economic self-interest.'"

4. 1. 3   DISCLOSURE OF FEES

In 2015, NASAA published an investor advisory regarding fees charged by broker-dealer firms for services and maintenance of investment accounts. The advisory followed research from NASAA, showing that investors are confused about brokerage services and maintenance fees and want clear and easy access to fee information from their broker-dealer firms. A national public opinion poll commissioned by NASAA found that fees are important to investors, but a general lack of standardization and clarity in their disclosures has left investors unaware of how much their broker-dealer firms charge for the service and maintenance of their investment accounts. Here are some ways that broker-dealers can make the disclosures easier for customers to follow:

- Fees are typically disclosed when a customer account is opened. If the firm changes the fee schedule, be clear about it, and be sure to use appropriate methods to give advance notification of the changes to the customer.

- Minimize the fine print, or at least make the fees and charges clear. Whether using a table, a chart, or a list, make sure it is easy for customers to determine what the fees and charges are and how they are computed.

- Use standardized and uncomplicated terms to describe service and maintenance fees in order to help clients compare fees between different firms.

TAKE NOTE   A working group convened by NASAA has developed a model fee disclosure schedule and related accessibility guidelines to help investors better understand and compare various broker-dealer service and maintenance-related fees. The template and guidelines make fee disclosure easily accessible for retail investors to use to understand and compare fees.

4. 1. 3. 1   Typical Broker-Dealer Fees

Examples of the more common fees that might be charged by a broker-dealer include the following:

- Issuance of a stock certificate. Although most securities are kept in street name, there could be instances where the customer wants delivery of the physical certificate. There is usually a charge for this service.

- Transferring an account. When a client decides to move the account from one broker-dealer to another, there is usually a charge to cover the administrative expenses of the transfer.

- Wiring funds. Although frequently waived for those with large account balances, if the client needs money wired out of the account, a charge, similar to that made by most banks, is levied against the account.

- Margin account interest. When purchasing on margin, money is borrowed and the rate of interest charged on the borrowed funds must be disclosed.

- Account maintenance fees. Similar to the monthly charge on your bank statement, many firms charge an annual account fee, particularly if a small account.

- Safekeeping of funds/securities. This is the charge made for maintaining custody of client assets, which is usually waived for larger accounts.

- Late settlement fee. This is similar to the late fee on a credit card. When a client's payment arrives after settlement date (or is returned due to insufficient funds), the broker-dealer may assess a fee.

- Postage and handling. Although many firms absorb the cost of normal mailings, express or overnight delivery at the request of the client is usually subject to a charge

This is not a complete list, but it includes the most common charges. What is most important for the exam is that all of the fees must be disclosed.

TEST TOPIC ALERT

Not included in the fee disclosure documents are:

- commissions,

- markups and markdowns, and

- advisory fees.

There are other documents where those disclosures are made.

---

4. 2   UNLAWFUL REPRESENTATIONS CONCERNING REGISTRATIONS

Misrepresentation is a prohibited practice. There are two areas covered: registration of the securities professional and registration of a security.

4. 2. 1   MISREPRESENTING A SECURITIES PROFESSIONAL'S REGISTRATION

Once you are registered, what can you say about that? Can you say the Administrator has *approved* of you or your registration? Not at all! Representing that your registration implies any kind of approval of you or your qualifications is a prohibited practice. What you can state is that you are a registered agent of ABC Broker-Dealer, or you are a registered investment adviser representative of the XYZ Investment Adviser.

4. 2. 2   MISREPRESENTING A SECURITY'S REGISTRATION

Similar to the above, it is prohibited to imply that registration of a security means that the Administrator (or any regulatory body) has *approved* of the issue. In fact, on the front page (or inside cover) of every prospectus is a statement called the disclaimer, which states that the security has not been approved or disapproved, and any representation to the contrary is a criminal offense.

1. Which of the following statements may be made by an issuer selling securities to the public that are registered with the Administrator?

    A. The Administrator has cleared this issue for sale to the public.
    B. The Administrator has passed on the adequacy of the information provided in the prospectus.
    C. The Administrator has approved the accuracy of the information contained in the prospectus.
    D. The Administrator has affirmed the merits of the security as an investment.

2. LMN Securities, a broker-dealer registered with the SEC in more than a dozen states, has just become a member firm of the New York Stock Exchange. It would be permitted for LMN to tell its customers that

    A. the membership in the NYSE is a testimony to the integrity of the firm
    B. they are now members of the NYSE
    C. they are now federal covered and will no longer have to register in those states where they do not maintain a place of business.
    D. this adds one more level of approval of the firm's business

3. Investment advisers and their representatives have an obligation to place their clients' needs ahead of their own. This is legally known as

    A. avoiding conflicts of interest
    B. making full disclosure
    C. fiduciary responsibility
    D. playing fair

Quick Quiz answers can be found at the end of the unit.

4. 3   PERFORMANCE GUARANTEES

There is little that can be guaranteed in this industry.

4. 3. 1   GUARANTEED SECURITY

As mentioned in the beginning of this course, a guaranteed security is where a party other than the issuer guarantees the payment of principal and interest (on a debt security) or dividend (on an equity security). The important thing about that guarantee is that there is no guarantee on the performance of the investment. That is, gains cannot be part of the guarantee.

4. 3. 2   GUARANTEE AGAINST LOSS

Unfortunately, it is not uncommon in the industry for a securities professional to tell a client something to the effect of, "If this stock doesn't earn X% within the next three months, I'll make up the difference," or, "I am so sure you won't lose on this investment that I'll buy it back from you at your cost plus 10%." Both of these are considered performance guarantees and are prohibited actions.

Perhaps the simplest statement regarding guarantees is found in the NASAA Model Rule on Unethical Business Practices of Investment Advisers, Investment Adviser Representatives, and Federal Covered Advisers, where it lists "Guaranteeing a client that a specific result will be achieved (gain or no loss) with advice which will be rendered" as one of the prohibitions.

TAKE NOTE
Although performance guarantees are prohibited, under certain circumstances, investment advisers can receive performance-based compensation. That means the advisory contract with the client can provide that investment return that is better than that of a selected index can result in a higher fee to the adviser. Of course, it must go both ways; if the performance of the account is below that of the index, the fee is reduced.

TEST TOPIC ALERT
If justified, a broker-dealer, but not an associated person of the firm, may correct a bona fide error. This does not apply to an associated person of a member because of the concern that any such payment may conceal individual misconduct.

---

4. 4   CUSTOMER AGREEMENTS

Opening an account with a broker-dealer involves a certain amount of paperwork. How could one make suitable recommendations without having some knowledge of the customer's financial condition and objectives? In addition, there are federal laws requiring broker-dealers to obtain enough information about a client to minimize the possibility of money laundering or other illegal practices. We will examine some of these agreements.

4. 4. 1   NEW ACCOUNT AGREEMENT

Opening an account requires the completion of the new account agreement. This is basically a contract between the broker-dealer and the customer explaining the rights and obligations of both and the charges for the services that will be rendered. Information that must be obtained from the client includes items such as:

■ does the client have the legal capacity to enter into agreements? That is, is the client of full legal age in the state of jurisdiction, and does she have the capacity to enter into the agreement?

■ employment information

■ the Customer Identification Program (CIP) notice. In order to help the government fight the funding of terrorism and money laundering activities, broker-dealers are required by federal law to obtain, verify, and record information that identifies each person who opens an account. That information includes the following four items:

— name,

— date of birth—note that the new account form only requires the account holder be of legal age while the CIP requires the actual date of birth,

— a residential or business street address (no mail receiving or P.O. boxes), and

— tax identification number (if a U.S. citizen, this is typically the Social Security number);

- citizenship or visa details; and
- financial information about the client.

4. 4. 1. 1 Investment Advisory Contracts

NASAA's Model Rule on Unethical Business Practices of Investment Advisers, Investment Adviser Representatives, and Federal Covered Advisers includes the following as one of the unethical business practices:

> Entering into, extending or renewing any investment advisory contract, unless such contract is in writing and discloses, in substance, the services to be provided, the term of the contract, the advisory fee, the formula for computing the fee, the amount of prepaid fee to be returned in the event of contract termination or non-performance, whether the contract grants discretionary power to the adviser and that no assignment of such contract shall be made by the investment adviser without the consent of the other party to the contract.

Another prohibition found in that Model Rule is "Indicating, in an advisory contract, any condition, stipulation, or provisions binding any person to waive compliance with any provision of the Uniform Securities Act or of the Investment Advisers Act of 1940."

TEST TOPIC ALERT   This point (waivers) sometimes comes up on the exam. What you have to know is that in all cases on the test (remember, this course is about the *test* world and not the *real* world), waivers are not permitted.

4. 4. 1. 1. 1 Performance-Based Compensation for Investment Advisers

The Uniform Securities Act also prohibits certain performance fee arrangements contingent on capital gains or appreciation being part of the advisory contract. There is an exception, however, from the performance fee provisions for contracts with a qualified client defined as:

- a natural person or company that immediately after entering into the contract has at least $1 million under the management of the investment adviser; or
- a natural person or company that the IA has reason to believe that immediately before entering into the contract has a net worth exclusive of the primary residence (in the case of individuals, assets held jointly with a spouse, but no one else, can be used) in excess of $2.1 million.

When computing the fee, both gains and losses must be considered (the fee cannot be based solely on gains).

Please note: A fee based on the average amount of money under management over a particular period is not considered a performance fee.

4. 4. 2 SPECIAL ACCOUNTS

Some clients will open margin accounts, options accounts, or both. In these cases, special requirements apply.

4. 4. 2. 1 Margin Accounts

Margin accounts allow investors to leverage their investment dollars. Through margin accounts, investors can borrow money from brokerage firms by pledging the purchased stock as collateral. Opening a margin account involves signing two agreements, with an optional third. Those are:

- the **credit agreement**, which discloses the terms of the credit extended by the broker-dealer, including the method of interest computation and situations under which interest rates may change as well as the stipulation that the broker-dealer may use the client's margin securities as collateral for the loan that it makes to the client;

- the **hypothecation agreement**, which gives permission to the broker-dealer to pledge customer margin securities as collateral. The firm hypothecates customer securities to the bank, and the bank loans money to the broker-dealer on the basis of the loan value of these securities; and

- the optional loan consent form, which gives permission to the firm to loan customer margin securities to other customers or broker-dealers, usually for short sales.

TAKE NOTE

In simple terms, there are two loans taking place:

- the loan from the BD to the client with the client's securities used as collateral—that is covered in the credit agreement; and

- the loan from a bank to the BD with the client's securities used as collateral for the BD's loan—the authorization for the BD to use those securities is found in the hypothecation agreement.

TEST TOPIC ALERT

NASAA's Statement of Policy on Dishonest or Unethical Business Practices of Broker-Dealers and Agents states that it is prohibited to execute any transaction in a margin account without securing from the customer a properly executed, written margin agreement promptly *after* the initial transaction in the account.

4. 4. 2. 1. 1 Margin Account Risk Disclosure Document

Although NASAA does not have one, FINRA rules (which most states view as practices to be followed by broker-dealers under their jurisdiction), do have a risk disclosure requirement for margin accounts. As part of opening a margin account, the broker-dealer must provide customers with a risk disclosure document. This information must also be provided to margin customers on an annual basis. The document discusses the risks associated with margin trading, some of which are listed below.

- You can lose more funds than you deposit in the margin account.

- The firm can force the sale of securities or other assets in your account(s) and do so without contacting you.

- You are not entitled to choose which securities can be sold if a call for additional funds is not met.

- You are not entitled to an extension of time to meet a margin call.

- The firm can increase its house maintenance margin requirements at any time and is not required to provide you advance written notice.

4. 4. 2. 2 Options Accounts

NASAA does not have a specific rule dealing with the opening of options accounts. So, just as we did with the margin account risk disclosure document, we will refer to FINRA's rules.

Because trading options (puts and calls) generally involves a higher degree of risk than stocks, bonds, or mutual funds, a designated supervisory person with knowledge about options must approve the account opening. In addition, there is a special Options Disclosure Document (ODD) that must be provided to any prospective options customer.

In approving a customer's account for options trading, a broker-dealer, or agent associated with the broker-dealer, must exercise due diligence to ascertain the essential facts relative to the customer, his financial situation, and his investment objectives. One question asked on a new options account form that is not required on a normal brokerage account opening is investment experience and knowledge (e.g., number of years, size, frequency, and type of transactions) for options, stocks and bonds, commodities, and other financial instruments. Based upon such information, the designated supervisory person shall specifically approve or disapprove in writing the customer's account for options trading.

The account approval will indicate the:

- date the options disclosure document (ODD) is furnished to the customer;

- nature and types of transactions for which the account is approved (e.g., buying, covered writing, uncovered writing, spreading, discretionary transactions);

- name of the agent assigned to the account;

- name of the supervisor approving the account;

- date of approval; and

- dates of verification of currency of account information.

4. 4. 2. 2. 1   Receipt of the Options Account Agreement

Within 15 days after a customer's account has been approved for options trading, the broker-dealer must obtain from the customer a written agreement that the customer is aware of and agrees to be bound by FINRA rules applicable to the trading of option contracts and that the customer has received a copy of the current ODD. Part of the agreement states that she is aware of and agrees to be bound by the rules of the Options Clearing Corporation.

4. 4. 2. 3 Discretionary Accounts

A discretionary account is one where the customer grants the power to a broker-dealer or investment adviser to make buy and sell decisions in the account without the need to have prior contact with the customer. Before a broker-dealer or agent can exercise discretion, a written discretionary authorization permitting such discretion must be received by the firm, and the account must be approved by a designated supervisor.

The rule for investment advisers is slightly different. In the case of an advisory client, oral authorization may be relied upon for the first 10 business days after the initial discretionary trade in the account. After that time, however, without a written authorization, no further discretion may be exercised. We'll learn more about discretionary accounts in the next unit.

QUICK QUIZ 4.B

1. In which of the following cases must the required documentation be received prior to any account activity?

    A. Discretionary account with a broker-dealer
    B. Discretionary account with an investment adviser
    C. Margin account
    D. Options account

2. Which of the following is NOT required under the Customer Identification Program when opening a new account for an individual?

    A. Date of birth
    B. Name of employer
    C. Social Security number
    D. Physical residential address

4. 5 CORRESPONDENCE AND SOCIAL MEDIA

It should be clear that disclosure and fairness are the primary themes underlying all communications with customers. Use of social media websites for business purposes should be treated no differently from any other business-related electronic communication. Firms must ensure they have sufficient systems, policies, and procedures to supervise, review, and retain business communications made using social media sites. In this final segment of this unit, we will address several of the specific methods used to communicate with both existing and prospective clients.

4. 5. 1 SOCIAL MEDIA INCLUDING ELECTRONIC COMMUNICATIONS (EMAILS AND TEXT MESSAGES)

Communication with customers has historically been through written correspondence, while the traditional way of reaching prospects has been through print, TV, and radio advertising. In the 21st century, however, snail mail has given way to email, texting, and the broker-dealer's website. Prospects are being reached through various social networks as well as the internet.

At the time of this printing, NASAA's primary concern with social media has been alerting investors to the risks. Although some of that may be tested, it is probable that the Series 63's focus will be on usage of social media by securities professionals. As has been done with other topics not directly addressed by NASAA, we will rely on the policies adopted by other regulators. But first, let's look at some of NASAA's comments regarding investor awareness.

4. 5. 1. 1 Investor Concerns Regarding Social Media

Social networking in the internet age allows people to connect to one another more quickly and easily than ever before. Investment promoters increasingly are logging on to find investors and their money.

The role of the securities professional is to help protect clients from falling prey to the many phony schemes found on social networks.

While social networking helps connect people with others who share similar interests or views, con artists infiltrate these social networks looking for victims. By joining and actively participating in a social network or community, the con artist builds credibility and gains the trust of other members of the group. In online social networks, a con artist can establish this trust and credibility more quickly. The scammer has immediate access to potential victims through their online profiles, which may contain sensitive personal information such as their dates or places of birth, phone numbers, home addresses, religious and political views, employment histories, and even personal photographs.

The con artist takes advantage of how easily people share background and personal information online and uses it to make a skillful and highly targeted pitch. The scam can spread rapidly through a social network as the con artist gains access to the friends and colleagues of the initial target.

TAKE NOTE Social media generally takes two forms: static and interactive. **Static content** remains posted until changed by the person who established the account on the site. Generally, static content is accessible to all visitors to the site. Examples of static content typically available through social networking sites include company websites, profiles, backgrounds, or walls.

Interactive content, as the name implies, has input from both the creator and the viewer. Common examples include Facebook, Twitter, Instagram, and LinkedIn.

4. 5. 1. 1. 1 Online Red Flags for Investors

■ **Promises of high returns with no risk.** Many online scams promise unreasonably high short-term profits. Guarantees of returns around 2% a day, 14% a week, or 40% a month are too good to be true. Remember that risk and reward go hand in hand.

■ **Offshore operations.** Many scams are headquartered offshore, making it more difficult for regulators to shut down the scam and recover investors' funds.

■ **E-currency sites.** If investors have to open an e-currency account to transfer money, use caution. These sites may not be regulated, and con artists use them to cover up money trails.

■ **Recruit friends.** Most cons will offer bonuses if investors recruit their friends into the scheme.

■ **Professional websites with little to no information.** These days anyone can put up a website. Scam sites may look professional, but they offer little to no information about the company's management, location, or details about the investment.

■ **No written information.** Online scam promoters often fail to provide a prospectus or other form of written information detailing the risks of the investment and procedures to get the investor's money out.

■ **Testimonials from other group members.** Scam artists frequently pay out high returns to early investors using money from later arrivals. This type of scam is a Ponzi scheme. Fraud aimed at groups of people who share similar interests is called affinity fraud.

4. 5. 1. 2   Regulatory Concerns About Social Media

Both the SEC and FINRA have established policies, most of which are used as the basis for disciplinary actions when the Administrator's staff conducts an examination of broker-dealers and investment advisers located in his state.

FINRA has offered guidance to broker-dealers and registered personnel in their notices to members regarding the use of different technologies and devices for the delivery of business communications. As the technology, communications platforms, and devices are ever-changing, so will be the guidance, and FINRA will continue to supply interpretive materials to assist in that respect. Currently, the use of email, instant messaging, chat rooms, blogs, bulletin boards, and websites—including social networking sites such as Facebook, LinkedIn, and Twitter—are all included within FINRA's guidance.

While the challenge is generally to determine which category of public communication any piece falls under to determine its supervisory and filing requirements (retail, correspondence, or institutional), FINRA has said that it will always be the **content** delivered that ultimately determines this, and not the technology, platform, or device used to deliver it. In this light, FINRA reminds broker-dealers that compliance responsibilities when communicating via the internet or other electronic media are the same as in face-to-face discussions or in written communications with the public. Therefore, all existing FINRA rules and regulations applicable to communications with the public would also be applicable to communications delivered electronically by any technology or device if the content is business related. In addition, registered representatives (agents) must be aware of internal firm policies and procedures that may restrict or prohibit the use of certain electronic communications, and in those instances, FINRA directs that employees of the firm must abide by the firm's internal policies.

E X A M P L E

Although social media has been around for some time, it has now caught the attention of the SEC (and every other regulator, for that matter). You might ask, "Why should I be concerned with my emails or Facebook posts?" Well, here are just a couple of examples of how and why the regulators react.

The problem for regulated financial institutions is that inappropriate use of email and other social media can mean non-compliance with government and industry regulations, resulting in hefty fines, potential loss of business, and fraud. A few years ago, a major international bank lost nearly €4.9 billion in fraudulent trades by a rogue employee that used instant messaging to manage the transactions. On a smaller level, in early 2016, an agent was fined $15,000 and suspended from association with any broker-dealer for a period of two years for sending an unapproved email to prospective clients. During the same time period, a broker-dealer was fined $1.1 million, and one of its agents was fined $50,000, for failure to retain emails as required. So, this is serious business to the regulators.

You need to know that agents are duty bound to follow the rules and regulations surrounding electronic communications, even during their own time, if they are identifiable as a representative of the securities firm. Members of the marketing team might understand what is appropriate to post to Facebook or what process to follow to post, but, without proper training, average agents may not. Their posts or photographs from weekend parties might not be suitable content.

4. 5. 1. 2. 1 Review and Supervision of Electronic Communications

When it comes to review and supervision, it is important to note that the terms *electronic communications*, *email*, and *electronic correspondence* may be used interchangeably and can include such forms of electronic communications as instant messaging and text messaging.

4. 5. 2 ADVERTISING

NASAA considers it to be an unethical business practice to use any advertising or sales presentation in such a fashion as to be deceptive or misleading. An example of such practice would be:

- a distribution of any nonfactual data;

- any material or presentation based on conjecture;

- unfounded or unrealistic claims in any brochure, flyer, or display by words, pictures, or graphs; or

- anything otherwise designed to supplement, detract from, supersede, or defeat the purpose or effect of any prospectus or disclosure.

One way in which this violation occurs is when a broker-dealer or agent prepares a sales brochure for a new issue but includes only the positive information from the prospectus. Leaving out risk factors and other potentially deal-killing information is prohibited. Somewhat related, and also prohibited, is **highlighting** or making any other marks on a prospectus to draw attention to key points.

As stated in the previous unit, under the Uniform Securities Act, the Administrator may by rule or order require the filing advertisement and sales literature unless the security or transaction is exempted or is a federal covered security.

4. 5. 2. 1 Broker-Dealer Advertising

Included in advertising is a firm's website. In Unit 1, we described the conditions related to determining if a broker-dealer was considered to have a place of business in the state (and required to register) or not. You should go back and review that material.

Whether through the website or other social media, an important form of communications with the public is the making of recommendations.

A logical question is, do recommendations made through social media come under the same suitability constraints as any other recommendation? The reply is just what you would expect: of course they do. But it is not always obvious when a particular communication constitutes a recommendation for purposes of the suitability rule. Because so much hinges on what is considered to be a recommendation, let's look further at some examples of what is and what is not a recommendation.

In addition to when a broker-dealer acts merely as an order-taker regarding a particular transaction (an unsolicited transaction, which we know is an exempt transaction—exempt from the registration and advertising filing requirements under the USA), the policy generally would view the following activities and communications as falling **outside** the definition of *recommendation*.

- A broker-dealer creates a website that is available to customers or groups of customers. The website has research pages or electronic libraries that contain research reports (which may include buy-sell recommendations from the author of the report), news, quotes, and charts that customers can obtain or request.

■ A broker-dealer has a search engine on its website that enables customers to sort through the data available about the performance of a broad range of stocks and mutual funds, company fundamentals, and industry sectors. The data is not limited to, and does not favor, securities in which the BD makes a market or has made a buy recommendation. Customers use and direct this tool on their own. Search results may display current news, quotes, and links to related sites.

■ A broker-dealer provides research tools on its website that allow customers to screen through a wide universe of securities (e.g., all exchange-listed and Nasdaq securities) or an externally recognized group of securities (e.g., certain indexes) and to request lists of securities that meet broad, objective criteria (e.g., all companies in a certain sector with 25% annual earnings growth). The BD does not control the generation of the list in order to favor certain securities. For instance, the BD does not limit the universe of securities to those in which it makes a market or for which it has made a buy recommendation.

■ A broker-dealer allows customers to subscribe to emails or other electronic communications that alert customers to news affecting the securities in the customer's portfolio or on the customer's watch list. The customer selects the scope of the information that the firm will send to him.

On the other hand, the regulators generally would view the following communications as falling **within** the definition of *recommendation*:

■ A broker-dealer sends a customer-specific electronic communication (e.g., an email or pop-up screen) to a targeted customer or targeted group of customers, encouraging the particular customer(s) to purchase a security.

■ A broker-dealer sends its customers an email stating that customers should be invested in stocks from a particular sector (such as technology) and urges customers to purchase one or more stocks from a list with buy recommendations.

■ A broker-dealer provides a portfolio analysis tool that allows a customer to indicate an investment goal and input personalized information such as age, financial condition, and risk tolerance. The BD, in this instance, then sends the customer a list of specific securities the customer could buy or sell to meet the investment goal the customer has indicated.

■ A broker-dealer uses data-mining technology (the electronic collection of information on website users) to analyze a customer's financial or online activity—whether or not it is known by the customer—and then, based on those observations, sends (or "pushes") specific investment suggestions that the customer purchase or sell a security.

It is important to keep in mind that these examples are meant only to provide guidance and are not an exhaustive list of communications that are or are not considered to be recommendations. The regulators recognize that many other types of electronic communications are not easily characterized. In addition, changes to the factual suppositions upon which these examples are based (or the existence of additional factors) could alter the determination of whether similar communications may or may not be viewed as recommendations.

Broker-dealers, therefore, should analyze all relevant facts and circumstances to determine whether a communication is a recommendation, and they should take the necessary steps to fulfill their suitability obligations.

4. 5. 2. 2   Investment Adviser Advertising

When it comes to investment advisers, the Model Rule states that publishing, circulating, or distributing any advertisement which does not comply with the Investment Advisers Act of 1940 would be prohibited.

An investment adviser should not publish, circulate, or distribute any advertisement that is inconsistent with federal rules governing the use of advertisements. Included in the prohibition are advertisements:

- containing untrue statements of material fact;

- that refer directly or indirectly to any testimonial of any kind;

- that refer to past specific recommendations of the investment adviser, unless certain conditions are met (such as including all recommendations, both winners and losers, for a period of at least the previous 12 months);

- that represent that a chart, formula, or other device being offered can, by itself, be used to determine which securities are to be bought or sold; or

- that contain a statement that any analysis, report, or service will be furnished for free when that is not the case.

These prohibitions are fundamental and sound standards that all investment advisers should follow.

An advertisement under state law is defined as a communication to more than one person. In addition, although the rules do not prohibit **testimonials** for broker-dealers, they are strictly forbidden for use by IAs. One thing to look for on the exam deals with investment advisers who advertise a charting or similar system—they must indicate that there are *limitations and difficulties* inherent in using such programs.

TAKE NOTE   In March 2014, the SEC published an interpretive release dealing with testimonials for investment advisers using social media. Included in that release is the statement that third-party use of the "like" feature on an investment adviser's social media site could be deemed to be a testimonial if it is an explicit or implicit statement of a client's experience with the adviser.

4. 5. 3   ISSUES RELATED TO AGENTS

While much of the supervisory burden revolves around broker-dealer use of various social media tools, the nitty-gritty, day-to-day work relates to their agents. Some things to be aware of include the following.

- In addition to computers in the office, personal devices (Blackberry, iPhone, Android, etc.) used to communicate with clients in a social media setting are covered by the rules.

- Depending on the nature of the media, prior approval by a supervisory person may or may not be required. For example, an "unscripted" participation in an interactive electronic forum (such as Twitter) comes within the definition of *retail communication*, which does not require prior supervisory approval. On the other hand, a LinkedIn page would probably require pre-approval.

- Look out for the red flags. Certain activities, such as linking to third-party sites or receiving data feeds from outside sources could contain information that NASAA considers objectionable.

- It is not the device or technology that determines if a piece delivered by a broker-dealer or any agent is subject to approval and recordkeeping. Rather, it should always be the *content* that determines if a piece delivered by an agent is subject to approval and recordkeeping.

- It is suggested that Twitter posts are easy to monitor, but sites such as Facebook are not, given what they've termed *entanglement* issues (i.e., the firm or its personnel is involved with the preparation of a third-party post) and the challenges they pose. Essentially, who is responsible for links to a third-party site, and who is responsible for third-party postings to an agent's Facebook page?

- Specifically regarding Twitter, posts do *not* need supervisory pre-approval except for an agent's initial tweet.

- LinkedIn is considered different from Facebook, as it is more of a business networking site than a social site. With that, it is believed that information limited to your current position, past positions, and job responsibilities allow the site to be left unmonitored as the firm would have no responsibility regarding that content for any individual. However, if testimonials are used on the site ("Joe is the best stockbroker in the world," or "I've made a ton of money because of Joe's recommendations"), or if recommendations are posted on the site, then that would make it a business site that the firm is now responsible for.

4. 5. 3. 1   Supervisory Actions to Be Taken by the Broker-Dealer

Prior to allowing associated persons to use social media for business purposes, a firm's policies and procedures must provide for personnel training and education relating to the parameters of permitted use. Both supervisory personnel and agents need to understand the difference between interactive and static content, between business and non-business communications, and whether the communication is a retail communication requiring pre-approval. A firm should consider requiring training in the use of social media prior to permitting use. At a minimum, a firm that permits use of social media sites must hold annual training as part of its continuing education obligations. Any such training will reinforce personnel understanding of the firm's policies and procedures as applied to this continuously evolving technology and, in turn, limit the firm's compliance risks.

One of the unintended consequences of the growth of social media has been exposure to privacy issues. The firm's social media policies should include relevant privacy issues. We will cover those in the next unit when we discuss cybersecurity and data protection.

To summarize, because the technology behind social media continues to advance at such a rapid pace, potential damage to both the firm and employee exist. To mitigate these, it is suggested that firm policies should:

- be committed to writing and communicated firmwide;

- be written in a clear and concise manner so as to eliminate confusion;

- define the responsibilities of all concerned parties, from registered representatives (agents) to principals, to minimize confusion and maximize expectations; and

- clearly describe the monitoring tools to be used by the firm.

Since social media technology continues to evolve, the potential for reputational and financial loss from any employee or firm mistake is difficult to quantify. Prior to venturing into any form of social media, firm policies should (1) be firmly established, (2) be precise, (3) clearly define the employees' responsibilities, (4) and explain how they are to be monitored on each electronic platform utilized by the firm. Until the law catches up with technology, a useful way to reduce and manage unforeseeable social media risk is to create a work environment that fosters a strong culture of compliance.

4. 5. 4   BROCHURE RULE

To provide some assurance that the act will not be violated, the regulators have recommended that each of the adviser's advisory clients be given a written statement (brochure) prepared by the adviser that makes all appropriate disclosures. The disclosure statement should include the nature and extent of any adverse interest of the adviser, including the amount of compensation he would receive in connection with the account. This is particularly important if the adviser will be receiving compensation from sources other than the agreed-upon advisory fee or that recommendations are limited to the firm's proprietary products. Furthermore, the adviser should, but is not required to, obtain a written acknowledgment from each of his clients of their receipt of the disclosure statement.

Because the brochure is really the only way the potential or existing client can learn about the investment adviser, disclosure must be made to all current clients and to prospective clients regarding material disciplinary action. The broadest definition of **material** would include any actions taken against the firm or management persons by a court or regulatory authority within the past 10 years. Required disclosure would include the following:

- State or regulatory proceedings in which the adviser or a management person was found to have violated rules or statutes that led to the denial, suspension, or revocation of the firm's or the individual management person's registration

- Court proceedings, such as a permanent or temporary injunction, against the firm or management person pertaining to an investment-related activity or any felony

- Self-regulatory organization proceedings in which the adviser or management person caused the business to lose its registration; the firm or individual was barred, suspended, or expelled; or a fine in excess of $2,500 or a limitation was placed on the adviser or management person's activities

Remember that in Unit 1 we mentioned that investment advisers registered with the Administrator use the Form ADV Parts 1 and 2. Unless otherwise provided in this rule, an investment adviser, registered or required to be registered under the Uniform Securities Act, must furnish each advisory client and prospective advisory client with:

- a brochure, which may be a copy of Part 2A of its Form ADV or written documents containing the information required by Part 2A of Form ADV;

- a copy of its Part 2B brochure supplement for each individual who

  — provides investment advice and has direct contact with clients in this state, or

  — exercises discretion over assets of clients in this state, even if no direct contact is involved;

- a copy of its Part 2A Appendix 1 wrap fee brochure if the investment adviser sponsors or participates in a wrap fee account;

- a summary of material changes, which may be included in Form ADV Part 2 or given as a separate document; and

- such other information as the Administrator may require.

TAKE ✓ NOTE   It may help you remember that the **A** in Part 2**A** tells us that that part is about the **A**dviser and the **B** in Part 2 is about the **B**odies (the people) who work there.

4. 5. 4. 1   Brochure Delivery Requirements

The NASAA Model Rule dealing with investment adviser brochures has very specific delivery requirements, both at the initial phase of contact and on an ongoing basis.

4. 5. 4. 1. 1   Initial Delivery

An investment adviser, except as discussed in the following, must deliver the Part 2A brochure and any Part 2B brochure supplements required by the rule to a prospective advisory client:

■ not less than 48 hours prior to entering into any advisory contract with such client or prospective client; or

■ at the time of entering into any such contract, if the advisory client has a right to terminate the contract without penalty within five business days after entering into the contract.

4. 5. 4. 1. 2   Annual Delivery

An investment adviser, except discussed in the following, must:

■ deliver within 120 days of the end of its fiscal year a free, updated brochure and related brochure supplements, which include or are accompanied by a summary of material changes; or

■ deliver a summary of material changes that includes an offer to provide a copy of the updated brochure and supplements and information on how the client may obtain a copy of the brochures and supplements.

TAKE NOTE   Investment advisers do not have to deliver a summary of material changes or a brochure to clients if no material changes have taken place since the last summary and brochure delivery.

4. 5. 4. 1. 3   Exceptions to the Brochure Delivery Requirements

Delivery of the brochure and related brochure supplements need not be made to:

■ clients who receive only impersonal advice and who pay less than $500 in fees per year; or

■ an investment company registered under the Investment Company Act of 1940.

TEST TOPIC ALERT   For the purpose of the brochure rule, *contract for impersonal advisory services* means any contract relating solely to the provision of investment advisory services:

■ by means of written material or oral statements that do not purport to meet the objectives or needs of specific individuals or accounts;

■ through the issuance of statistical information containing no expression of opinion as to the investment merits of a particular security; or

■ any combination of the above services.

4. 5. 4. 1. 4   *Electronic Delivery of the Brochure*

Delivery of the brochure and related supplements may be made electronically if the investment adviser:

- in the case of an initial delivery to a potential client obtains verification that a readable copy of the brochure and supplements were received by the client;
- in cases other than initial deliveries obtains each client's prior consent to provide the brochure and supplements electronically;
- prepares the electronically delivered brochure and supplements in the format prescribed in the instructions to Form ADV Part 2;
- delivers the brochure and supplements in a format that can be retained by the client in either electronic or paper form; and
- establishes procedures to supervise personnel transmitting the brochure and supplements and prevent violations of this rule.

EXAMPLE

Many students get confused over the 90-day and 120-day requirements. This example should help:

Which of the following statements accurately describes the time limits for investment adviser documents?

I.   Filing of the annual updating amendment to Form ADV with the appropriate regulatory body is within 90 days of the end of the adviser's fiscal year.

II. Filing of the annual updating amendment to Form ADV with the appropriate regulatory body is within 120 days of the end of the adviser's fiscal year.

III. Delivery of the investment adviser's brochure to the customer is due within 90 days of the end of the adviser's fiscal year.

IV. Delivery of the investment adviser's brochure to the customer is due within 120 days of the end of the adviser's fiscal year.

A. I and II
B. I and IV
C. II, III, and IV
D. IV only

The answer would be choice **B**, I and IV. Some logic here might help. The investment adviser must get its paperwork into the state (or SEC) prior to the end of the 90-day period. Then, the IA has another 30 days to get the information into the brochure to be sent to the clients.

QUICK QUIZ 4.C

1. Which of the following is NOT a factor when a communication to be distributed to the public is either being reviewed or approved by the broker-dealer?

   A. Whether statements of benefits are balanced with statements of potential risks
   B. The nature of the audience to which the communication is intended to be distributed
   C. Whether the piece will be distributed in written form or on the firm's website
   D. Whether the communication is targeting existing customers or prospective ones

2. The regulatory bodies consider which of the following social media sites to be predominately used for business rather than personal communications?

   A. Facebook
   B. Instagram
   C. LinkedIn
   D. Twitter

UNIT TEST

1. LMN Widgets, Inc., has filed a registration statement with the SEC. Once the registration is effective, an agent can state that
   A. the issue may legally be sold
   B. the SEC has guaranteed the issue
   C. the SEC has endorsed the issue
   D. the SEC has guaranteed the accuracy of the information in the prospectus

2. The statement, generally found on the cover of a prospectus, that states the SEC's non-approval of a security's registration is known as the
   A. disclaimer
   B. non-approval clause
   C. representation statement
   D. effective date

3. If a broker-dealer is selling shares of an affiliated company, under which of the following conditions could the broker-dealer sell these shares to an account over which the broker-dealer has discretion?
   A. If normal discretionary papers are filled out and the account has been accepted in writing by a principal of the broker-dealer
   B. If specific authorization is received from the customer
   C. If written disclosure of the affiliation has been given to the customer no later than with the confirmation
   D. Under no circumstances may these shares be sold to discretionary accounts

4. Disclosure to customers of control relationships is required in
   A. principal transactions
   B. agency transactions
   C. primary offerings
   D. all of the above

5. A customer of a broker-dealer purchases 100 shares of KAPCO common stock. The trade confirmation sent to the customer must include
   A. the client's social security number
   B. the amount of the next expected dividend
   C. whether the broker-dealer acted as agent or principal
   D. the amount of the commission, if the broker-dealer acted in a principal capacity

6. When a broker-dealer engages in a customer transaction from its own account, which of the following statements are TRUE?
   I. Partners of the broker-dealer are trading in their personal accounts.
   II. The broker-dealer is trading from its inventory with customers.
   III. The broker-dealer must disclose its capacity as a principal in the transaction.
   IV. The broker-dealer must disclose its capacity as agent in the transaction.
   A. I and III
   B. I and IV
   C. II and III
   D. III and IV

7. An investment adviser is a member of the board of directors of a privately held corporation that has just gone public. The adviser would like to recommend the stock to several of his advisory clients. Which of the following statements are TRUE?
   I. The adviser can do so without restriction.
   II. The adviser must disclose the existence of a control relationship.
   III. The adviser may base his recommendation on all information at his disposal.
   IV. The adviser must base his recommendation on publicly available information.
   A. I and III
   B. I and IV
   C. II and III
   D. II and IV

8. Which of the following actions by an agent of a broker-dealer would be an unethical business practice?

   A. Recommending securities that result in negative returns in the customer's account

   B. Indicating, when opening the account, that, in order to maximize account performance, it will sometimes be necessary to waive compliance with certain provisions of the Uniform Securities Act

   C. Splitting compensation with a sales assistant who is registered as an agent with the same firm

   D. Failing to enter a sell order for a security when its price is falling and when the agent has discretionary authority.

9. Which of the following statements concerning conflicts of interest under NASAA's Model Rule on Unethical Business Practices of Investment Advisers, Investment Adviser Representatives, and Federal Covered Advisers is NOT true?

   A. Where a conflict of interest exists, an adviser must decline taking on the client.

   B. A conflict of interest is defined as anything that may impair the impartiality of the advice being rendered.

   C. An investment adviser who receives a fee for investment advice, and whose investment adviser representatives are paid commissions from broker-dealers, presents a conflict of interest that must be disclosed.

   D. The existence of the fiduciary relationship with clients strengthens the requirement for disclosure of any potential conflict of interest.

10. NASAA studies reveal that many clients of broker-dealers are confused about the fees they are charged. All of the following are ways in which these fees and charges may be disclosed EXCEPT

   A. a chart

   B. a list

   C. a phone call

   D. a table

11. A client of a state-registered investment adviser would expect that the advisory contract would be

   A. oral

   B. written

   C. oral or written

   D. vague

12. Alfred Mortensin is an agent with a major Midwestern broker-dealer. Alfred has done some personal research on the OxyCarbon Chemical Company (OCCC) and is of the opinion that it is an appropriate investment for some of his clients. In order to ease the fear that some clients have, Alfred offers to buy back any shares of OCCC for a period of 6 months at a price no lower than 5% below the client's purchase price. Under the NASAA Statement of Policy on Dishonest or Unethical Business Practices of Broker-Dealers and Agents,

   A. this would be permitted because by offering to buy the shares back at a price lower than the purchase price, Alfred is not guaranteeing a profit.

   B. this would be permitted because Alfred is not charging clients for the research he performed

   C. this would not be permitted because Alfred is guaranteeing results

   D. this would not be permitted because Alfred is not willing to give them back their full purchase price.

13. It is legal under the USA for an agent to tell a client that

   A. a registered security may lawfully be sold in that state

   B. an exempt security is not required to be registered because it is generally regarded as being safer than a nonexempt security

   C. the agent's qualifications have been found satisfactory by the Administrator

   D. a registered security has been approved for sale in the state by the Administrator

14. A client has a cash account at his broker-dealer. Now, he wishes to open a margin account as well. Which of the following best describes the action that must be taken?

   A. Oral instructions to open the account are sufficient because the customer relationship already exists.

   B. The customer must make the request in writing, either by mail or by fax.

   C. The firm must obtain a properly executed written margin agreement promptly after the initial transaction in the account.

   D. The customer must physically present himself at the agent's office and sign the appropriate papers.

15. The purpose of the Customer Identification Program (CIP) is to

   A. enable a broker-dealer to form a reasonable belief that it knows the true identity of each customer

   B. enable a broker-dealer to know how to contact a customer in the event of an emergency

   C. provide a method by which broker-dealers could assist customers laundering money

   D. provide broker-dealers with sufficient client information to make suitable recommendations

16. Opening a new account at a broker-dealer involves completing a new account form. Which of the following is NOT a required question on that form?

   A. Is the client of legal age?

   B. What is the client's citizenship?

   C. Where is the client employed?

   D. What is the client's marital status?

17. When an existing client opens a margin account, there are additional documents to be completed. Which of the following are mandatory?

   I. The credit agreement

   II. The hypothecation agreement

   III. The loan consent agreement

   IV. The new account agreement

   A. I and II

   B. I, II, and IV

   C. II and III

   D. III and IV

18. A client wishing to open an options account must be furnished with a copy of the

   A. broker-dealer's options prospectus

   B. OCC

   C. ODD

   D. put and call directory

19. The regulatory bodies are concerned about agents using social media to communicate with clients when they are using their

   I. office desktop computers

   II. personal tablets

   III. smartphones

   IV. personal laptop from homes

   A. I and II

   B. I and IV

   C. II, III, and IV

   D. I, II, III, and IV

20. One of your clients approaches you to get your evaluation of an investment opportunity that was received through a Facebook post sent by a friend. The investment promises a monthly return in excess of 1% and claims that it is registered with an offshore regulatory body. You should explain to your client that

   A. these are reasonable expectations based on the investment and the location of the issuer

   B. your firm does not sell that security and, as a result, you cannot make any comments about the issue

   C. it is important to check with the friend to find out more about the deal

   D. these are red flags and are a clear warning to stay away from this investment.

ANSWERS AND RATIONALES

1. **A.** The SEC (or the Administrator) does not approve, disapprove, endorse, or guarantee a registration statement's accuracy.

2. **A.** The disclaimer is the statement which must appear on every prospectus. It states that the SEC has not approved or disapproved of the issuer, nor has it passed on the accuracy or adequacy of the information contained therein.

3. **B.** Normally, disclosure of the broker-dealer's control relationship with the affiliate would be sufficient. However, a sale to a discretionary account requires specific approval of the customer.

4. **D.** The nature of any control relationship or conflict of interest must be disclosed to customers. This includes both primary (new issue) and secondary transactions, whether the firm acts as agent or principal.

5. **C.** A customer confirmation must always disclose the capacity in which the broker-dealer acted (agent or principal). Commissions are only shown when acting in an agency capacity; principal (dealer) transactions involve markup or markdown.

6. **C.** The Uniform Securities Act defines a broker-dealer as a legal person (entity) engaging in the business of effecting securities transactions for the account of others or for its own account. In this context, trading for its own account means that the broker-dealer is trading from its inventory with customers. The broker-dealer has an ethical responsibility to disclose its capacity as a principal in the transaction. When trading for its own account, a broker-dealer is functioning as a principal or dealer. When trading for the accounts of others with no participation as a direct party to the trade, a broker-dealer functions in an agency capacity.

7. **D.** As a director of a public company, the adviser is an insider and must disclose this relationship to any clients that were recommended the stock. Further, as an insider, the adviser must be careful to base any recommendations on publicly available information or there would likely be a violation of the insider trading rules.

8. **B.** It is very clear that waivers of this type are never permitted; you just can't waive compliance with the laws. An agent's securities recommendations that result in losses are not a violation of the Uniform Securities Act. Splitting compensation with a fellow licensed employee is not a violation of the Uniform Securities Act. An agent with discretionary authority is not under an obligation to sell a security simply because it is declining in price.

9. **A.** Conflicts of interest could impair the rendering of unbiased and objective advice but, as long as disclosed and agreed to by the client, the account may be accepted. Conflicts of interest include, but are not limited to, receiving compensation from sources other than clients' fees (such as a salary or commission from a broker-dealer) as a result of providing investment advice. Such conflicts of interest must be disclosed to a client in writing before the investment advisory contract is signed.

10. **C.** Suggested methods of disclosing fees and charges include charts, lists, and tables. It is unreasonable to think that the kind of detail involved could be disclosed on a phone call.

11. **B.** Under the Uniform Securities Act, all advisory contracts must be in writing.

12. **C.** It makes no difference that the agent is only guaranteeing at least purchase price less 5%. Guaranteeing performance of a security is never permitted.

13. **A.** An agent may indicate that a security is registered or is exempt from registration. All of the other statements are illegal.

14. **C.** Opening a margin account is far more detailed than opening a cash account. There are a number of different agreements that have to be signed. The firm must obtain a properly executed written margin agreement promptly after the initial transaction in the account. The presence of an existing cash account is meaningless here.

15. **A.** The CIP is part of the USA PATRIOT Act, and its primary concern is to make sure that broker-dealers (and other financial institutions, such as banks) know exactly who the customer is. Money laundering is an illegal activity, and the CIP does not provide the kind of information necessary for making suitability judgments.

16. **D.** Marital status is important to know for suitability purposes, but it is not one of the required pieces of information on the new account form (even though most firms do ask it).

17. **A.** Only the credit and hypothecation agreements are mandatory when an existing client opens a margin account. The loan consent agreement is optional and, as an existing client, the new account form has already been completed—it does not have to be filled out again.

18. **C.** The options disclosure document, or ODD (technically called the "Characteristics & Risks of Standardized Options"), is required before a client can begin trading options.

19. **D.** The format is not what counts; it is the content that matters.

20. **D.** Unreasonably high returns and not being registered in the U.S. are two items on the list of red flag warnings to investors published by NASAA.

QUICK QUIZ ANSWERS

Quick Quiz 4.A

1. **A.** The Administrator does not approve or disapprove of securities. Rather, the Administrator reviews registrations for omission of material facts and clarity of information and makes certain that all supporting documentation is included. If these requirements are met, the Administrator clears or releases the security for sale to the public.

2. **B.** When it comes to the registration of any securities professional, any statement relating to approval or something similar is prohibited. There is no such thing as a federal covered broker-dealer, and becoming a member of a national stock exchange has no impact on the state registration of a broker-dealer.

3. **C.** The obligation of investment advisers and IARs to place clients' interests ahead of their own is known as acting in a fiduciary capacity.

Quick Quiz 4.B

1. **A.** No trading may take place in a discretionary account with a broker-dealer before the signed authorization form has been received. In the case of an investment adviser, the written form must be received no later than 10 business days after the initial trade. For margin accounts, the documentation must be received promptly after the initial trade, and in options accounts, the customer agreement must be received within 15 days after the account opening.

2. **B.** The name of the client's employer is part of the new account form, but is not one of the requirements of the CIP as are the other items.

Quick Quiz 4.C

1. **C.** The format is not what counts; it is the content that matters.

2. **C.** LinkedIn is viewed as a site used far more for business purposes than the others.

5

Ethical Practices and Obligations

The Uniform Securities Act was drafted for two primary reasons: (1) to eliminate conflicts in state securities legislation and make state securities laws uniform, and (2) to protect the public from unethical securities practices and fraud. Understanding ethical practices, and securities professionals' obligations to follow them, is the subject of this unit. This unit addresses what constitutes unethical and prohibited business practices, as defined in the Statement of Policy on Dishonest or Unethical Business Practices of Broker-Dealers and Agents issued by NASAA (the North American Securities Administrators Association), as well as what are considered fraudulent practices under securities laws.

Recognizing that the industry is a dynamic rather than static one, this unit will also deal with the modern challenges of cybersecurity and data protection.

Fraudulent, dishonest, and unethical practices are very heavily tested topics. They make up 25% of the exam. You must know what these practices are and be able to apply the principles that guide ethical behavior to specific situations presented in the exam.

The Series 63 exam will include 15 questions on the material presented in this unit. ∎

When you have completed this unit, you should be able to:

■ **recognize** conflicts of interest and other ethical issues;

■ **describe** the different forms of compensation earned by securities professionals;

■ **identify** the procedures to be followed when taking responsibility for customer funds and securities; and

■ **list** steps to be taken to increase cybersecurity and data protection.

5. 1 ANTIFRAUD PROVISIONS OF THE USA

Fraudulent activity may occur when conducting securities sales or when providing investment advice. In general, **fraud** means the deliberate or willful attempt to deceive someone for profit or gain. As mentioned in previous units, if it is a security, exempt or not, it is covered under the USA's antifraud provisions. However, these provisions only apply to securities. Therefore, if the inappropriate activity occurs during the offer or sale or rendering of advice relating to something that is *not* a security, these antifraud provisions do not apply.

5. 1. 1 FRAUDULENT PRACTICES

Although there is a legal difference between a fraudulent practice and one that is unethical or prohibited, it is highly unlikely that you will have to know that for the exam. About the only significant testable concern is that you can go to jail for committing fraud (a criminal offense) while the punishment for engaging in a practice that is prohibited or unethical is generally limited to a fine, suspension, or revocation. Most of the exam will deal with practices that are unethical, but let's point out what the Uniform Securities Act considers fraud.

State securities laws modeled on the USA address fraud by making it unlawful for any person, when engaged in the offer, sale, or purchase of any security, directly or indirectly, to:

- employ any device, scheme, or artifice to defraud;
- make any untrue statement of a material fact or omit to state a material fact necessary to make a statement not misleading; or
- engage in any act, practice, or course of business that operates as a fraud or deceit on a person.

TEST TOPIC ALERT   The law defines **material** as information used by a prospective purchaser to make an informed investment decision. Omitting a material fact or misstatement of such would be considered fraudulent behavior.

TAKE NOTE   As long as it involves a security, there are no exceptions to the antifraud provisions of state securities laws. They pertain to any person or transaction, whether the person or transaction is registered, exempt, or federal covered. Prevention of fraud is one of the few areas of securities law over which the states have full authority to act.

The following is a list of the fraudulent acts most likely to be tested on your exam.

5. 1. 1. 1 Misleading or Untrue Statements

The willful act of telling a lie or making a misleading statement in connection with the offer or sale of a security is considered fraudulent activity. The following are some examples of acting in a fraudulent manner:

- **Inaccurate market quotations**—Telling a client a stock is up when the reverse is true is obviously an improper action. However, it would not be considered fraud if the inaccuracy resulted from a malfunction of the quote machine or an unintended clerical error. To be considered fraud, the action must be deliberate.

- **Misstatements of an issuer's earnings or projected earnings or dividends**—Telling a client that earnings are up, or that the dividend will be increased when that is not the case, is a fraudulent practice. However, it would not be fraud if you were quoting a published news release that was incorrect.

- **Inaccurate statements regarding the amount of commissions, markup, or markdown**—There are circumstances where the amount of commission or markup may be higher than normal. That is permissible, as long as it is disclosed properly. However, telling a client that it costs him nothing to trade with your firm because you never charge a commission, and not informing him that all trades are done on a principal basis with a markup or markdown, is fraud.

TEST TOPIC ALERT   You might see a question where you have to know that it could be considered fraudulent activity for an agent or IAR to use social media (i.e., posting a tweet) to make a false announcement about a company in order to affect the stock price.

TEST TOPIC ALERT   It is important to understand that, other than in the above circumstance where commissions may be higher than normal, a broker-dealer is not obligated to disclose the amount of commission on any offer to sell *before* the transaction. However, commissions are always required to be disclosed on the trade confirmation.

- **Stating or implying that the agent has inside information when that is not the case**—As we will see shortly, the use of material non-public inside (MNPI) information is a fraudulent practice. But what about the agent who attempts to boost her credibility to clients by inferring that what she is about to tell them is "inside information" and, once released, will have a major impact on the stock? Since it isn't true, she isn't acting on inside information, but she is still guilty of making untrue statements.

- **Telling a customer that a security will be listed on an exchange without concrete information concerning its listing status**—Making any statement relating to a change in marketplace for the security is only permitted if, in fact, you have knowledge that such change has been announced.

- **Informing a client that the registration of a security with the SEC or with the state securities Administrator means that the security has been approved by these regulators**—Registration never implies approval.

- **Misrepresenting the status of customer accounts**—This behavior is fraudulent. Many people are not motivated to pay strict attention to their monthly account statements, making it relatively easy for an unscrupulous agent to fraudulently claim increasing values in the account when the opposite is true. Doing so would be a fraudulent action.

- **Promising a customer services without any intent to perform them or without being properly qualified to perform them**—You say, "Yes, I can" to your client, even if you know you cannot deliver. For instance, the client asks you to analyze his bond portfolio to determine the average duration. Even though you do not know how to do that, you agree to do so. Under the USA, you have committed fraud.

- **Representing to customers that the Administrator approves of the broker-dealer's or agent's abilities**—This is another case of using the word *approve* improperly. A broker-dealer or agent is registered, not approved.

TEST TOPIC ALERT Merely learning the terms is not enough to get you through the exam. On the exam, you must be able to identify situations in which the above violations occur. Be able to apply the concepts of fraud and unethical behavior to scenarios that are likely to occur in everyday business.

EXAMPLE **Making Leading or Untrue Statements**

Here is a case when an agent made multiple statements that were improper:

An agent contacts a client with the news that the largest holding in her portfolio has been approved for listing on the NYSE and will begin trading on that market in one week. The effect of the listing should be a noticeable appreciation in the stock's price. While on the topic, the agent exaggerates the company's earnings by $1 per share to make the client more receptive to the suggestion that she increase the size of her position. A final statement is made that the broker-dealer will be saving her money by not charging any commission on the trade because they already have the stock in inventory.

If you were to see a question like this on your exam, what would you find to be wrong with this agent's actions?

There is nothing wrong with telling a client that a stock has been approved for listing on the NYSE when that is true, but it is misleading to imply that the listing will have an impact on the stock's market price. Furthermore, there is never a time when earnings can be misstated—that is fraudulent behavior. Finally, implying that the purchase will be free of transaction costs is a problem because sales out of inventory carry a mark-up rather than a commission.

5. 1. 1. 2   Failure to State Material Facts

The USA does not require an agent to provide all information about an investment, but only information that is material to making an informed investment decision. However, the agent must not fail to mention material information that could affect the price of the security. In addition, the agent may not state facts that in and of themselves are true but, as a result of deliberately omitting other facts, render the recommendation misleading under the circumstances. It is the agent's responsibility to determine what is material.

TEST TOPIC ALERT Full disclosure also applies when filling out an order to purchase or sell securities, referred to as an order ticket. Each order ticket must disclose the account ID, a description of the security (including the number of shares if a stock, and total par value if a bond), the terms and conditions of the order (market or limit), the time of order entry and execution, the execution price, and the identity of the agent who accepted the order or is responsible for the account. We do not need the client's name or address on the order ticket.

5. 1. 1. 3   Using Inside Information

Making recommendations on the basis of material inside information about an issuer or its securities is prohibited. Should an agent come into possession of inside information, the agent must report the possession of the information to a supervisor or compliance officer.

TAKE NOTE

Material non-public inside (MNPI) information under securities law is any information about a company that has not been communicated to the general public and that would likely affect the value of a security. Generally, but not exclusively, this information comes from officers or other insiders of the issuer who have access to financial or other relevant records. Your firm's internally generated research report on a company could also be considered MNPI if it was likely that release of the report would impact the market price of the stock. Even if you acquire the information accidentally, you cannot use it until it becomes public.

TEST TOPIC ALERT

The exam may ask you to identify who is guilty of insider trading violations—a corporate officer of the issuer who divulges material inside information to a friend, but no transaction takes place, or an agent who executes a trade for a client who is acting on inside information? Simply giving someone inside information, although imprudent, is not a violation of the law. Only when the information is used for trading does a violation occur. In this question, the agent is in violation for accepting an order on the basis of material nonpublic information that results in a trade.

EXAMPLE

Using Inside Information

Because the potential rewards are so great, this is one of the most commonly violated rules by both investors and securities professionals. Some go to extreme lengths to try to hide the activity in an effort to make it difficult to uncover.

As an example of the type of returns that can be made, Mr. H, a convenience store employee has a sister whose boyfriend worked for a company that was about to be bought out by another company. The boyfriend mentioned that to the sister who told her brother. The day before the announcement was made public, Mr. H. took his life savings of $8,000 and invested in that company. The next day, after the announcement and the jump in price, he sold and reaped a profit of over $295,000 (almost 37 times his investment in 1 trading day). Yes, he was caught (which is how we know the story) and had to return his profits and then some interest.

Another case involved getting access to a law firm's computer. The law firm specialized in mergers and acquisitions, and those with access were able to learn of upcoming takeover bids being made at prices significantly higher than the current trading price. To avoid being noticed, the trades were placed through the account of one of the participant's mother who was based in China. Total penalties in this case were almost $6 million plus interest of about $125,000.

In our first example, Mr. H wasn't looking for the information, but when it came his way, he used it. In the second example, the perpetrators hacked into the computers with malice aforethought.

EXAMPLE

The exam might present a question about insider trading in the following manner:

Which of the following employees of a publicly traded company would most likely have access to MNPI?

A. VP of Human Resources
B. Receptionist
C. Chief Financial Officer (CFO)
D. VP of Marketing

Choice **C** is correct. Although any of these employees could obtain access to MNPI, because the CFO is the individual who sees the financial numbers first, it is part of the job to have access to earnings numbers before anyone else.

5. 1. 1. 4 Market Manipulation

Effecting any transaction in, or inducing the purchase or sale of, any security by means of any manipulative, deceptive, or fraudulent device, practice, plan, program, design, or contrivance.

Securities legislation is designed to uphold the integrity of markets and transactions in securities. However, market integrity is violated when transactions misrepresent actual securities prices or market activity. The most common forms of market manipulation are matched orders and wash trades.

Matched orders occur when market participants agree to buy and sell securities among themselves to create the appearance of activity or trading in a security. Increased volume in a security can induce unsuspecting investors to purchase the security, thereby bidding up the price. As the price rises, participants who initiated the matched orders sell their securities at a profit.

A **wash trade** is an attempt to manipulate a security's price by creating an apparent interest in the security that really does not exist. This is done by an investor buying in one brokerage account and simultaneously selling through another. No beneficial change in ownership has occurred (because the buyer and seller are the same person), but to the marketplace, it appears that volume or price is increasing.

TAKE NOTE

Arbitrage is the simultaneous buying and selling of the same security in different markets to take advantage of different prices; it is not a form of market manipulation. Simultaneously buying a security in one market and selling it in another forces prices to converge and, therefore, provides uniform prices for the general public.

TEST TOPIC ALERT

Although matched orders and wash trades are the two most common examples of market manipulation on the exam, there are other ways in which broker-dealers and their agents can deceive clients through unethical business practices such as disseminating false trading information, front running, and withholding shares of an IPO (explained later in this SOP).

5. 2   DISHONEST OR UNETHICAL BUSINESS PRACTICES OF BROKER-DEALERS AND AGENTS

In 1983, NASAA released a Statement of Policy on Dishonest or Unethical Practices of Broker-Dealers and Agents (SOP) enumerating a large number of business practices that, when engaged in by broker-dealers or agents, they deemed dishonest or unethical. Subsequently, they have issued several Model Rules that have expanded the list. Most students report seeing a number of questions on their Series 63 exam that are drawn from the following material, especially those relating uniquely to agents. In most cases, the listed prohibition is logical common sense, "Don't lie, don't cheat, and don't steal." However, due to the nature of this exam and its legal interpretations, particularly for those of you without a securities or law background, further explanations will be supplied.

The premise of the policy is that all broker-dealers and agents should observe high standards of commercial honor and just and equitable principles of trade in the conduct of their business. Acts and practices, including but not limited to those enumerated below, are considered contrary to such standards and may constitute grounds for denial, suspension, or revocation of registration, or such other action authorized by the Uniform Securities Act. You will need to know that it is a dishonest or unethical business practice if a broker-dealer is doing any of the following (those that apply to agents as well are marked with an *).

5. 2. 1   DELIVERY DELAYS

Engaging in a pattern of unreasonable and unjustifiable delays in the delivery of securities purchased by any of its customers or in the payment upon request of free credit balances reflecting completed transactions of any of its customers. A free credit balance is just like a credit balance on your charge card—it is your money and must be sent to you upon request. In the event that the client requests a certificate for the security purchased, it would be considered an unethical business practice for the firm to delay delivering it to the client.

5. 2. 2   CHURNING*

Inducing trading in a customer's account that is excessive in size or frequency in view of the financial resources, objectives, and character of the account. A key here is the word *excessive*. By definition, anytime something is excessive, it is too much. The regulators understand that different clients have different needs and ability to take risks, so what is excessive for the 80-year-old pensioner is probably not going to be so for the 40-year-old partner in a major law firm.

5. 2. 3   UNSUITABLE RECOMMENDATIONS*

Recommending to a customer the purchase, sale, or exchange of any security without grounds to believe that such transaction or recommendation is suitable for the customer, based upon reasonable inquiry concerning the customer's investment objectives, financial situation and needs, and any other relevant information known by the broker-dealer.

Agents must always have reasonable grounds for making recommendations to clients. Before making recommendations, the agent must inquire into the client's financial status, investment objectives, and ability to assume financial risk. What about the client who refuses to give any financial information or discuss objectives? In that case, all the agent can do is accept unsolicited orders because there is no basis for making any recommendation.

The following practices violate the suitability requirements under the USA as well as the rules of fair practice that regulatory agencies have developed. A securities professional may not:

- recommend securities transactions without regard to the customer's financial situation, needs, or investment objectives;

- induce transactions solely to generate commissions (churning), defined as transactions in customer accounts that are excessive in size or frequency in relation to the client's financial resources, objectives, or the character of the account;

- recommend a security without reasonable grounds;

- fail to sufficiently describe the important facts and risks concerning a transaction or security; and

- make blanket recommendations.

TAKE NOTE
What would be considered a *blanket recommendation*? It will almost always be unsuitable if the same security is recommended to the majority of your clients. How could all of them have the same needs? Some are looking for income, some for growth, and some for safety, and no one security can provide all three.

TAKE NOTE
What do you do when you think you've made a totally appropriate recommendation to your client, but your client is not happy with it? Upon reflection, you realize the client's problem is a lack of understanding of both the recommendation and the marketplace. What should you do? Most would agree that the first step would be to attempt to impart some education to the client in an effort to make your recommendation clearer. However, as with all customer issues, the client is the one who has to make the final decision.

5. 2. 3. 1   Free Lunch Seminars

Although not specifically included in the NASAA Statement of Policy, recent rules regarding unfair business practices, especially with regard to seniors, may be included on your exam. The most common instance is the so-called free lunch seminar. These seminars are widely offered by financial services firms seeking to sell financial products, and they often include a free meal for attendees. Even though many of these seminars are promoted as being educational workshops accompanied by the statement, "Nothing will be sold at this meeting," the seminars are clearly intended to result in the attendees opening new accounts with the sponsoring firm and, ultimately, in the sale of investment products, if not at the seminar itself, then in follow-up contacts with the attendees.

If not clearly presented, NASAA will consider both the sponsoring firm and those agents involved in the delivery of the seminar to be committing a prohibited business practice.

5. 2. 4 UNAUTHORIZED TRANSACTIONS*

Executing a transaction on behalf of a customer without authorization to do so. Unless discretionary authorization (see following) has been received, broker-dealers and their agents may never enter an order for a client on their own volition, even when it is in the best interest of the client. You may be asked a question where a spouse of a client or other person with a strong personal relationship contacts the agent with transaction instructions, allegedly on behalf of the client. Unless there is a written third-party trading authorization on file, no activity can take place.

Somewhat related to this activity is deliberately failing to follow a customer's instructions. In this case, the client has given the terms of the order and if the agent decides to purchase more or less than ordered, or in any other way change the nature of the order, it is a prohibited practice.

5. 2. 4. 1 Third-Party Trading*

Placing an order to purchase or sell a security for the account of a client upon instruction of a third party without first having obtained a written third-party trading authorization from the client.

It is sound business practice for a broker-dealer or an agent not to place an order for the account of a customer on instruction of a third party without first knowing that the third party has obtained authority from the client for the order. For example, it would be important for an agent to know that a lawyer had power of attorney over an estate whose account the agent was managing prior to placing any order on instruction of the lawyer. Placing orders under such circumstances could result in substantial civil liability, besides being an unethical practice.

5. 2. 5 EXERCISING DISCRETION*

Exercising any discretionary power in effecting a transaction for a customer's account without first obtaining written discretionary authority from the customer, unless the discretionary power relates solely to the time or price for the executing of orders.

Agents of broker-dealers may not exercise discretion in an account without prior written authority (power of attorney) from the client. Prior written authority is also known as trading authorization.

Discretion is given to an agent by the client when the client authorizes (in writing) the agent to act on his own and use his discretion in deciding the following for the client:

- Asset (security)
- Action (buy or sell)
- Amount (how many shares)

However, merely authorizing an agent to determine the best price or time to trade a security is not considered to be discretion, particularly for purposes of the financial requirements, such as bonding or, in the case of an investment adviser, minimum net worth.

CASE STUDY   **Discretionary Trading Authorization**

What exactly does it mean when a securities professional can exercise discretion in a client's account? Simply, that person can make decisions regarding securities trading in the client's account without prior consultation with the client. As long as the securities professional can select the specific security (the asset), or whether to buy or sell (the action), or the size of the order (the amount), the person has discretionary authority. In most cases, the party using discretion selects all three of these. Other than an exception applying to investment advisers (see 5.3.7), written discretionary authority from the client must be in hand prior to exercise of discretion. An example of a test question might go something like this:

All of the following client orders would require discretionary authorization EXCEPT

A. "Buy me 100 shares of a stock with a dividend of at least 4%."
B. "I need a tax write-off, so sell something out of my portfolio to general a capital loss."
C. "I'm going to need some cash, so sell something I own."
D. "Please buy 300 shares of XYZ stock for me when you think the price is right."

Choice **D** is correct because the client has specified the name of the asset, the action, and the amount. All the client is asking is that the agent determine the right price. Determining price or time (assuming the other items are present) is not considered the use of discretion requiring written authorization.

5. 2. 6 MARGIN DOCUMENTS*

Executing any transaction in a margin account without securing from the customer a properly executed written margin agreement promptly *after* the initial transaction in the account.

5. 2. 7 COMMINGLING OF CUSTOMER AND FIRM ASSETS

Failing to segregate customers' free securities or securities held in safekeeping. Customers' "free" securities are those which have no lien against them, unlike those which have been pledged in a margin account (just like you might have a lien against your car).

Securities that are held in a customer's name must not be **commingled** (mixed) with securities of the firm.

If a firm has 100,000 shares of ABC common stock in its own proprietary account, and its clients separately own an additional 100,000 shares, the firm may not place customer shares in the firm's proprietary account.

To mix shares together could jeopardize the security of client securities in the event of default.

5. 2. 8 IMPROPER HYPOTHECATION

Hypothecating a customer's securities without having a lien thereon, unless the broker-dealer secures from the customer a properly executed written consent promptly after the initial transaction. There are strict rules to be followed, the details of which will not be tested.

5. 2. 9 UNREASONABLE COMMISSIONS OR MARKUPS*

Entering into a transaction with or for a customer at a price not reasonably related to the current market price of the security or receiving an unreasonable commission or profit.

There is one way that a broker-dealer might make a very large profit and it would *not* be considered unreasonable: When acting in a dealer (or principal) capacity, broker-dealers sell out of inventory. What would be the situation if a firm bought some securities for their inventory and, several months later, the value of those securities had doubled or tripled? What would be a fair price to charge customers? The rules make it clear that quotes are always based on the current market so, in this case, the broker-dealer would make a substantial profit. By the way, this goes both ways. If the firm had stock in inventory that decreased greatly in value, the firm would not be able to pass any of the loss to clients—any sales would take place based on the current depressed market prices.

5. 2. 9. 1 Higher-Than-Normal Commissions

In some cases, a particular transaction may involve more expense to the broker-dealers, particularly in a thinly traded security, and that could justify a charge that is higher than normal. Of course, all charges must be clearly disclosed to clients. If not, a violation has occurred.

5. 2. 10 TIMELY PROSPECTUS DELIVERY*

Failing to furnish to a customer purchasing securities in an offering, no later than the due date of confirmation of the transaction, either a final prospectus or a preliminary prospectus. Here is further detail from the USA that might answer a question on the exam:

The Administrator may require that a prospectus for a security registered under Qualification be sent or given to each person to whom an offer is made prior to the sale of the security rather than no later than the due date of the confirmation.

5. 2. 11 UNREASONABLE SERVICING FEES

Charging unreasonable and inequitable fees for services performed, including miscellaneous services such as collection of monies due for principal, dividends or interest, exchange or transfer of securities, appraisals, safekeeping, custody of securities, and other services related to its securities business. NASAA recognizes that not all broker-dealers offer the same level of services and that those who offer a large array of services to their clients may charge more without it being considered an unethical business practice. As discussed in the previous unit, these fees must be disclosed.

5. 2. 12 DISHONORING QUOTES

Offering to buy from or sell to any person any security at a stated price unless such broker-dealer is prepared to purchase or sell, as the case may be, at such price and under such conditions as are stated at the time of such offer to buy or sell.

In other words, if a broker-dealer quotes a stock at $20.60 to $20.75, it had better be ready to sell at least the minimum trading unit (usually 100 shares) to a client at $20.75 per share (his ask or offering price), or buy from a client at $20.60 (his bid price).

5. 2. 13 CONTROLLED MARKET

Representing that a security being offered to a customer is "at the market price" or a price relevant to the market price, unless such broker-dealer knows or has reasonable grounds to believe that a market for such security exists other than that made, created, or controlled by himself. When your firm is the only market maker in a security, it determines the price, not the normal supply and demand in a marketplace where there are competing firms.

5. 2. 14 GUARANTEEING AGAINST LOSS*

Guaranteeing a customer against loss in any securities account of such customer carried by the broker-dealer or in any securities transaction effected by the broker-dealer with or for such customer.

Securities professionals may not guarantee a certain performance, nor may they guarantee against a loss by providing funds to the account. One common example of this on the exam is when an agent is so sure that a stock's price will go up, he offers to buy it back from the client at a price higher than the original sale price.

TEST TOPIC ALERT

The term *guaranteed* under the USA means "guaranteed as to payment of principal, interest, or dividends." It is allowable to refer to a guaranteed security when an entity other than the issuer is making the guarantee. However, the regulatory agencies of the securities industry prohibit securities professionals from guaranteeing the performance returns of an investment or portfolio.

5. 2. 15 DISSEMINATING FALSE TRADING INFORMATION*

Publishing or circulating, or causing to be published or circulated, any notice, circular, advertisement, newspaper article, investment service, or communication of any kind which purports to report any transaction as a purchase or sale of any security, unless such broker-dealer believes that such transaction was a bona fide purchase or sale of such security; or which purports to quote the bid price or asked price for any security, unless such broker-dealer believes that such quotation represents a bona fide bid for or offer of such security. This would be considered a form of market manipulation.

5. 2. 16 DECEPTIVE ADVERTISING PRACTICES*

Using any advertising or sales presentation in such a fashion as to be deceptive or misleading. An example of such practice would be a distribution of any nonfactual data, material, or presentation based on conjecture; unfounded or unrealistic claims or assertions in any brochure, flyer, or display by words, pictures, or graphs; or anything otherwise designed to supplement, detract from, supersede, or defeat the purpose or effect of any prospectus or disclosure.

5. 2. 17 FAILING TO DISCLOSE CONFLICTS OF INTEREST

Failing to disclose that the broker-dealer is controlled by, controlling, affiliated with, or under common control with the issuer of any security before entering into any contract with or for a customer for the purchase or sale of such security. If such disclosure is not made in writing, it must be supplemented by the giving or sending of written disclosure at or before the completion of the transaction. One of the most common examples of a conflict of interest that must be disclosed is when the agent is offering a proprietary product, such as a house fund (a mutual fund where the underwriter or adviser is affiliated with the broker-dealer) or a limited partnership offering (DPP) where the sponsor is an affiliate of the broker-dealer.

Check the previous Unit for a more complete discussion on conflicts of interest.

5. 2. 18 WITHHOLDING SHARES OF A PUBLIC OFFERING

Failing to make a bona fide public offering of all of the securities allotted to a broker-dealer for distribution, whether acquired as an underwriter, a selling group member, or from a member participating in the distribution as an underwriter or selling group member. If the firm is fortunate to be part of the underwriting of one of these IPOs that rockets in price because the issue is *oversubscribed*, they better be sure to allocate the shares to clients in an equitable manner and not keep any for themselves.

5. 2. 19 RESPONDING TO COMPLAINTS*

Failure or refusal to furnish a customer, upon reasonable request, information to which he is entitled, or to respond to a formal written request or complaint.

When a written complaint is received by the firm (and only written complaints are recognized), action must be taken. The complainant (customer) would be notified that the complaint had been received and an entry would be made in the firm's complaint file. If an agent were the subject of the complaint, the agent would be notified, but would *not* be given a copy of the complaint (agents do not have recordkeeping requirements). If the complaint is received by the agent rather than the firm, the agent must report the complaint to the appropriate supervisor. If the complaint is sent by email, that is considered *in writing*.

5. 2. 19. 1 Reporting Errors

In order to keep from generating complaints, any trade or other operational error, once discovered, must be reported by the agent to the appropriate supervisory person.

5. 2. 20 FRONT RUNNING*

Front running is the unethical business practice of a broker-dealer or one of its representatives placing a personal order ahead of a previously received customer order. It occurs most frequently when the firm has received an institutional order of sufficient size to move the market, generally referred to as a *block* order. By running in front of the order, the firm or representative can profit on that movement.

EXAMPLE   **Front Running**

In the industry, the term generally used is *front running of block transactions*. FINRA, in their Rule 5270, basically defines front running of blocks as:

No broker-dealer or associated person of that broker-dealer shall cause to be executed an order to buy or sell a security when such person causing such order to be executed has material, non-public market information concerning an imminent block transaction in that security prior to the time information concerning the block transaction has been made publicly available or has otherwise become stale or obsolete.

Because of the size of block transactions (generally a minimum of 10,000 shares), their execution can potentially cause large movements in the market price of the stock. Getting in ahead of that jump (or out ahead of the drop if a block sale) can lead to earning profits in an unethical and prohibited manner.

For example, Paula, an agent with a large broker-dealer has just received an order to purchase 20,000 shares of STU common stock. In essence, Paula has information that the market doesn't know yet and, based on the average daily trading volume of STU, knows that this order will cause a jump in STU's market price. Paula purchases 1,000 shares for her own account and then enters the block order. The execution of that large trade causes STU to now trade $2 per share higher than when Paula bought hers. She immediately sells her shares and secures a profit of about $2,000 using this unethical business practice.

5. 2. 21 SPREADING RUMORS*

Any agent hearing a rumor must report it to the appropriate supervisor. Broker-dealers must ensure that rumors they become aware of are not spread or used in any way, particularly not as the basis for recommendations.

5. 2. 22 BACKDATING RECORDS*

All records and documents must reflect their actual dates. Although there can be tax or other benefits to clients when their trade confirmations are backdated, it is an unethical business practice to do so.

5. 2. 23 AGREEING TO WAIVERS

The USA makes it clear that any condition, stipulation, or provision binding any person acquiring any security or receiving any investment advice to waive compliance with any provision of the act or any rule or order hereunder is void. For exam purposes, if you are given a question where clients agree to waive their rights to sue, the agreement is null and void.

5. 2. 24 INVESTMENT COMPANY SALES*

In 1997, NASAA adopted the NASAA Statement of Policy titled, "Dishonest or Unethical Business Practices by Broker-Dealers and Agents in Connection with Investment Company Shares." Several of those items are currently being tested. Under this policy, any broker-dealer or agent who engages in one or more of the following practices shall be deemed to have engaged in "dishonest or unethical practices in the securities business," as used in the Uniform Securities Act, and such conduct may constitute grounds for denial, suspension, or revocation of registration or such other action authorized by statute.

5. 2. 24. 1 Sales Load Communications

In connection with the solicitation of investment company shares, stating or implying to a customer that the shares are sold without a commission, are "no load" or have "no sales charge" if there is associated with the purchase of the shares:

- *any* front-end load;
- *any* contingent deferred sales load (CDSC); or
- a Rule 12b-1 fee or a service fee if such fees in total exceed .25% of average net fund assets per year.

5. 2. 24. 2 Breakpoints

In connection with the solicitation of investment company shares, failing to disclose to any customer any relevant:

- sales charge discount on the purchase of shares in dollar amounts at or above a breakpoint; or
- letter of intent feature, if available, which will reduce the sales charges.

5. 2. 24. 3 Unfair Comparisons

It is considered an unethical business practice to compare or in any way imply that money market mutual funds are similar to savings accounts at insured banks. Although generally quite safe, money market funds do not have FDIC insurance, and there is no guarantee that their principal will not fluctuate.

5. 2. 24. 4   Selling Dividends

In connection with the solicitation of investment company shares, stating or implying to a customer that:

- the purchase of such shares shortly before an ex-dividend date is advantageous to such customer, unless there are specific, clearly described tax or other advantages to the customer; or

- a distribution of long-term capital gains by an investment company is part of the income yield from an investment in such shares.

5. 2. 24. 5   Share Classes

Related to the solicitation of investment company shares, recommending to a customer the purchase of a specific class of investment company shares in connection with a multi-class sales charge or fee arrangement, without reasonable grounds to believe that the sales charge or fee arrangement associated with such class of shares is suitable and appropriate, based on the customer's investment objectives, financial situation and other securities holdings, and the associated transaction or other fees.

5. 2. 24. 6   Switching Funds

In connection with the solicitation of investment company shares, recommending to a customer the liquidation or redemption of investment company shares for the purpose of purchasing shares in a different investment company portfolio having similar investment objectives and policies, without reasonable grounds to believe that such recommendation is suitable and appropriate, based on the customer's investment objectives, financial situation and other securities holdings, and any associated transaction charges or other fees.

5. 2. 25   LENDING OR BORROWING*

Engaging in the practice of lending to or borrowing money or securities from a customer.

Securities professionals may not borrow money or securities from a client unless the client is a broker-dealer, an affiliate of the professional, or a financial institution engaged in the business of loaning money.

Securities professionals may not loan money to clients unless the firm is a broker-dealer or financial institution engaged in the business of loaning funds or the client is an affiliate.

EXAMPLE   **Borrowing Money or Securities from Clients**

One of the more confusing areas relates to borrowing money from (or lending money to) clients. Part of the reason for the confusion is that FINRA rules (most students taking the Series 63 exam have taken a FINRA test) permit borrowing (lending) to clients under certain conditions that are more liberal than those of NASAA.

The first point to emphasize is that this prohibition only applies when the other side is a client. Securities professionals may borrow (or lend) as much as they want to those who are not clients, but once there is a client relationship, the NASAA policy takes effect. So, which clients can you borrow from?

■   A bank or other financial institution in the business of making loans (e.g., credit union)

■   A broker-dealer in a margin account

■   A fellow employee of your firm (or one affiliated with it)

Which clients can't you borrow from?

■   The employee at the lending institution who processes or approves your loan

■   The agent at the broker-dealer who services your margin account

■   A mortgage broker (only arranges the loan)

■   A family member, unless employed by the same or an affiliated firm

Lending arrangements between registered agents and their customers are permitted if the customer

A.   is a member of the representative's immediate family
B.   is the mortgage broker who arranged for the mortgage on your home
C.   was your roommate in college and remains you best friend
D.   works at the desk next to yours

The correct choice is **D**. You can borrow from or lend to another employee of your firm. You can also borrow from clients who are in the money-lending business. Remember, mortgage brokers don't lend the money, they put together the lender and the home buyer. If you'd like to borrow from an immediate family member, unless that individual works for the same or an affiliated firm, the only way to do that is to terminate the client relationship.

TEST TOPIC ALERT   As a former president of the United States once said, "Let me make one thing perfectly clear." When it comes to borrowing or lending money, you cannot borrow from *any* client (including your mother), unless that client is a lending institution such as a bank or credit union. Likewise, as an agent, you can never lend money to any client unless the client has some kind of affiliation with your firm. If your broker-dealer handles margin accounts, then, of course, money can be loaned to clients. Don't take this personally, just get the questions right on the exam.

5. 2. 26   PRACTICES SOLELY RELATED TO AGENTS

5. 2. 26. 1   Selling Away

Effecting securities transactions not recorded on the regular books or records of the broker-dealer that the agent represents, unless the transactions are authorized in writing by the broker-dealer prior to execution of the transaction. These are sometimes referred to as *private securities transactions* (not to be confused with a private placement).

EXAMPLE   **Selling Away**

The NASAA policy is very simple—agents wishing to sell a security without the transaction going through their broker-dealer can only do so if the transaction is authorized in writing by the BD prior to the trade being executed. How do violations occur? Certainly, there are cases where the agent deliberately flaunts the rule. One of the most common examples on the exam is when the agent is approached by a friend who is raising money for a new enterprise and suggests that the agent might have some clients for whom this would be an appropriate investment. If the agent gets written authorization from the employing broker-dealer, this would be permitted, but if not, a violation has occurred.

Many times, the problem arises because the agent does not understand that the product being offered is a security. For example, agents are increasingly targeted by issuers, promoters, and marketers to sell short-term promissory notes to their customers. Although, in almost all instances, these notes are securities, promoters of these products are marketing them to registered persons as non-securities products that do not have to be sold through a broker-dealer by a registered person. In a significant number of cases, agents have sold these notes to their customers away from their firms and without prior firm approval as required. When in doubt, ask your supervisor.

Here is how that might happen in real life (and on the exam as well).

While at your Tuesday night bowling league, one of the team members introduces you to a friend of hers who is also in the financial business. This individual invites you out to lunch and describes a potential investment for your clients. The product is a promissory note that the issuer's lawyers insist is not a security and you will be compensated nicely for any sales you make. You should:

A. thank your bowling partner for making this great introduction
B. start contacting clients for whom you believe this promissory note is a suitable investment
C. buy some of the notes yourself first before recommending them to clients
D. check with your supervisor to be sure you would not be violating the selling away rules

Maybe these promissory notes really aren't securities, but if they are, and you offer them to clients without the consent of your firm, you are in violation, which is why choice **D** is the correct answer.

TEST TOPIC ALERT   The exam may refer to this as a trade made off the books of the broker-dealer. Just remember that it is considered to be a prohibited practice anytime an agent effects securities transactions not recorded on the regular books or records of the broker-dealer the agent represents, unless the transactions are authorized in writing by the broker-dealer before execution of the transaction.

5. 2. 26. 2 Fictitious Accounts

Establishing or maintaining an account containing fictitious information in order to execute transactions which would otherwise be prohibited. Examples of this kind of conduct sometimes given on the exam are *beefing up* a client's net worth to enable him to engage in margin or options trading, or making him appear to have more investment experience than is true.

5. 2. 26. 3 Sharing in Accounts

Sharing directly or indirectly in profits or losses in the account of any customer without the written authorization of the customer and the broker-dealer that the agent represents.

Agents cannot share in the profits or losses of client accounts unless the client and the broker-dealer supply prior written approval.

TEST TOPIC ALERT   Unlike agents, broker-dealers, investment advisers, and investment adviser representatives are never permitted to share in the profits or losses in their clients' accounts.

5. 2. 26. 4 Splitting Commissions

Dividing or otherwise splitting the agent's commissions, profits, or other compensation from the purchase or sale of securities with any person not also registered as an agent for the same broker-dealer, or for a broker-dealer under direct or indirect common control. It is not necessary to disclose to an agent's client that he is splitting commissions with another agent *unless* it increases the transaction cost to the client.

QUICK QUIZ 5.A   Write **U** for unlawful or prohibited activities and **L** for lawful activities.

_____   1. An agent guarantees a client that funds invested in mutual funds made up of government securities cannot lose principal.

_____   2. A nondiscretionary customer calls his agent and places a buy order for 1,000 shares of any hot internet company. Later in the day, the agent enters an order for 1,000 shares of Global Internet Services.

_____   3. An agent receives a call from his client's spouse, advising him to sell her husband's securities. Her husband is out of the country and requested that his wife call the agent. The agent refuses because the wife does not have trading authorization, and she complains vigorously to his manager.

_____   4. A client writes a letter of complaint to his agent regarding securities that the agent had recommended. The agent calls the client to apologize and then disposes of the letter because the client seemed satisfied.

_____ 5. A registered agent borrows $10,000 from a credit union that is one of her best customers.

_____ 6. An agent is convinced that Internet Resources will rise significantly over the next 3 months. She offers to buy the stock back from her customers at 10% higher than its current price at any time during the next 3 months.

_____ 7. An agent receives an order for the purchase of an obscure foreign security. The agent informs the client that the commissions and charges on this purchase will be much higher than those of domestic securities.

_____ 8. An agent who works for a small broker-dealer that employs no securities analysts assures her clients that she can analyze any publicly traded security better than any analyst and that she will do it personally for each security purchased by a client, regardless of the industry.

_____ 9. An agent recommends that her client buy 1,000 shares of Internet Consultants, Inc., an unregistered nonexempt security with a bright future.

Quick Quiz answers can be found at the end of the unit.

5. 3   UNETHICAL BUSINESS PRACTICES OF INVESTMENT ADVISERS

The fraudulent and prohibited practices described in the previous section relate to the sale of securities and apply primarily to broker-dealers and agents. The USA also prohibits fraudulent and unethical activities by persons providing investment advice.

The USA makes it unlawful for any person who receives compensation (directly or indirectly) for advising another person (whether through analyses or reports) on the value of securities to use any device, scheme, or artifice to defraud the other person. Additionally, that person may not engage in any act, practice, or course of business that operates or would operate as fraud or deceit upon the other person or engage in dishonest or unethical practices as the Administrator may define by rule.

We will review a few of the practices deemed unethical for those giving investment advice. You will notice some overlap with the unethical practices previously covered for broker-dealers and agents.

5. 3. 1   SUITABILITY OF RECOMMENDATIONS

Recommending to a client to whom investment advice is provided the purchase, sale, or exchange of any security without reasonable grounds to believe that the recommendation is suitable for the client, on the basis of information furnished by the client after reasonable inquiry concerning the client's investment objectives, financial situation and needs, and any other information known by the investment adviser.

Because investment advisers have a **fiduciary** responsibility to their clients, even more than a broker-dealer (or agent), an adviser (or IAR) has a fundamental obligation to analyze a client's financial situation and needs prior to making any recommendation to the client. The fiduciary relationship means that the client's interest must always come first. By failing to make reasonable inquiry or by failing to make recommendations that are in line with the financial situation, investment objectives, and character of a client's account, an investment adviser has not met its fiduciary responsibility.

TAKE NOTE

What about the client who refuses to give any financial information or discuss objectives? In that case, the investment adviser will probably refuse to do business with the person. This is different than the same scenario with an agent. An agent's only job is to effect securities transactions, while that of the IA or IAR is to give advice—it's part of that fiduciary responsibility. How can you possibly give advice if you have no idea what would be appropriate for the client?

TEST TOPIC ALERT

It is possible you might have a test question where the investment adviser (or IAR) recommends the same security to most or all of its customers. This would generally be prohibited because it is highly unlikely that the same security would be suitable for all clients. This practice could also be referred to as blanket recommendations.

5. 3. 2   MISREPRESENTING QUALIFICATIONS

To misrepresent to any advisory client, or prospective advisory client, the qualifications of the investment adviser or any employee of the investment adviser, or to misrepresent the nature of the advisory services being offered or fees to be charged for such service, or to omit to state a material fact regarding qualifications, services, or fees.

When an investment adviser offers its services to a prospective client or when providing services to an existing client, the qualifications of the investment adviser or any employee of the investment adviser and the nature of the advisory services and the fees to be charged must be disclosed in such a way as to not mislead. Overstating the qualifications of the investment adviser or disclosing inaccurately the nature of the advisory services to be provided or fees to be charged are not ethical ways to either acquire or retain clients.

5. 3. 3   UNREASONABLE ADVISORY FEES

Charging a client an unreasonable advisory fee.

This rule is intended to prohibit an investment adviser from charging an excessively high advisory fee. *Unreasonable*, as used in this rule, means unreasonable in relation to fees charged by other advisers for similar services. Although no two advisory services are exactly alike, comparisons can be drawn. In those instances where an advisory fee is out of line with fees charged by other advisers providing essentially the same services, an investment adviser should justify the charge. It would be very difficult for a client to compare various advisory services to evaluate those services and the fees charged. This rule will allow state Administrators to research the competitiveness of an adviser's services and fees to make a determination as to whether the fees being charged are unreasonably high.

5. 3. 4 CONFLICTS OF INTEREST

Failing to disclose to clients in writing, before any advice is rendered, any material conflict of interest relating to the adviser or any of its employees that could reasonably be expected to impair the rendering of unbiased and objective advice, including:

■ compensation arrangements connected with advisory services to clients, which are in addition to compensation from such clients for such services; and

■ charging a client an advisory fee for rendering advice when a commission for executing securities transactions pursuant to such advice will be received by the adviser or its employees.

This rule is designed to require disclosure of all material conflicts of interest relating to the adviser or any of its employees that could affect the advice that is rendered. The two examples cited in the rule pertain to compensation arrangements that benefit the adviser and that are connected with advisory services being provided. However, full disclosure of all other material conflicts of interest, such as affiliations between the investment adviser and product suppliers, are also required to be made under the rule.

5. 3. 5 UNAUTHORIZED DISCLOSURES

Disclosing the identity, affairs, or investments of any client unless required by law to do so, or unless consented to by the client.

An investment advisory firm has a responsibility to ensure that all information collected from a client be kept confidential. The only exception to the rule should be in instances where the client authorized the release of such information or when the investment advisory firm is required by law to disclose such information.

TAKE NOTE   If the account is a joint one, such as with a spouse, the adviser does not need consent to discuss account matters with either party.

5. 3. 6 IMPROPER CUSTODY

Taking any action, directly or indirectly, with respect to those securities or funds in which any client has any beneficial interest, where the investment adviser has custody or possession of such securities or funds when the adviser's action is subject to and does not comply with the requirements of the NASAA Model Rule on Custody.

In instances where an investment adviser has custody or possession of clients' funds or securities, it should comply with the NASAA Model Rule on Custody designed to ensure the safekeeping of those securities and funds. The rules under the act specifically provide that securities of clients be segregated and properly marked, that the funds of the clients be deposited in separate bank accounts, that the investment adviser notify each client as to the place and manner in which such funds and securities are being maintained, that an itemized list of all securities and funds in the adviser's possession be sent to the client not less frequently than every three months, and that all such funds and securities be verified annually by actual examination by an independent CPA on a surprise basis. The rule establishes very conservative measures to safeguard each client's funds and securities held by an investment adviser.

5. 3. 7   OTHER UNETHICAL BUSINESS PRACTICES

Just as with broker-dealers and agents, investment advisers and their representatives are prohibited from engaging in unethical business practices, which include the following:

■ Exercise unauthorized discretion in advisory accounts. One odd difference is that investment advisers are permitted oral discretion for the first 10 business days after the initial discretionary transaction. After that, written authorization must be in hand.

■ Engage in excessive trading (churning). There are many situations where an investment adviser may receive commissions, or be affiliated with a person that receives commissions, from the securities transactions that are placed by the investment adviser. This creates a potential reward for increased securities trading, which is not allowed.

■ Placing an order to purchase or sell a security for the account of a client without authority to do so

■ Placing an order to purchase or sell a security for the account of a client upon instruction of a third party without first having obtained a written third-party trading authorization from the client

■ Borrowing money from or lending money to clients unless meeting the same conditions applying to broker-dealers and agents (affiliate or in the money lending business)

■ Guaranteeing a client that a specific result will be achieved (gain or no loss) with advice that will be rendered

■ Using testimonials in advertisements (this does not apply to broker-dealers and agents)

5. 4   FIDUCIARY RESPONSIBILITIES WHEN PROVIDING INVESTMENT ADVICE

When securities professionals act in an investment advisory capacity, they act as fiduciaries and are held to higher ethical standards than when they are engaged in the sales of securities. Fiduciary responsibility exceeds that which is normally required of ordinary business relationships because the fiduciary is in a position of trust. A fiduciary must act for the benefit of the client and place the interests of clients above their own. When securities professionals provide advice for a fee, they have a higher level of responsibility as fiduciaries.

An IA or an IAR may be placed in the specific fiduciary position of trustee of a corporate retirement plan. Not only must they act solely for the benefit of the plan participants (the employees and the employer), but they must be careful to avoid engaging in any prohibited transactions. One of the most common examples used on the exam is when a C-level officer of the company (CEO, CFO, and so forth) approaches the trustee (IA or IAR) and suggests that the plan lend money to the company to help out with a short-term cash deficiency. That is not acceptable.

5. 4. 1   IAR AS AN AGENT

The securities laws do not prohibit a registered investment adviser representative from being an employee of a registered broker-dealer. However, there would be a duty on the part of both the broker-dealer and the soliciting advisers to inform advisory clients of their ability to seek execution of transactions with broker-dealers other than those who have employed the advisers.

5. 4. 2   CUSTODY OF CLIENT FUNDS AND SECURITIES

Under the NASAA Model Rule on Custody, it is unlawful for an investment adviser to have custody of client funds and securities if:

■ the Administrator in the state prohibits, by rule, investment advisers from having custody;

■ in absence of a rule, an adviser fails to notify the Administrator that it has custody; and

■ the investment adviser fails to supply clients, no less frequently than quarterly, with a statement of account activity and the location and amount of their assets.

TEST TOPIC ALERT   If an investment adviser wishes to maintain custody of customer funds or securities, and state law does not prohibit doing so, the adviser must give written notice to the Administrator. Do not choose the answer on the exam that states, "must obtain permission from the Administrator." All that is required is notification.

5. 4. 2. 1   Definition of Custody

Custody means holding, directly or indirectly, client funds or securities, or having any authority to obtain possession of them. The investment adviser has custody if a related person (any person, directly or indirectly, controlling or controlled by the investment adviser; and any person that is under common control with the investment adviser) holds, directly or indirectly, client funds or securities, or has any authority to obtain possession of them, in connection with advisory services the investment adviser provides to clients.

Custody includes:

■ possession of client funds or securities, unless received inadvertently and returned to the sender within three business days of receiving them;

■ any arrangement (including a general power of attorney) under which you are authorized or permitted to withdraw client funds or securities maintained with a custodian upon your instruction to the custodian; and

■ any capacity (such as general partner of a limited partnership, managing member of a limited liability company or a comparable position for another type of pooled investment vehicle, or trustee of a trust) that gives you or your supervised person legal ownership of or access to client funds or securities.

Custody does *not* include:

■ receipt of checks drawn by clients and made payable to unrelated third parties if forwarded to the third party within three business days of receipt; and

■ having investment discretion over the client's account.

Custody is the physical possession or control of funds and securities. Many advisers do not have custody because their client funds and securities are maintained at a bank or brokerage house. The adviser makes investment decisions under an advisory contract even though the client's funds and securities are placed in a custodial account at a commercial bank. Most Administrators will require advisers who maintain custody to provide a surety bond or meet certain net worth standards.

TEST TOPIC ALERT

Most investment advisers do not take custody and, therefore, are unable to accept direct delivery of customer securities or funds except under the limited conditions described in this section. However, broker-dealers are not constrained by this rule; they are only required to provide receipts any time they accept customer assets.

QUICK QUIZ 5.B

True or False?

_____ 1. An Administrator may not prevent custody of securities or funds if an adviser notifies the Administrator before taking custody.

_____ 2. Under USA antifraud provisions, an investment adviser is bound by the same restrictions that apply to sales practices when engaged in sales activities.

5. 4. 3   UNIFORM PRUDENT INVESTORS ACT OF 1994 (UPIA)

Beginning with the dynamic growth of the stock markets in the late 1960s, the investment practices of fiduciaries experienced significant change. As a result, the Uniform Prudent Investor Act (UPIA) was passed in 1994 as an attempt to update trust investment laws in recognition of those many changes. One of the major influences on this legislation was the growing acceptance of modern portfolio theory. The basic standards for anyone, not just an investment adviser, who has a fiduciary role are found in this act, which has been adopted by almost all states. Under the UPIA, fiduciaries are required to use skill and caution when making investment decisions with other people's money. The UPIA makes five fundamental alterations in the former criteria for prudent investing.

Those changes are as follows.

- The standard of prudence is applied to any investment as part of the total portfolio, rather than to individual investments. In this context, the term *portfolio* means all of the trust's or estate's assets; it is the *total return* of the portfolio that is measured, not the return of any of the individual assets.

- The trade-off in all investments between risk and return is identified as the fiduciary's primary consideration.

- All categorical restrictions on types of investments have been removed; the trustee can invest in anything that plays an appropriate role in achieving the risk/return objectives of the trust and that meets the other requirements of prudent investing.

- The well-accepted requirement that fiduciaries diversify their investments has been integrated into the definition of prudent investing.

- The much-criticized former rule forbidding the trustee to delegate investment functions has been reversed. Delegation is now permitted, subject to safeguards.

With greater numbers of trustees delegating investment decisions to investment advisers, NASAA has determined that you must know how the UPIA affects their role. Here are some thoughts that will help you on the exam.

■ A trustee must invest and manage trust assets as a prudent investor would, by considering the purposes, terms, distribution requirements, and other circumstances of the trust. In satisfying this standard, the trustee must exercise reasonable care, skill, and caution.

■ A trustee's investment and management decisions about individual assets must be evaluated, not in isolation but in the context of the total portfolio and as a part of an overall investment strategy with risk and return objectives that are reasonably suited to the trust.

■ A higher standard applies to the trustee who is an expert (a *prudent* expert) because he is assumed to have special skills.

■ Judging if a trustee has acted with prudence is based upon conduct and not the performance of the portfolio.

What conduct by a trustee demonstrates prudence? The following five-step process encompasses all of the requirements of the UPIA:

■ Analyze current position

■ Design optimal investment portfolio structure

■ Formalize investment policy

■ Implement investment policy

■ Monitor and supervise

5. 4. 4   AGENCY CROSS TRANSACTIONS

In an **agency cross transaction**, the investment adviser (or IAR acting on behalf of the firm) acts as agent for both its advisory client and the party on the other side of the trade. The USA will permit an investment adviser to engage in these transactions provided the adviser obtains prior written consent for these types of transactions from the client that discloses the following:

■ The investment adviser will be receiving commissions from both sides of the trade.

■ There is a potential conflict of interest because of the division of loyalties to both sides.

■ On at least an annual basis, the investment adviser furnishes a statement or summary of the account identifying the total number of such transactions and the total amount of all remuneration from these transactions.

■ The disclosure document conspicuously indicates that this arrangement may be terminated at any time.

■ No transaction is effected in which the same investment adviser or an investment adviser and any person controlling, controlled by, or under common control with that investment adviser recommended the transaction to both any seller and any purchaser.

These requirements do not relieve advisers of their duties to obtain best execution and best price for any transaction.

In addition to the prior consent, at or before the completion of each agency cross transaction, the client must be sent a written trade confirmation that includes:

■ a statement of the nature of the transaction;

■ the date, and if requested, the time of the transaction; and

■ the source and amount of any remuneration to be received by the IA (or IAR) in connection with the transaction.

EXAMPLE

An adviser has a client who is conservative and another who generally looks for more aggressive positions. The conservative client calls and expresses concerns about the volatility of First Tech Internet Services, Inc., stating that he thinks this may be the best time to exit his position. The adviser agrees and mentions that he has a risk-taking client for whom First Tech is suitable and he'd like to "cross" the security between the two clients, charging a small commission to each of them. With the permission of both parties, this is not a violation.

TEST TOPIC ALERT

In an agency cross transaction, the adviser may not recommend the transaction to both parties of the trade. As you can see in the previous example, the conservative client initiated the discussion about the sale, and the adviser recommended the transaction only to one side: the aggressive client.

TAKE NOTE

In the case of agency cross transactions, permission to engage in them must be obtained in writing prior to the first transaction. In essence, the client is giving blanket authority to engage in this activity. In the case of acting as a principal or agent, as described previously, no blanket authorization is permitted and oral, rather than written consent must be obtained prior to the completion of the transaction.

5. 5 SECTION 28(E) SAFE HARBOR

Research is the foundation of the money management industry. Providing research is one important, long-standing service of the brokerage business. Soft-dollar arrangements have developed as a link between the brokerage industry's supply of research and the money management industry's demand for research. What does that mean and how does it work? To find the answers, we must review the provisions of Section 28(e) of the Securities Exchange Act of 1934.

Broker-dealers typically provide a bundle of services, including research and execution of transactions. The research provided can be either proprietary (created and provided by the broker-dealer, including tangible research products as well as access to analysts and traders) or third party (created by a third party but provided by the broker-dealer). Because commission dollars pay for the entire bundle of services, the practice of allocating certain amounts of these dollars to pay for the research component has come to be called *soft dollars*. The SEC has defined soft-dollar practices as arrangements under which products or services other than execution of securities transactions are obtained by an adviser from or through a broker-dealer in exchange for the direction by the adviser of client brokerage transactions to the broker-dealer, frequently referred to as *directed transactions* on the exam. Under traditional fiduciary principles, a fiduciary cannot use assets entrusted by clients to benefit itself. As the SEC has recognized, when an adviser uses client commissions to buy research from a broker-dealer, it receives a benefit because it is relieved from the need to produce or pay for the research itself.

In addition, when transactions involving soft dollars involve the adviser receiving executions at inferior prices, advisers using soft dollars face a conflict of interest between their need to obtain research and their clients' interest in paying the lowest commission rate available and obtaining the best possible execution.

Congress created a safe harbor under Section 28(e) of the Securities Exchange Act of 1934 to protect advisers from claims that they had breached their fiduciary duties by causing clients to pay more than the lowest available commission rates in exchange for research and execution. Because of the conflict of interest that exists when an investment adviser receives research, products, or other services as a result of allocating brokerage on behalf of clients, the SEC requires advisers to disclose soft-dollar arrangements to their clients. Section 28(e) provides that a person who exercises investment discretion with respect to an account will not be deemed to have acted unlawfully or to have breached a fiduciary duty solely by reason of his having caused the account to pay more than the lowest available commission if such person determines in good faith that the amount of the commission is reasonable in relation to the value of the brokerage and research services provided.

In adopting Section 28(e), Congress acknowledged the important service broker-dealers provide by producing and distributing investment research to money managers. Section 28(e) defines when a person is deemed to be providing brokerage and research services, and states that a person provides brokerage and research services insofar as he:

- furnishes advice directly or through publications or writing about the value of securities, the advisability of investing in, purchasing, or selling securities, or the availability of purchasers or sellers of securities;

- furnishes analyses and reports concerning issuers, industries, securities, economic factors and trends, portfolio strategy, and performance of accounts; or

- effects securities transactions and performs functions incidental thereto (such as clearance, settlement, and custody).

TEST TOPIC ALERT

What this all comes down to is knowing what is and what is not included in the safe harbor. Here are some of the items that, if received as soft-dollar compensation, would likely fall under 28(e)'s safe harbor:

- Research reports analyzing the performance of a particular company or stock
- Financial newsletters and trade journals could be eligible research if they relate with appropriate specificity
- Quantitative analytical software
- Seminars or conferences with appropriate content
- Effecting and clearing securities trades

The following would be likely to fall out of the safe harbor (**not** be allowable):

- Telephone lines
- Office furniture, including computer hardware
- Travel expenses associated with attending seminars
- Rent
- Any software that does not relate directly to analysis of securities
- Payment for training courses for this exam
- Internet service

1. Which of the following would NOT be included in the safe harbor provisions of Section 28(e) of the Securities Exchange Act of 1934?

   A. Proprietary research
   B. Third-party research
   C. Rent
   D. Seminar registration fees

2. When an investment adviser with discretion over a client's account directs trade executions to a specific broker-dealer and uses the commission dollars generated to acquire software that analyzes technical market trends, it is known as

   A. hard-dollar compensation
   B. indirect compensation
   C. investment discretion
   D. soft-dollar compensation

5. 6 SALES OF SECURITIES AT FINANCIAL INSTITUTIONS

The 1990s saw a proliferation of broker-dealer services being offered on the premises of financial institutions, particularly banks. In response to the potential for confusion as well as conflicts of interest, NASAA prepared Model Rules for sales of securities at financial institutions, which were adopted October 6, 1998. Here are the key points for you to know.

No broker-dealer shall conduct broker-dealer services on the premises of a financial institution where retail deposits (deposits from ordinary customers like you and me) are taken unless the broker-dealer complies initially and continuously with the following requirements.

5. 6. 1 SETTING

Wherever practical, broker-dealer services should be conducted in a physical location distinct from the area in which the financial institution's retail deposits are taken. In situations where there is insufficient space to allow separate areas, the broker-dealer has a heightened responsibility to distinguish its services from those of the financial institution. The broker-dealer's name should be clearly displayed in the area in which the broker-dealer conducts its services.

5. 6. 2 CUSTOMER DISCLOSURE AND WRITTEN ACKNOWLEDGMENT

At or prior to the time that a customer's securities brokerage account is opened by a broker-dealer on the premises of a financial institution where retail deposits are taken, the broker-dealer must:

■ disclose, **orally** and **in writing**, that the securities products purchased or sold in a transaction with the broker-dealer

— are not insured by the Federal Deposit Insurance Corporation (FDIC),

— are not deposits or other obligations of the financial institution and are not guaranteed by the financial institution, and

— are subject to investment risks, including possible loss of the principal invested; and

■ make reasonable efforts to obtain from each customer, during the account opening process, a written acknowledgment of the disclosures.

5. 6. 3   COMMUNICATIONS WITH THE PUBLIC

The following logo format disclosures may be used by a broker-dealer in advertisements and sales literature, including material published or designed for use in radio or television broadcasts, Automated Teller Machine (ATM) screens, billboards, signs, posters, and brochures, to comply with the requirements, provided that such disclosures are displayed in a conspicuous manner:

■ Not FDIC Insured

■ No Bank Guarantee

■ May Lose Value

As long as the omission of the disclosures would not cause the advertisement or sales literature to be misleading in light of the context in which the material is presented, such disclosures are not required with respect to messages contained in:

■ radio broadcasts of **30 seconds** or less;

■ electronic signs, including billboard-type signs that are electronic, time, and temperature signs and ticker tape signs, but excluding messages contained in such media as television, online computer services, or ATMs; and

■ signs, such as banners and posters, when used only as location indicators.

5. 6. 4   SIPC COVERAGE

While most people are familiar with FDIC insurance and the role it plays insuring client accounts at banks, insurance from the Securities Investors Protection Corporation (SIPC) is less well known. SIPC provides protection to clients of broker-dealers in the event the BD enters bankruptcy proceedings. SIPC (not the Administrator) appoints a trustee whose job is to return assets owned by clients but held at the BD. SIPC does *not* protect against a decline in the value of the client's portfolio. As with FDIC, there are limits to the coverage, but those will not be tested.

5. 7   CURRENCY TRANSACTION REPORTS (CTRS)

The Bank Secrecy Act requires every financial institution to file a Currency Transaction Report (CTR) on FinCEN Form 112 for each cash transaction that exceeds $10,000. This requirement applies to cash transactions used to pay off loans, the electronic transfer of funds, or the purchase of certificates of deposit, stock, bonds, mutual funds, or other investments.

5. 8   CYBERSECURITY AND DATA PROTECTION

Hardly a day goes by without news of a hacking attempt that has compromised the security of a company, its clients, or both. There are steps that can be taken by securities professionals to reduce the potential for loss to the firm and its clients.

5. 8. 1   CYBERSECURITY POINTS TO BE ADDRESSED:

In September 2014, NASAA released results of a pilot survey designed to better understand the cybersecurity practices of state-registered investment advisers. Based on that survey, in setting up a cybersecurity program, NASAA suggests addressing the following points:

- **Cyber preparedness:** Has the firm addressed which cybersecurity threats and vulnerabilities may impact its business?
- **Cybersecurity compliance program:** Does the firm have written policies, procedures, or training programs in place regarding safeguarding client information?
- **Cybersecurity and social media:** Does the firm have written policies, procedures, or training programs in place relating to the use of social media for business purposes (e.g., Linkedin, Twitter, Facebook)?
- **Cyber insurance:** Does the firm maintain insurance coverage for cybersecurity?
- **Cyber expertise:** Has the firm engaged an outside consultant to provide cybersecurity services for your firm?
- **Cyber confidentiality:** Does the firm have confidentiality agreements with any third-party service providers with access to the firm's information technology systems?
- **Cyber incident:** Has the firm ever experienced a cybersecurity incident where, directly or indirectly, theft, loss, unauthorized exposure, use of, or access to customer information occurred? If so, has the firm taken steps to close any gaps in its cybersecurity infrastructure?
- **Cyber disposal:** Does the firm have a procedure for the disposal of electronic data storage devices?
- **Cyber continuation:** What are the plans for your firm's continued operation during a cyber-event or cybersecurity incident?
- **Cyber losses:** Are there plans for treating the loss of electronic devices (e.g., loss of a laptop containing personal and confidential client information)?
- **Cybersecurity safeguards:** Does the firm use safeguards, such as encryption and antivirus or anti-malware programs? Does the firm contact clients via email or other electronic messaging, and if so, does the firm use secure email or any procedures to authenticate client instructions received via email or electronic messaging, to work against the possibility of a client being impersonated?

5. 8. 1. 1   Safeguarding Client Information

Broker-dealers have a great deal of information about their clients that would be highly valuable to persons with evil intentions. Our primary concern here is with identity theft, which may be used to falsify client requests for funds and/or securities. In order to combat identity theft, securities professionals must be aware of the red flags.

TAKE NOTE
Identity theft means a fraud committed or attempted using the identifying information of another person without authority. *Red flag* means a pattern, practice, or specific activity that indicates the possible existence of identity theft.

The regulators are concerned when broker-dealers (or other financial professionals) maintain what are referred to as "covered accounts." The term *covered account* is defined as:

■ an account that a financial institution offers or maintains—primarily for personal, family, or household purposes—that involves or is designed to permit multiple payments or transactions (not a business account—it is felt that there is much less identity theft risk there); and

■ any other account that the financial institution offers or maintains for which there is a reasonably foreseeable risk to customers or to the safety and soundness of the financial institution from identity theft, including financial, operational, compliance, reputation, or litigation risks.

TAKE NOTE
The definition includes a margin account as an example of a covered account. Also included is a brokerage account with a broker-dealer or an account maintained by a mutual fund (or its agent) that permits wire transfers or other payments to third parties.

Investment advisers who have the ability to direct transfers or payments from accounts belonging to individuals to third parties upon the individuals' instructions, or who act as agents on behalf of the individuals, are susceptible to the same types of risks of fraud as other financial institutions. Individuals who hold accounts with these investment advisers bear the same types of risks of identity theft and loss of assets as consumers holding accounts with other financial institutions. If such an adviser does not have a program in place to verify investors' identities and detect identity theft red flags, another individual may deceive the adviser by posing as an investor.

It is required that each financial institution that offers or maintains one or more covered accounts must develop and implement a written program designed to detect, prevent, and mitigate identity theft in connection with the opening of a covered account or any existing covered account. These provisions also require that each program be appropriate to the size and complexity of the financial institution and the nature and scope of its activities.

The program must include reasonable policies and procedures to:

■ identify relevant red flags for the covered accounts that the financial institution offers or maintains and incorporate those red flags into its program;

■ detect red flags that have been incorporated into the program of the financial institution;

■ respond appropriately to any red flags that are detected to prevent and mitigate identity theft; and

■ ensure the program (including the red flags determined to be relevant) is updated periodically to reflect changes in risks to customers and to the safety and soundness of the financial institution or creditor from identity theft.

5. 8. 1. 2 Identity Theft Red Flags

Following is a list of some of the most common warnings that firms should include in their identity theft programs as is appropriate to the nature of the firm's business:

■ Alerts, notifications, or other warnings received from consumer reporting agencies or service providers, such as fraud detection services or a notice of credit freeze in response to a request for a consumer report;

■ Presentation of suspicious documents, such as documents that appear to have been altered or forged;

■ The photograph or physical description on the identification is not consistent with the appearance of the applicant or customer presenting the identification;

■ Presentation of suspicious personal identifying information, such as a suspicious address change;

■ Unusual use of, or other suspicious activity related to, a covered account;

■ Notice from customers, victims of identity theft, law enforcement authorities, or other persons regarding possible identity theft in connection with covered accounts held by the financial institution;

■ Personal identifying information provided by the customer is not consistent with other personal identifying information provided by the customer (e.g., there is a lack of correlation between the SSN range and date of birth);

■ Personal identifying information provided is of a type commonly associated with fraudulent activity as indicated by internal or third-party sources used by the financial institution. For example

— The address on an application is fictitious, a mail drop, or a prison, or

— The phone number is invalid or is associated with a pager or answering service;

■ For financial institutions that use challenge questions (what is the name of your first pet, etc.), the person opening the covered account or the customer cannot provide authenticating information beyond that which generally would be available from a wallet or consumer report; and

■ Mail sent to the customer is returned repeatedly as undeliverable although transactions continue to be conducted in connection with the customer's covered account.

Please note, this is not meant to be an exhaustive list. Your firm will make you aware of its program and the specific red flags they are addressing. The exam is more concerned about concept than an actual list, although you should be able to recognize obvious patterns of misuse in an account.

5. 8. 2 METHODS FOR PROTECTING THE FIRM AND ITS CUSTOMERS

What are the methods of authentication used by customers or employees to access electronic data storage devices, which allow access to client communications, client information, or both?

■ Single-factor authentication (e.g., ID/ Password)

■ Dual-factor authentication (e.g., Key FOBS, secure IDs)

■ Adaptive-factor authentication (e.g., challenge questions)

- Biometric authentication (e.g., fingerprint scan)
- Antivirus software installed on electronic devices used to access client information

Some questions to ask regarding the security methods used include the following.

- How often are updates downloaded to antivirus software?
- Does your firm utilize encryption on its files or devices?
- Does your firm utilize online or remote backup of electronic files?
- Does your firm allow remote access to servers or workstations via a virtual private network (VPN) or similar technology?
- Does your firm use free Cloud services such as iCloud, Dropbox, or Google Drive, to store personal and confidential client information?
- Does your firm utilize your firm's website to use or access client information data?
- Does your firm's website include a client portal?

As you can see from the many questions posed, protecting data is not a simple issue. Although the decision as to what will be used and how it will be used is that of the firm, agents must be aware of the tools being employed and how they work. That is why so much emphasis is placed on initial and continual training.

QUICK QUIZ 5.D

1. Protection of customer confidential information is an obligation of the

     I. agent servicing the customer's account
     II. broker-dealer maintaining the account
     III. customer
     IV. investment adviser in an advisory account

     A. I and II
     B. II and IV
     C. III and IV
     D. I, II, III, and IV

2. A broker-dealer's cybersecurity procedures should address all of the following EXCEPT

     A. the music played while customers are placed on hold
     B. office desktop computers
     C. agent's personal smartphones used on occasion to communicate with clients
     D. remote access to servers or workstations via a virtual private network (VPN)

UNIT TEST

1. Market manipulation is one of the prohibited practices under the Uniform Securities Act. Which of the following is an example of a broker-dealer engaging in market manipulation?

   I. Churning
   II. Arbitrage
   III. Wash trade
   IV. Matched orders

   A. I and II
   B. I, III, and IV
   C. III and IV
   D. IV only

2. Your customer called to check on her account value at 9:00 am. You were unavailable at the time. It is now 2:00 pm, and you are able to call her back. Between 9:00 am and 2:00 pm, her account value dropped from $11,500 to $10,000. What should you say to her?

   A. "At the time you called, your account had a value of $10,000."
   B. "Your account value cannot be determined until the market closes."
   C. "Your account is valued at $10,000 at this time."
   D. "Your account was down to $9,700 earlier today but is now up to $10,000."

3. All of the following are prohibited practices under the USA EXCEPT

   A. borrowing money or securities from the account of a former banker with express written permission
   B. failing to identify a customer's financial objectives
   C. selling unregistered non-exempt securities to a closed-end investment company
   D. supplying funds to a client's account only when or if it declines below a previously agreed-upon level

4. A customer is upset with her agent for not servicing her account properly and sends him a complaint letter about his actions. Under the Uniform Securities Act, the agent should

   A. call the customer, apologize, and attempt to correct the problem
   B. tell the customer he is willing to make rescission
   C. do nothing
   D. bring the customer complaint to his employer immediately

5. In which of the following cases is an agent NOT considered to have acted in a prohibited or unethical manner?

   A. The agent borrows money from his wealthy clients' accounts with their written consent.
   B. The agent solicits orders for non-exempt, unregistered securities from institutional clients.
   C. The agent buys and sells securities in accounts to generate a high level of commissions.
   D. The agent alters market quotations to induce a client to invest in an attractive growth stock.

6. According to the USA, which of the following is an example of market manipulation?

   A. Creating the illusion of active trading
   B. Omitting material facts in a presentation
   C. Guaranteeing performance of a security
   D. Transacting in excess of a customer's financial capability

7. In 1998, NASAA promulgated a Model Rule covering the sales of securities at financial institutions. Under that rule, an advertisement by a broker-dealer would be exempt from meeting certain disclosure requirements of that rule if

   A. it was distributed to a limited demographic group
   B. the broker-dealer and the bank were affiliated
   C. it were a radio ad not exceeding 30 seconds, as long as the omission of the required disclosures would not cause the advertisement to be misleading in light of the context in which the material is presented
   D. the advertisement only related to NYSE-listed stocks

8. Which of the following practices is prohibited under the USA?

   A. Participating in active trading of a security in which an unusually high trading volume has occurred
   B. Offering services that an agent cannot realistically perform because of his broker-dealer's limitations
   C. Altering the customer's order at the request of a customer, which subsequently results in a substantial loss
   D. Failing to inform the firm's principal of frequent oral customer complaints

9. An agent hears a rumor concerning a security and uses the rumor to convince a client to purchase the security. Under the USA, the agent may

   A. recommend the security if it is an appropriate investment
   B. recommend the investment if the rumor is based on material inside information
   C. recommend the security if the source of the rumor is reliable
   D. not recommend the security

10. If an agent thought that a technology stock was undervalued and actively solicited 75% of his customers to buy the stock, the agent

    A. did not violate the USA if all material facts were disclosed
    B. committed an unethical sales practice because the firm has not recommended this technology stock
    C. has probably committed the unethical business practice known as blanket recommendations
    D. did not commit a violation if all clients were accurately informed of the price of the stock

11. Which of the following transactions are prohibited?

    I. Borrowing money or securities from a high net worth customer
    II. Selling speculative issues to a retired couple of modest means on a fixed income
    III. Failing to follow a customer's orders so as to prevent investment in a security not adequately covered by well-known securities analysts
    IV. Backdating confirmations for the benefit of the client's tax reporting

    A. I and II
    B. I, II, and III
    C. II and III
    D. I, II, III, and IV

12. An agent omits facts that a prudent investor requires to make informed decisions. Under the Uniform Securities Act, this action is

    A. fraudulent for nonexempt securities only
    B. fraudulent for exempt securities only
    C. fraudulent for both exempt and nonexempt securities
    D. not fraudulent if there was willful intent to omit the information

13. Which of the following actions is NOT a prohibited practice under the NASAA Statement of Policy on Dishonest or Unethical Business Practices of Broker-Dealers and Agents?

    A. An agent places an order to purchase a stock ahead of a large institutional order he has just received for that stock.

    B. An agent receives an unsolicited order from a client to purchase 200 shares of XYZ 10 seconds after he has turned in his own order for that stock. It turns out that the agent acquired the shares for less than the client and does not make up the difference.

    C. A principal of a broker-dealer allows a rumor to spread that ABC is going to acquire LMN; after a few days, the broker-dealer sells ABC short for its own account.

    D. An agent sells a customer's stock at the bid price and makes up the difference with a personal check.

14. Which of the following is(are) prohibited under the USA?

    I. Recommending tax shelters to low-income retirees

    II. Stating that a state Administrator has approved an offering on the basis of the quality of information found in the prospectus

    III. Soliciting non-institutional orders for unregistered, nonexempt securities

    IV. Employing any device to defraud

    A. I only
    B. I and II
    C. I, II, and III
    D. I, II, III, and IV

15. According to the Uniform Securities Act, an investment adviser may have custody of a customer's funds and securities if

    A. it has received the permission of the Administrator
    B. it has received permission from the SEC
    C. it does not share in the capital gains of the account
    D. the Administrator has been informed of the custody

16. According to the NASAA Statement of Policy on Dishonest or Unethical Business Practices of Broker-Dealers and Agents, which of the following is a prohibited activity?

    A. The agent enters into an agreement to share in the profits and losses of the customer's account without the written consent of his broker-dealer.

    B. The agent and his spouse jointly own their own personal trading account at the firm.

    C. The agent, with his firm's and the client's written permission, participates in the profits and losses of the customer's account.

    D. An agent refuses a client's request to share in the performance of the client's account.

17. ZAP Brokerage has 5 partners. Raymond Zap, Jr., is a minor partner. He violates the USA because he did not perform his job of making sure that the firm maintained the minimum required capital. Which of the following are TRUE?

    I. Only Raymond will have his license suspended.

    II. The Administrator may revoke the entire firm's right to sell securities.

    III. A revocation of ZAP's registration would cause each of its agent's registrations to be terminated.

    IV. The firm could be fined up to $5,000 but incur no suspension.

    A. I and II
    B. II and III
    C. III and IV
    D. I, II, III, and IV

18. Under the Uniform Prudent Investors Act (UPIA) of 1994,

    A. investment advisers are prohibited from accepting delegation of investment decision making from trustees

    B. those in a fiduciary capacity are not permitted to charge for their services

    C. diversification of investments as a concept has been integrated into the definition of prudent investing

    D. those acting in a fiduciary capacity are eligible for the transaction exemption offered under the Uniform Securities Act of 1956

19. Under the Uniform Securities Act, all of the following are prohibited practices EXCEPT

    A. making recommendations on the basis of material, nonpublic information

    B. making recommendations on the basis of material information after that information has been publicly released

    C. making recommendations without having reasonable grounds for believing they are suitable

    D. stating that recommendations have been approved by the Administrator

20. Under the NASAA Statement of Policy on Dishonest or Unethical Business Practices of Broker-Dealers and Agents, all of the following are prohibited business practices EXCEPT

    A. failing to indicate that securities prices are subject to market fluctuation

    B. ignoring an order to buy a stock immediately at the market price because the price is falling and the customer will likely get a better price by waiting

    C. telling a customer that commission, taxes, and other costs will be higher than normal, even when you do not know exactly how high they will be

    D. wash trades and matching orders to create the appearance of market activity

21. Potential cybersecurity threats can come from

    I. agents using social media to communicate with customers

    II. weak passwords

    III. allowing employees to take office laptop computers home

    IV. infrequent updating of antivirus software

    A. I and II

    B. I and III

    C. II, III and IV

    D. I, II, III, and IV

22. Making recommendations on the basis of material inside information about an issuer or its securities, when this information has not been made public, is prohibited. Therefore, an agent or broker-dealer doing which of the following would be engaging in a fraudulent practice?

    I. Giving inside information to privileged clients without a fee

    II. Informing other issuers about the inside information with the intent of collectively taking advantage of the information

    III. Having your relatives in another state invest heavily in this security when it appears in the market

    IV. Investing large sums of the firm's money in this issue with the written consent of all partners

    A. I and III

    B. I and IV

    C. II and IV

    D. I, II, III, and IV

23. You have a wealthy client who complains to you about the extremely low rates currently being offered by his bank on CDs. You tell him that you are willing to borrow up to $100,000 for 2 years at prime +1 and will deposit securities you own as collateral. Under the NASAA Statement of Policy on Dishonest or Unethical Business Practices of Broker-Dealers and Agents

    A. it is prohibited to borrow money from a client unless the client is in the money lending business

    B. it is always prohibited to pay a client more than a bank CD rate

    C. it could be permitted if the proper disclosures were made

    D. approval of the appropriate supervisor of your firm would be required

24. Broker-dealer A wants to promote and reward teamwork. The firm plans to pay out a small percentage of year-end profits to the clerical staff as a bonus for their hard work. Under the Uniform Securities Act, is this permitted?

    A. Yes, if the bonuses are equally divided

    B. Yes, if all the agents agree to it

    C. Yes, if the clerical staff are all registered agents of the firm

    D. Yes, as long as the compensation is not sales related

25. A great concern to broker-dealers is the theft of the identity of a client. To reduce the possibility of a client's assets being improperly taken, most firms would consider all of these to be a red flag EXCEPT

    A. almost 1 year since your last contact with your client, you receive a phone call requesting that funds be wired to an offshore account

    B. a client regularly visits your office to pick up a check representing the proceeds of recently settled transactions

    C. when running a credit report on a new client's applications, there is a discrepancy between the home address listed on the report and the one on the new account form

    D. the photograph on the identification documents provided does not resemble the individual opening the account

ANSWERS AND RATIONALES

1. **C.** A wash trade, the practice of attempting to create the appearance of trading activity by entering offsetting buy and sell orders, is a form of market manipulation. Matched orders occur when market participants agree to buy and sell securities among themselves to create the appearance of heightened market activity; this is also a form of market manipulation. Although churning is a prohibited practice, it does not involve manipulating the market, and arbitrage is the perfectly legal practice of buying a security in one marketplace and simultaneously selling it in another to benefit from a price disparity.

2. **C.** All other choices are clearly a misrepresentation of account status.

3. **C.** It is permissible to sell unregistered, non-exempt securities to an institutional buyer, such as an investment company, because that would be an exempt transaction. Borrowing money or securities from other than a bank or broker-dealer in the business of lending, failing to identify a customer's financial objectives, and guaranteeing a customer's account against losses are all prohibited practices.

4. **D.** Failure to bring customers' written complaints to the attention of the agent's broker-dealer is prohibited.

5. **B.** Transactions with institutions are exempt. Even a non-exempt security is excused from registering with the state when the transaction is exempt. An agent can only borrow money from a client who is in the money-lending business or an affiliate of the broker-dealer. Trading an account for the purpose of generating commissions is the prohibited action known as *churning* and it would never be permitted to alter market quotations.

6. **A.** Creating the illusion of trading activity is market manipulation. Guaranteeing performance of a security and omitting material facts are prohibited practices but do not constitute market manipulation. Trades too large for a customer are also prohibited because they are not suitable, but they are not market manipulation.

7. **C.** Under this Model Rule, certain disclosures must be made. They include statements that even though the investments are being sold on the premises of a financial institution (typically a bank), they are not FDIC insured, may lose money, and are not an obligation of the bank. However, an exception from those required disclosures is made in the case of a short (no longer than 30 seconds) radio advertisement, as long as there is nothing in that ad that could be construed as misleading without those disclaimers.

8. **B.** An agent may not offer services that he cannot perform. An agent may participate actively in trading a security in which an unusually high trading volume has occurred, provided the trading is not designed to create a false appearance of high volume. At the client's request, an agent can alter a client's order, even if the change results in a loss. An agent is only required to report written complaints to his employing principal, although it would be wise to report repeated oral complaints.

9. **D.** The use of information that has no basis in fact, such as a rumor, is prohibited.

10. **C.** Agents must always determine suitability before soliciting purchases or sales. The key here is that the agent recommended this stock to such a high percentage of his clients. One investment cannot be suitable for the majority of your clients. This is sometimes referred to as a "blanket" recommendation.

11. **D.** All of the practices are prohibited. An agent may not borrow money or securities from a customer unless that customer is a bank or broker-dealer in the business of lending money and/or securities. Selling speculative issues to a retired couple of modest means is an unsuitable transaction because it is not consistent with the objectives of the client. An agent must follow legal orders of the customer, even if the agent believes the order is an unwise one. An agent may not backdate confirmations (or any other records for that matter) for the benefit of the client.

12. **C.** Material facts are facts that an investor relies on to make investment decisions. The omission of a material fact in the sale, purchase, or offer of a security is fraudulent. This applies whether the security offered is exempt or nonexempt.

13. **B.** A securities professional may enter a personal order ahead of a client just by happenstance. There is no obligation to get the client the better price. Had the order been solicited, then we must be sure to place our customer's orders ahead of our own. Allowing a rumor to spread and then trading in response to it is a prohibited practice. Selling stock at the bid price and making up the difference with a personal check is a prohibited practice. Filling a firm's proprietary order ahead of a customer's order is a prohibited practice called front running.

14. **D.** Recommending tax shelters to low-income retirees is an example of an unsuitable transaction. Stating that an Administrator has approved an offering on the basis of the quality of information in the prospectus, soliciting retail orders for unregistered nonexempt securities, and employing a device to defraud are all prohibited practices under the USA.

15. **D.** As long as retaining custody of funds is not prohibited, an investment adviser may have custody of a customer's account after providing notice to the Administrator.

16. **A.** It is a prohibited practice under the NASAA Statement of Policy on Dishonest or Unethical Business Practices of Broker-Dealers and Agents for an agent to share in the profits or losses of a customer's account unless the customer and the employer have given written consent. Unlike FINRA rules, there is no requirement that the sharing be proportionate. Also, this type of sharing is only permitted for agents, not any of the other three securities professionals. An agent is permitted to jointly own a personal account at the firm and can refuse to share in a customer's account.

17. **B.** Although Raymond is certainly in trouble and may have his registration revoked or suspended, the firm may also have problems. First, the Administrator may close the firm because of inadequate capital. It is also possible that the firm may face disciplinary action because of failure to properly supervise Raymond. Thirdly, the actions of a partner of a firm can lead to action against the firm. An agent cannot be an agent without representing a dealer, so this action would automatically terminate the licenses of all the agents who work for this firm.

18. **C.** Those in a fiduciary capacity (trustees, executors, and investment advisers, among others) are required to act in the best interest of the client. The UPIA of 1994 revised previous versions and declared the importance of diversification as well as permitted delegation of investment decision making to qualified persons. Although fiduciary transactions are exempt under the USA, that has nothing to do with the UPIA.

19. **B.** Nonpublic (inside) information of a material nature never may be used. All recommendations must be suitable, and recommendations are never approved by the Administrator.

20. **C.** It is appropriate to tell a customer that certain costs will be higher than normal, even if it is not known how much higher. In fact, it would be a prohibited practice to fail to inform the customer of such higher costs before the trade. All of the other choices are prohibited actions.

21. **D.** Cybersecurity threats can come from almost anywhere that digital media is used.

22. **D.** All the answer choices involve fraudulent trading in response to insider information. Material information not available to the investing public cannot be used by anyone when making investment decisions.

23. **A.** You can never borrow money from a client who is not in the money lending business.

24. **D.** USA rules permit bonuses to nonregistered personnel as long as the compensation is not directly tied to sales of securities.

25. **B** There is nothing wrong with a client picking up a check for the proceeds of a securities transaction, even if done on a regular basis (some folks don't trust the mail). Each of the other choices should raise a red flag as being something needing further investigation.

QUICK QUIZ ANSWERS

Quick Quiz 5.A

1. **U.** It is unlawful to guarantee the performance of any security. Even though the government securities are guaranteed, the mutual fund investment is not.

2. **U.** It is unlawful to exercise discretion without prior written authorization. Because the client was a nondiscretionary client, the agent could not, on his own initiative, select which internet company to invest in.

3. **L.** An agent must refuse orders from anyone other than the customer unless that person has prior written trading authority.

4. **U.** All written customer complaints must be forwarded to a designated supervisor of the agent's employing broker-dealer.

5. **L.** Agents may borrow from banks or financial institutions that are in the business of lending money to public customers. Agents may not borrow money from customers who are not in the business of lending money.

6. **U.** An agent may not guarantee the performance of a security.

7. **L.** It is lawful to charge extra transaction fees when justified, as long as the customer is informed before the transaction.

8. **U.** It is unlawful to promise services that an agent cannot reasonably expect to perform or that the agent is not qualified to perform.

9. **U.** It is unlawful to solicit unregistered nonexempt securities.

Quick Quiz 5.B

1. **F.** An Administrator may, by rule or order, prevent an adviser from taking custody. If an Administrator prevents custody, an adviser cannot overrule the Administrator by notifying the Administrator first.

2. **T.** Investment advisers are bound by the regulations that apply to sales activities as well as those that apply to advisory activities. The reverse is also true. When a sales agent engages in investment advisory activities, the agent is bound by the rules that apply to providing investment advice to others as well as those that apply to sales practices.

Quick Quiz 5.C

1. **C.** Section 28(e) provides a safe harbor for those expenses paid with soft dollars that offer a direct research benefit. Rent is not included in the list of acceptable items coming under that safe harbor.

2. **D.** Soft-dollar compensation is when an investment adviser derives an economic benefit from the use of a client's commission dollars. Software of the type mentioned here is allowable under the safe harbor provisions of Section 28(e) of the Securities Exchange Act of 1934. It is true that this is indirect compensation and that this is a discretionary account, but the answer that best matches the question is soft dollar. Many times on the exam, you'll have to select the best of the choices given.

Quick Quiz 5.D

1. **D.** Although any securities professional handing a customer account is obligated to follow all necessary procedures to protect client data, customers themselves also bear a responsibility. Customers ignoring the cybersecurity safeguards put not only their own data at risk, but also that of other customers, by potentially opening the door to hackers.

2. **A.** It is hard to imagine how the music on hold would present a security risk. All of the others clearly offer potential for loss.

Glossary

Numerics

12b-1 plan A section of the Investment Company Act of 1940 that permits an open-end investment company (mutual fund) to levy an ongoing charge for advertising and sales promotional expenses. This fee may not exceed .75% and, if above .25%, the fund may not describe itself as no-load.

A

accredited investor Any institution or individual meeting minimum requirements for the purchase of securities qualifying under the Regulation D registration exemption, as defined in Rule 501 of Regulation D.

An accredited investor generally is accepted to be one who:

- has a net worth, exclusive of the net equity in a primary residence, of $1 million or more; or

- has had an annual income of $200,000 or more in each of the two most recent years (or $300,000 jointly with a spouse) and who has a reasonable expectation of reaching the same income level in the current year.

Administrator The official or agency administering the securities laws of a state.

adoption A social media term used to describe the firm's endorsement or approval of the content of a third-party site. This is not prohibited, but the relationship must be disclosed.

advertisement Any material designed for use by newspapers, magazines, radio, television, telephone recording, or any other public medium to solicit business. The firm using advertising has little control over the type of individuals being exposed to the advertising.

affiliate A person in a position to influence the policies of a corporation. This includes partners, officers, directors, and entities who control more than 10% of the voting stock.

agency cross transaction For an advisory client, a transaction in which a person acts as an investment adviser in relation to a transaction in which that investment adviser, or any person controlling, controlled by, or under common control with that investment adviser, acts as broker for both an advisory client and for another person on the other side of the transaction.

agency transaction A transaction in which a broker-dealer acts for the accounts of others by buying or selling securities on behalf of customers.

agent (1) A securities salesperson who represents a broker-dealer or an issuer when selling or trying to sell securities to the investing public. This individual is considered an agent whether he actually receives or simply solicits orders. (2) A person acting for the accounts of others.

annuity A contract between an insurance company and an individual; it generally guarantees lifetime income to the individual on whose life the contract is based in return for either a lump sum or a periodic payment to the insurance company. The contract holder's objective is usually retirement income. Fixed annuities (where the monthly payout doesn't change) are not securities, but variable annuities (where the monthly payout varies based on the performance of the separate account portfolio) are securities.

arbitrage The purchase of securities on one market and the simultaneous resale on another market to take advantage of a price discrepancy. This is not a form of market manipulation and is completely legal.

assessable stock Stock issued below par, carrying with it the option on the part of the issuer or creditors to assess the owner for the remainder. A gift of assessable stock is considered a sale under the Uniform Securities Act.

assignment Transferring an investment advisory contract to another firm. This may not be done without written consent of the customer. A change in the majority interest in an investment advisory firm organized as a partnership is also considered assignment.

associated person Any employee, manager, director, officer, or partner of a member broker-dealer or another entity (e.g., issuer or bank), or any person controlling, controlled by, or in common control with that member, is considered an associated person of that member.

B

bank holding company A holding company whose primary asset is a commercial bank. *See also* holding company.

blue sky (v.) To qualify a securities offering in a particular state.

blue-sky laws The commonly used term for state regulations governing the securities industry.

bona fide From the Latin term for good faith. A bona fide offer is a sincere one.

breakpoint In the sale of mutual funds, the price points at which purchasers are entitled to a reduction in sales charge. One method of taking advantage of breakpoints is through the use of a letter of intent. *See* letter of intent, front-end load.

brochure rules An investment adviser must provide its customer with its brochure (Parts 2A and 2B of Form ADV) at least 48 hours before having him sign the contract. If delivery is made after that, (but no later than the finalization of the contract), the customer must be given five days to void the contract without penalty.

broker The role of a broker-dealer firm when it acts as an agent for a customer and charges the customer a commission for its services.

broker-dealer A firm that acts for the securities accounts of others (acting as a broker) or its own account (acting as a dealer) in trades. Excluded from the definition are:

- agents (registered representatives);

- issuers;

- banks, savings institutions, and trust companies; and

- firms that fit the definition, but (1) have no office in the state and (2) effect transactions only with accredited investors such as issuers, banks, insurance companies, or other broker-dealers, with non-residents of the state, or with existing clients who have fewer than 30 days' residency in the state.

C

cancellation Nonpunitive termination of registration by the Administrator. Reasons include the registrant's death, the registrant ceasing to do business, mental incompetence on the part of the registrant, or the Administrator's inability to locate the registrant.

cash account An account with a broker-dealer where securities purchases are paid for in full. *See* margin account.

CDSC Conditional deferred sales charge. Sometimes called a back-end load (conditional deferred sales load, or CDSL) to differentiate between it and a front-end load. Instead of charging a load on each purchase, there is no sales charge unless the investor redeems shares too early. These charges begin reducing after the first year and generally decline to zero between the sixth and eighth year after purchase. *See* front-end load.

cease and desist Used by the Administrator when it appears that a registered person has or is about to commit a violation. May be issued with or without a prior hearing.

churning A prohibited practice in which a salesperson effects transactions in a customer's account that are excessive in size or frequency in relation to the size and character of the account.

closed-end management company An investment company that issues a fixed number of shares in an actively managed portfolio of securities. The shares may be of several classes, and they are traded in the secondary marketplace, either on an exchange or over the counter. The market price of the shares is determined by supply and demand and not by NAV. *Syn.* publicly traded fund.

commercial paper An unsecured, short-term promissory note issued by a corporation for financing accounts receivable and inventories. It is usually issued at a discount reflecting prevailing market interest rates. Maturities range up to 270 days.

commingling Mixing broker-dealer or investment adviser cash and securities with customer cash and securities in the same account. This is a prohibited practice.

commission A broker's fee for handling transactions for a client in an agency capacity.

confirmation A printed document that states the trade, settlement date, and money due from or owed to a customer; it is sent or given to the customer on or before the settlement date. *Syn.* trade confirmation.

consent to service of process A legal document entered into by all registrants, whereby the Administrator is given the power to accept legal papers on behalf of the registrant.

covered adviser *See* federal covered adviser.

covered security *See* federal covered security.

custody Maintaining possession of a customer's money and/or securities. Many states prohibit investment advisers from keeping custody. The others require the adviser to notify the Administrator if it intends to do so. An adviser is also considered to have custody if the customer has authorized it to receive and disperse funds and securities from his bank account.

customer Any person who opens a trading account with a broker-dealer. A customer may be classified in terms of account ownership, trading authorization, payment method, or types of securities traded.

customer agreement (margin agreement) A document that a customer must sign when opening a margin account with a broker-dealer; it allows the firm to liquidate all or a portion of the account if the customer fails to meet a margin call.

customer ledger The accounting record that lists separately all customer cash and margin accounts carried by a firm.

cybersecurity Sometimes referred to as information technology security, it focuses on protecting computers, networks, programs, and data from unintended or unauthorized access, change, or destruction.

D

dealer A firm acting as a principal, for its own account, in a trade. Such a firm actually owns the securities during the trade and charges its customer a markup (if the firm is selling the securities) or a markdown (if the firm is buying them).

delivery The change in ownership or control of a security in exchange for payment. Delivery takes place on the settlement date.

direct participation program (DPP) These programs are direct investments in limited partnerships and limited liability corporations. Real estate, oil and gas, and equipment leasing are examples of direct participation assets. Investors in DPPs allow for direct participation in cash flow as well as tax benefits. Under both state and federal law, these are securities.

discretion The authority for someone other than the beneficial owner of an account to make investment decisions for that account regarding the security, the number of shares or units, and whether to buy or sell. Decisions concerning only timing and price do not constitute discretion.

discretionary account An account in which the customer authorizes in writing a broker-dealer or investment adviser to use his judgment in buying and selling securities, including selection, timing, amount, and price. Judgment as to time or price only is not considered discretion. Discretionary trades must always be suitable for the customer.

Dodd-Frank bill The general term by which the Wall Street Reform and Consumer Protection Act of 2010 is known. Considered to be the most significant legislation impacting the securities industry since the 1930s.

DPP *See* direct participation program.

E

effective date The date on which a security can be offered publicly if no stop order is submitted to the issuer by the Administrator.

electronic storage An acceptable method of recordkeeping, generally on computer disc. Among the requirements is that it cannot be altered and can be used to generate a paper copy upon request.

enjoin A person who is the subject of a court-ordered injunction is said to be enjoined.

entangled A social media term sometimes referred to as entanglement. This is where the firm participates in the development of the content of a third-party site. This is not prohibited, but the relationship must be disclosed.

executor A person given fiduciary authorization to manage the affairs of a decedent's estate.

exempt Not being required to do something that others are required to do.

exempt security A security that need not be in formal compliance with a given piece of legislation, such as the Securities Act of 1933 or the Uniform Securities Act as adopted by a state. Examples are U.S. government and municipal securities. No security is exempt from the antifraud provisions of any securities legislation.

exempt transaction A transaction exempt from registration, sales literature, and advertising requirements under the Uniform Securities Act. Examples of exempt transactions include:

- isolated nonissuer transactions;
- transactions with financial institutions (e.g., banks, savings institutions, trust companies, insurance companies, pension or profit-sharing plans, broker-dealers);
- unsolicited transactions;
- fiduciary transactions;
- private placement transactions;
- transactions between an issuer and its underwriters; and
- transactions with an issuer's employees, partners, or directors if no commission is paid directly or indirectly for the soliciting.

F

federal covered adviser An adviser regulated under the Investment Advisers Act of 1940. The person is either required to register with the SEC or is excluded from the definition of investment adviser under that act. A federal covered adviser has a federally imposed exemption from state securities regulation. The exam will frequently just use the term covered adviser.

federal covered security Under the NSMIA of 1996, a new definition was created: covered security, sometimes referred to as a federal covered security on the exam. State securities registration requirements were preempted with respect to covered securities, other than the ability to require notice filing, particularly in the case of registered investment companies. The most tested federal covered securities include those listed on the major U.S. exchanges and Nasdaq, as well as investment companies registered with the SEC and securities offered pursuant to the provisions of Rule 506 of Regulation D under the Securities Act of 1933 (private placements).

fiduciary A person legally appointed and authorized to represent another person and act on that person's behalf.

Financial Industry Regulatory Authority (FINRA)
The largest regulator for securities firms doing business in the United States. It oversees approximately 635,000 registered representatives. Overseen by the SEC, FINRA's primary role is to maintain the fairness of U.S. capital markets.

foreign government securities Securities issued by the sovereign government of a country other than the United States. If the United States has diplomatic relations with that foreign country, such securities are exempt from federal and state registration, but the foreign equivalent of municipal securities is nonexempt.

Form ADV The document used by an investment adviser to register with the appropriate authority. It consists of two basic parts, Part 1 and Part 2, with each of those divided into two parts, 1A and 1B and 2A and 2B. Part 1 is used to disclose information to the regulators, and Part 2 is used to meet the brochure requirements for disclosures to clients.

fraud The deliberate concealment, misrepresentation, or omission of material information or the truth to deceive or manipulate another party for unlawful or unfair gain.

front-end load When discussing the sale of mutual fund shares, the amount of sales charge levied on each purchase. The maximum permitted load is 8.5% of the offering price, but most funds today charge 5% or less. This load can be reduced by reaching a breakpoint. *See* breakpoint, letter of intent, CDSC.

front running Taking action to profit from a customer order before executing the order. For example, if the customer places a large order for a particular stock, the agent might purchase calls on the stock before placing the order and then profit from any price rise caused by the order. This is a prohibited practice.

G

government security An obligation of the U.S. government, backed by the full faith and credit of the government, and regarded as the highest grade or safest issue (i.e., default risk free). The U.S. government issues short-term Treasury bills, medium-term Treasury notes, and long-term Treasury bonds.

guaranteed Securities that have a guarantee, usually from a source other than the issuer, as to the payment of principal, interest, or dividends, but not capital gains.

guardian A fiduciary who manages the assets of a minor or incompetent for the benefit of that person.

H

home state If an investment adviser is registered with a state Administrator (state-registered adviser), the firm's home state is the state where it maintains its principal office and place of business. The investment adviser is required to meet the bonding, net worth, and record-keeping requirements of its home state, even if it is registered in other states with more severe requirements.

hypothecation When securities are purchased in a margin account, they are pledged as collateral for the loan made by the broker-dealer to the client. When these securities are pledged, they are said to be hypothecated. Clients must sign a written hypothecation agreement promptly after the initial margin transaction in their account. *See* margin account.

I

identity theft A fraud committed or attempted using the identifying information of another person without authority.

impersonal investment advice Investment advisory services that do not purport to meet the objectives or needs of specific individuals or accounts.

initial public offering (IPO) The first sale of securities by a corporation to the public.

injunction A court order requiring a person to do or omit doing a specific action. It is an extraordinary remedy that courts utilize in special cases where preservation of the status quo or taking some specific action is required in order to prevent possible injustice. A person who has been given adequate notice of an injunction but fails to follow the court's orders may be punished for contempt of court.

inside information Material and nonpublic information a person obtained or used for the purpose of trading in securities. *See also* material fact.

insider Any person who has nonpublic knowledge (material information) about a corporation. Insiders include directors, officers, and stockholders who own more than 10% of any class of equity security of a corporation.

institutional account An account held for the benefit of others. Examples include banks, trusts, pension and profit-sharing plans, mutual funds, and insurance companies.

institutional investor Institutional investors are covered by fewer protective regulations because it is assumed that they are more knowledgeable and better able to protect themselves. The Uniform Securities Act includes in its definition of institutional clients a bank, savings institution, trust company, insurance company, investment company (as defined in the Investment Company Act of 1940), or employee benefit plan with assets of not less than $1 million.

interactive content Social media format in which content is supplied by both the creator and the viewer(s).

investment adviser Any person who, for compensation (a flat fee or a percentage of assets managed), is in the business of offering investment advice on securities.

investment adviser representative Any partner, officer, director, or other individual employed by or associated with an investment adviser who (1) gives investment advice or makes recommendations, (2) manages client accounts or portfolios, (3) determines which investment recommendations or advice should be given, (4) offers or sells investment advisory services, or (5) supervises employees involved in any of these activities.

Investment Advisers Act of 1940 Legislation passed by Congress that requires certain investment advisers to register as such with the SEC, to abide by the Investment Advisers Act of 1940 and all other applicable federal acts, and to treat its customers in a fair and equitable manner.

investment banker A broker-dealer in the business of raising capital for corporations and municipalities.

investment company A company engaged primarily in the business of investing and trading in securities, including face-amount certificate companies, unit investment trusts, and management companies.

Investment Company Act of 1940 Congressional legislation enacted to regulate investment companies that requires any investment company in interstate commerce to register with the SEC.

isolated nonissuer transaction An exempt transaction between individual investors, conducted privately. The exempt nature of the transaction must be established by a principal for each separate trade.

issuer (1) The corporation, government, or other entity that offers its securities for sale. (2) According to the USA, any person who issues or proposes to issue any security. When a corporation or municipality raises additional capital through an offering of securities, that corporation or municipality is the issuer of those securities.

L

letter of intent A non-binding agreement between a purchaser of mutual funds and the fund underwriter that allows the investor up to 13 months to reach a specified dollar purchase. In so doing, the client receives the sales charge reduction applicable to that breakpoint with the first and subsequent purchases. *See* breakpoint, front-end load.

M

margin The use of borrowed money to purchase securities.

margin account An account with a broker-dealer where the firm lends 50% of the purchase price to the client, with the client putting up the balance. Such accounts use leverage and carry greater risk than cash accounts. *See* cash account, hypothecation.

markdown The profit made by a dealer when purchasing a security from a customer. *See* markup.

market maker A dealer willing to accept the risk of holding securities to facilitate trading in a particular security.

markup The profit made by a dealer when selling a security to a customer. Just as in any business, dealers purchase at one price and sell to their clients at a higher one. That difference is the markup. *See* markdown.

matched orders Simultaneously buying and selling a security to give its trading volume a falsely high appearance. This is a prohibited practice.

material fact Information required to be included in a registration statement that a knowledgeable investor would deem significant in making an investment determination. *See also* inside information.

municipal security Exempt debt security issued by some level of government other than the federal to raise money for a public project. Interest payable on these instruments is not federally taxable.

N

National Conference of Commissioners on Uniform State Laws (NCCUSL) The NCCUSL, founded in 1892, is an organization composed of lawyers who draft and propose template state legislation where uniformity in law among the states is deemed to be desirable. It was the NCCUSL that wrote the Uniform Securities Act. The organization does not, of course, actually write laws, but rather proposes legislation that a state may adopt if it chooses.

National Securities Markets Improvement Act of 1996 (NSMIA) Federal legislation designed to clarify the demarcation between federal and state securities law and to improve the efficiency of the securities markets in the United States. Some securities, known as federal covered securities, and some advisory firms, known as federal covered advisers, were removed from state purview to eliminate duplication of regulatory effort.

net capital The amount of cash and SEC-approved assets readily convertible into cash that a broker-dealer owns in excess of its liabilities. The SEC (or the state) sets net capital requirements to ensure that broker-dealers have enough capital to deal responsibly with the investing public.

new account form The form that must be filled out for each new account opened with a brokerage firm. The form specifies, at a minimum, the account owner, trading authorization, payment method, and types of securities appropriate for the customer.

no-load The term used to describe a mutual fund whose shares are offered without any sales charge. The term may not be used if the fund has a 12b-1 plan with a charge in excess of .25% or has any front-end load or CDSC.

nonexempt Obligated, not free from complying.

nonexempt security A security whose issue and sale must be in compliance with the Uniform Securities Act and/or the various federal securities acts. Most corporate securities are nonexempt.

nonissuer A person other than the issuer of a security. In a nonissuer securities transaction, for example, the issuer is not one of the parties in the transaction, and the transaction is not, according to the law, directly or indirectly for the benefit of the issuer. When the USA refers to a nonissuer transaction, it is referring to a transaction in which the proceeds of the sale go to the selling stockholder. Most nonissuer transactions also are called secondary transactions.

North American Securities Administrators Association (NASAA) The NASAA, founded in Kansas in 1919, is the oldest international investor protection organization. Its current membership is 67 Administrators from the territories, districts, and states of the United States, from Mexico, and from the provinces of Canada. The Series 63 is written by the NASAA and administered by FINRA.

notice filing (1) Method by which a registered investment company and certain other federal covered securities file records with state securities Administrators. (2) SEC-registered advisers (federal covered) may have to provide state securities authorities (the Administrator) with copies of documents that are filed with the SEC and pay a filing fee.

NSMIA *See* National Securities Markets Improvement Act of 1996.

O

OCC *See* Options Clearing Corporation

ODD Prior to buying or selling an option, investors must read a copy of the Characteristics & Risks of Standardized Options, better known as the options disclosure document (ODD). It explains the characteristics and risks of exchange-traded options.

offer (1) Under the USA, every attempt to solicit a purchase or sale in a security for value. (2) An indication by an investor, trader, or dealer of a willingness to sell a security or commodity.

Options Clearing Corporation An organization that acts as both the issuer and guarantor for option contracts. The Options Clearing Corporation (OCC) operates under the jurisdiction of the U.S. Securities and Exchange Commission (SEC).

OTC Bulletin Board (OTCBB) The OTCBB is a regulated interdealer quotation system owned by FINRA. It displays real-time quotes, last-sale prices, and volume information for OTC equity securities not listed or traded on an exchange. OTCBB securities include national, regional, and foreign equity issues, warrants, units, ADRs, and DPPs. These are not federal covered securities (unless senior to one from the issuer, that is).

oversubscribed The term used to describe a new security issue where the demand for the shares greatly exceeds the available supply. These issues usually appreciate rapidly on the first day of trading, and failure to properly allocate them is a prohibited practice.

P

painting the tape Spurious trading in a particular security among a group of collaborating investors to give a falsely high appearance of interest in the security. This is a prohibited practice.

pecuniary Of or relating to money, such as operating for pecuniary profit.

person In general, any entity that can be held to a contract; an individual, corporation, trust, government, political subdivision, and unincorporated association are all examples.

preorganization certificate Agreement for the future purchase of the stock of a corporation when it is eventually formed. Distribution of preorganization certificates is an exempt transaction, provided certain conditions are met.

principal office and place of business The firm's executive office from which the firm's officers, partners, or managers direct, control, and coordinate the activities of the firm.

principal transaction A transaction in which a broker-dealer either buys securities from customers and takes them into its own inventory or sells securities to customers from its inventory. Dealers cannot act as both principal and agent in the same transaction.

private placement The USA's private placement provision allows an exemption from full state registration for a security that is offered in that state to no more than 10 noninstitutional investors within a 12-month period.

probity Being morally and ethically above reproach; having integrity. A necessary trait for someone in this business.

promissory note A financial instrument, included in the definition of a security, that contains a written promise by one party to pay another party a definite sum of money, either on demand or at a specified future date. The most common form on the exam is commercial paper.

proscribed A term commonly used in legal situations to describe a prohibited action.

prospectus The legal document that must be given to every investor who purchases registered securities in an offering. It describes the details of the company and the particular offering.

prudent investor rule Legally known as the Uniform Prudent Investors Act of 1994 (UPIA). A modern adaptation of the prudent man rule, which, as a result of the development of modern portfolio theory, applies the standard of prudence to the entire portfolio rather than to individual investments. It requires the fiduciary to measure risk with respect to return.

Q

quotation The price given for a security. It consists of two numbers, the bid and the ask (or offer). The bid price is what the dealer is willing to pay a customer who is selling the security, and the ask is the selling price by a dealer to a customer who is buying. *Syn.* quote.

R

red flags Term used to describe potential warnings about an investment. Examples of red flags are promises of high returns with low risk and "don't miss this opportunity; get in now." The term is also used in conjunction with protecting against identity theft.

registered investment company An investment company, such as an open-end management company (mutual fund) or closed-end management company, that is registered with the SEC and exempt from state registration and regulation.

registration by coordination A security is eligible for blue-sky registration by coordination in a state if the issuer files for registration of that security under the Securities Act of 1933 and files duplicates of the registration documents with the state Administrator. The state registration becomes effective at the same time the federal registration statement becomes effective.

registration by qualification A security is eligible for blue-sky registration by qualification in a state if all of the offering is to be sold in a single state or if the security is not eligible for another method of state registration. Net worth and disclosure requirements apply, and registration does not become effective until the Administrator so orders.

registration statement Before nonexempt securities can be offered to the public, they require registration under the Securities Act of 1933 and/or the Uniform Securities Act. The registration statement must disclose all pertinent information concerning the issuer and the offering. This statement is submitted to the SEC and/or Administrator in accordance with the requirements of their respective laws. If the securities are to be sold in only a single state, by qualification, only that state's registration requirements apply.

rescission Buying back, from the customer, a security that was inadvertently sold unlawfully. The price is generally the customer's purchase price plus the state's legal rate of interest, less any income received. The customer has 30 days to accept or reject the offer.

retail investor An individual or noninstitutional investor.

S

Section 28(e) A code section of the Securities Exchange Act of 1934 that deals with soft-dollar compensation. *See also* soft-dollar compensation.

Securities Act of 1933 The federal legislation requiring the full and fair disclosure of all material information about the issuance of new securities.

Securities and Exchange Commission (SEC) The commission Congress created to protect investors, which enforces the Securities Act of 1933, the Securities Exchange Act of 1934, the Investment Company Act of 1940, the Investment Advisers Act of 1940, and other securities laws.

Securities Exchange Act of 1934 The federal legislation establishing the Securities and Exchange Commission that regulates securities exchanges and over-the-counter markets and protects investors from unfair and inequitable practices.

Securities Investor Protection Corporation (SIPC) A nonprofit membership corporation created by an act of Congress to protect clients of brokerage firms that are forced into bankruptcy. Membership is composed of all brokers and dealers registered under the Securities Exchange Act of 1934, all members of national securities exchanges, and most FINRA members. SIPC provides customers of these firms up to $500,000 coverage for cash and securities held by the firms (coverage of cash is limited to $250,000).

security An investment instrument represented by a certificate or other securitized document, ownership of which yields unpredictable profits or losses that stem from the actions of a third party, usually the issuer of the security. Examples are stocks, bonds, notes, certificates of interest in investment or marketing plans, and options on commodities or on other securities. Whole life insurance, with its table of guaranteed cash values, is not a security, but variable life is. A fixed annuity, with its guaranteed monthly payout, is not a security, but a variable annuity is. A futures contract, with its set terms, is not a security, but an option on that contract is.

self-regulatory organization (SRO) An entity that is accountable to the SEC for the enforcement of federal securities laws, as well as for the supervision of securities practices, within an assigned field of jurisdiction. Examples are FINRA, the various stock exchanges, the Municipal Securities Rulemaking Board, and the Chicago Board Options Exchange.

sell The act of conveying ownership of a security or other property for money or other value; every contract to sell a security or an interest in a security. Sales include the following.

■ Any security given or delivered with, or as a bonus for, any purchase of securities is considered to have been offered and sold for value.

■ A gift of assessable stock is considered to involve an offer and sale.

■ Every sale or offer of a warrant or right to purchase or subscribe to another security is considered to include an offer of the other security.

Sales do not include bona fide pledges or loans or stock dividends if nothing of value is given by the stockholders for the dividend.

selling away An associated person engaging in private securities transactions without the knowledge and consent of the employing broker-dealer. This violates NASAA's Statement of Policy on Dishonest or Unethical Practices of Broker-Dealers and Agents.

separate account The account that holds funds paid by variable annuity contract holders. The funds are kept separate from the insurer's general account and are invested in a portfolio of securities that matches the contract holders' objectives. This is what makes a variable annuity a security.

settlement date The business day on which delivery of a security and payment of money is to be made through the facilities of a registered clearing agency in connection with the sale of a security.

social media The collective online communications channels dedicated to community-based input, interaction, content-sharing, and collaboration. Websites and applications dedicated to forums, microblogging, social networking, and wikis are among the different types of social media. When used by securities professionals, great care must be taken to ensure compliance with relevant regulations.

soft-dollar compensation Noncash compensation received by an investment adviser from a broker-dealer, generally in exchange for directed brokerage transactions. Must always be disclosed and should come under the safe harbor provisions of Section 28(e). *See also* safe harbor.

solicited order An order resulting from a broker-dealer recommendation. The resulting trade must be suitable for the investor.

static content Social media format in which the content can only be changed by the originator.

stop order Action the Administrator takes to prevent a registration of a security in his state. Unlike cease and desist orders, stop orders require prior notice to the affected party and a hearing with a written finding.

street name The security is registered in the name of the broker-dealer on the issuer's books, and the BD firm holds the security for clients in "book-entry" form. "Book-entry" simply means that clients do not receive a certificate. Instead, the BD keeps a record in its books showing who owns that particular security.

suitability A determination made by a registered representative as to whether a particular security matches a customer's objectives and financial capability. The representative must have enough information about each customer to make this judgment. *See* suitable transaction.

suitable transaction A transaction that meets or takes into account the investment needs of the customer. All solicited transactions must be suitable.

surety bond A bond required for many employees, officers, and partners of broker-dealers and investment advisers to protect clients against acts of misplacement, fraudulent trading, and check forgery.

T

testimonial A statement in an advertisement or other promotional release, usually by a client, indicating great satisfaction with the provider of goods or services. Testimonials may never be used by investment advisers or their representatives.

thinly traded A security with a low trading volume, usually traded in the OTC market, with a wide spread between the quoted bid and ask prices.

trade confirmation A printed document that contains details of a transaction, including the settlement date and amount of money due from or owed to a customer. It must be sent to the customer on or before the settlement date. It is not a security.

trade date The date on which a securities transaction is executed.

transfer agent A person or an organization responsible for recording the names of registered stockholders and the number of shares owned, seeing that the certificates are signed by the appropriate corporate officers, affixing the corporate seal, and delivering the securities to the transferee.

U

underwriter The entity responsible for marketing stocks, bonds, mutual fund shares, and so forth.

Uniform Securities Act (USA) Template legislation written by the NCCUSL to serve as the basis for a state's securities legislation if the state wished to adopt it. It regulates securities, persons (broker-dealers and their agents and investment advisers and their representatives), and transactions in the securities markets within the state. All but a few of the states have adopted the USA in some form.

unit investment trust (UIT) An investment company that sells a fixed number of redeemable shares in a professionally selected portfolio of securities. It is organized under a trust indenture, not a corporate charter.

unsolicited order An order originated by the customer, not the result of a broker-dealer recommendation. The resulting trade is an exempt transaction, though written customer acknowledgment of its unsolicited nature may be required by the Administrator.

unsuitable transaction A transaction that does not meet the investment needs of the customer. An example is purchase of a municipal bond for a low-income customer seeking growth.

V

vacate When used in a legal context (such as on this exam), it means to cancel or annul a judgment or penalty.

W

wash trade When a customer enters a purchase order and a sale order for the same security at the same time. It creates a false appearance of activity in a security and is a prohibited practice.

withdrawal Voluntary termination of registration on the part of the registrant, through submission of Form ADV-W. Withdrawal is effective within 30 days under the Uniform Securities Act unless the Administrator makes a contrary finding.

wrap account An investment advisory account in which all management fees and commissions are combined and paid, usually quarterly, as a percentage of assets under management.

Index

Notes

Notes

Notes

Notes

Notes

Notes

Notes

Notes

Notes

Notes

Notes

Notes

Notes

Notes